JUMP FOR JOY

JUMP FOR JOY

JAZZ, BASKETBALL, AND BLACK CULTURE IN 1930S AMERICA

GENA CAPONI-TABERY

UNIVERSITY OF MASSACHUSETTS PRESS Amherst

LC 2008003492
ISBN 978-1-55849-663-7 (paper); 662-0 (library cloth)

Designed by Richard Hendel
Set in FF Quadraat with Eagle Bold display by dix!
Printed and bound by Thomson-Shore, Inc.

Library of Congress Cataloging-in-Publication Data

Capona-Tabery, Gena.
Jump for joy : jazz, basketball, and Black culture in 1930s America /
Gena Caponi-Tabery.
    p.   cm.
Includes bibliographical references and index.
ISBN 978-1-55849-663-7 (pbk. : alk. paper)—
ISBN 978-1-55849-662-0 (library cloth : alk. paper)
1. African Americans—Intellectual life—20th century.
2. Jazz—Social aspects—United States—History—20th century.
3. Sports—Social aspects—United States—History—20th century.
4. Social change—United States—History—20th century.
5. African Americans—Politics and government—20th century.
6. African Americans—Civil rights—History—20th century.
7. African Americans—History—1877–1964.
8. United States—Race relations—History—20th century.
I. Title.
E185.6.C265 2008
305.896′0730904 3—dc22
                                                        2008003492

British Library Cataloguing in Publication data are available.

FOR RON,
who does not jump,
but soars.

Mama exhorted her children at every opportunity to "jump at de sun." We might not land on the sun, but at least we would get off the ground.

—ZORA NEALE HURSTON, *Dust Tracks on a Road* (1942)

"I'm a good jumper," he said, "but I'm not so good at landing."

"Maybe you should stay closer to the ground then," I said.

And he shook his head and said the ground was the whole problem in the first place.

—BRIAN ANDREAS, "Good Jumper" (1997)

For what is ultimately at stake is morale, which is to say the will to persevere, the disposition to persist and perhaps prevail; and what must be avoided by all means is a failure of nerve.

—ALBERT MURRAY, *Stomping the Blues* (1976)

✦ CONTENTS

Illustrations follow page 100

In 1932 Duke Ellington made history with a recording that captured the feel of the entire swing era. "It Don't Mean a Thing (If It Ain't Got That Swing)" represented an energetic defiance of a depressingly downward spiral in national and world events. Nine years later, in 1941, the Duke brought to the stage a musical revue that likewise called on a style of music and dance that had rapidly escalated in popularity in the United States and was about to go global. This musical, *Jump for Joy*, drew from and celebrated several forms of black culture of the late 1930s, from music and dance to comedy and dress. It capped a period of black cultural achievement and exuberance unprecedented in American history and possibly not since matched. And when the country entered the war in December of that year, the dance and music that had incubated in 1930s America became a fad worldwide. In the 1960s, when San Francisco demonstrators challenged Ellington to make a statement on civil rights, he answered, "I made my statement in 1941 in *Jump for Joy* and I stand by it." [1]

But I am jumping ahead of myself. The question is: Why jumping? And why the 1930s?

It all started with jazz. And basketball.

It's easy to find parallels between jazz and basketball. Both are ensemble performances depending on fundamental knowledge of the art but also on the ability to improvise in the moment. Anyone can score; anyone can solo. And the most interesting part of the game or the music often takes place away from the ball or the melody. The abilities of individual players have taken the sport and the art to places that the original composers or creators of the game could never have envisioned. The slam dunk, for instance, is like those wonderful, transcendent moments in jazz when a performer does something so unexpected and unnecessary but so gratifying that it seems to lift the whole room—not just the player but everyone in the place.

There's much criticism today, as always, of unnecessary showmanship and celebration, self-aggrandizement, and over-the-top virtuosity in sports and jazz. But I don't mind showy moments—I live for them. A lot of people do. Moments of performance that might seem self-congratulatory actually do a lot for the spiritual well-being of the audience. They create a world of virtual time that not only raises us above our ordinary lives but also cements people together, gives us a feeling of having experienced something rare and valuable: something that makes us us.

The slam dunk is possibly just for show. Sometimes the artistry of the dunk works at cross-purposes with actually scoring. But there are showy moments in basketball that are transformative, elevating the practical to a thing of beauty. Like the jump shot, for instance. It's not really necessary to jump—not every time—to make a basket. But people do. Furthermore, there were no jump shots in the early years of the game. Who started doing it? And when?

The origin of the jump shot is the Holy Grail of basketball history. All the historians involved in this search mention the same few players in the later 1940s and early 1950s—and all are white. Not one historian mentions the 1937 rules change that completely altered the game and probably made jump shots possible. What about that rules change? Until 1937, after every score, players had to return to mid-court for a tip-off. Games were slow and low-scoring, often in the low 20s. In practice, up until 1937, basketball was a half-court game.

But in 1937 the National Basketball Committee eliminated the center tip-off after goals. Now players could run from one end of the court to the other, and faster, running teams immediately had the advantage. Players began to shoot from a running position, which meant they no longer planted both feet on the ground and launched a two-handed set shot. Instead, they left their feet and shot on the run with one hand and began to love the freedom of this shot.

I started thinking about that jump, about speed, and height, and skyscrapers, and jazz. I had in mind a piece by the Count Basie Orchestra, a piece called "One O'Clock Jump," the first of many swing pieces that were called "jumps." Brian Rust's Jazz Records, 1897–1942 indexes every jazz recording produced from the end of the nineteenth century to World War II, when a shortage of materials temporarily halted recording in this country. I looked up Basie's piece in this book and discovered that he recorded "One O'Clock Jump" on July 7, 1937, the same year basketball removed the center tip-off. Poring over Rust's book page by page, I counted 135 records containing the word "jump" in the title. Of these, 124 were recorded between 1937 and 1942. Many more actual "jump" recordings were produced during this time—too many to count. But it is clear that in these post-1937 song titles the word "jump" means something special—energetic dancing, partying—mostly, having fun.

What kind of dancing? Mainly it was the Lindy Hop, called in the later years of the decade the jitterbug. Charles Lindbergh's 1927 flight was newsworthy because aviation was so new, and he remained airborne longer than anyone had dreamed possible. But even more significant at the time, Lindbergh flew across the ocean, bridging a gap between two continents separated by a vast expanse of water. It wasn't the height but the distance of Lindy's flight that made it distinctive and important—not going up, but going *across* the ocean. The Lindy Hop at first, too, was more or less horizontal, a dance that moved across the floor with kicks to the side. The partners came together and gently pushed apart; distance was increased and diminished, and the gap was bridged.

But dancers began experimenting with what they called "air steps," in which the male dancer threw his partner over his head or back while she jumped. The first documented instance was at a dance contest at the Savoy Ballroom in 1936. From that moment on, any dancer who hoped to win a Lindy competition had to include air steps. Adding air steps moved the Lindy to a new—and higher—level of energy and complexity.

Not only did all three different forms of jumping begin at more or less the same time, but also they often happened in the same place: at combination basketball-dances. Many gymnasiums were closed to black athletes, who had to play wherever they could. The top black basketball teams of the 1920s and 1930s—the New York Renaissance and the Savoy Big Five (who became the Harlem Globetrotters)—took their names from their home courts, the Renaissance Casino in New York and the Savoy Ballroom in Chicago.[2] Basketball players and promoters found that ballrooms offered two of the most important ingredients of their game—hardwood floors and crowds. Basketball was a young sport, and games were short. But fans felt they had been cheated if the evening was over in less than two hours. So, as Eyre Saitch of the New York Renaissance said, "we had to have a dance afterward, or else nobody would come to the damn thing."[3]

Jump blues, the Lindy Hop's air steps, and basketball's fast break and jump shot all burst out of the same arenas and were soon embraced by white

America. Jump blues evolved into rhythm and blues and then rock and roll. The Lindy Hop changed American social dance completely and remains the foundation of most rock dancing. In the 1990s swing dance experienced a tremendous revival. And while it was possible as late as the 1950s to be benched for taking a jump shot—because it was associated with African American ballplayers—today, when basketball is the most popular sport among American teenagers, it is impossible to imagine the game without fast breaks, jump shots, and slam dunks, all introduced by black players.

Was there any plain old jumping going on? Well, yes. You don't have to look further than the 1936 Olympics, when nine African American athletes brought home thirteen medals, all in sprinting and jumping events, an explosion of black achievement in track and field. The spectacular performance of the 1936 African American Olympians started a revolution in American sports: by 1945 nearly all American sprint and jumping event records were held by black athletes. For countless African Americans, the accumulation of public victory upon public victory created an aggregate cultural permission to achieve, excel, and express themselves increasingly in public arenas.

Within two years there came three more extraordinary and public victories. In June 1937 boxer Joe Louis defeated James Braddock to become world heavyweight champion. A little more than a month later, the only all-black union in the country, the Brotherhood of Sleeping Car Porters, secured a labor contract with the Pullman Company—the first such contract ever signed with black union members. Then in June 1938 Joe Louis defended his championship against the German fighter Max Schmeling in a stunning battle that lasted only two and a half minutes. Across the globe, Louis was celebrated as the champion of democracy over totalitarianism, and for the first time in history Americans of all colors claimed a black man as their hero.

Political leaders can harness ideas and energy, but they seldom create them. The best, most powerful political leaders know how and when to seize existing movements, even if they might not be apparent but rather are lying just under the surface of a community. The jump of the late 1930s was a cultural expression that symbolized something important about the politics of that time. It symbolized hope, and optimism, and a willingness to act on that hope. Political leaders such as Adam Clayton Powell Jr. and A. Philip Randolph harnessed that energy and used it to fuel organized political action. But they weren't the source of the energy. The energy came from people's bodies and hearts and voices. It jumped out of them on dance floors and basketball courts, in gymnasiums and band halls.

The velocity of this change was and remains astonishing. In a few short years a new form of music appeared, dance steps evolved from stomps and shuffles to tosses and leaps, African American athletes astounded the world; and because the world called these achievements American, Americans began to think of them as their own as well. African Americans who were asserting themselves in places of leisure and recreation also won important political and civil victories. In the space of a decade, this country went from its first public acknowledgment of an all-black union to desegregating its defense industry and then its entire armed forces. Both literally and symbolically, the jump displaced a former cultural stasis, and cultural change accelerated.

Through sound and movement—through their bodies—musicians, dancers, and athletes enact the formative ideas of the age. Cultural production is political. And intellectual. Ordinary people matter, and they have ideas about their lives and how they might or should be lived. They express ideas through their work and their play, their living and their loving, and they enthusiastically support the artists and athletes who express these things more publicly and skillfully. And even if that cultural stuff isn't important to the scholars and historians of later decades, it certainly was important to the people who lived it.

In this book, I look at both the extraordinary and the ordinary African Americans of the 1930s who took music, dance, and sports to the air, those who laid the groundwork for postwar cultural *and* political expression. The African American cultural innovators I discuss here grabbed hold of something literally in the air at the time—a cultural obsession with height, flight, and speed—and through their exploration and celebration they achieved a fundamental form of social, and eventually political, elevation. At a time when international events made global heroes of Olympic athletes, Joe Louis, jazz musicians, and Lindy Hoppers, African Americans began to believe that if they counted for something in the eyes of the world—if, indeed, they stood for America—perhaps America itself might be ready to grant them full citizenship.

Chapter 1 gives an overview of the basketball-dance, a celebration of African American cultural life in a racist society. I try to furnish some context for the celebration, including the racism it had to transcend. The 1936 Olympics, the 1937 victory of the Brotherhood of Sleeping Car Porters, and Joe Louis's back-to-back championship wins over James Braddock and Max Schmeling in 1937 and 1938 gave African Americans a sense of accomplishment and power at a time when systematic discrimination was a fact of life in the United States.

In chapter 2 I discuss the American obsession with flying and with height and the real and imaginary superheroes who embodied these qualities for Americans in the 1930s. The mere quarter-century history of flight before Charles Lindbergh reminds us why his 1927 trans-Atlantic flight was so monumental. Meanwhile, an ongoing race to build the tallest skyscraper in America paralleled aeronautical innovations. When an economic depression put an end to the construction of tall buildings, a comic book superhero took to jumping skyscrapers and then soaring over them. At the same time, African American athletes became the fastest and highest ordinary mortals on the planet, mimicking the skyward trend of the urban physical environment and demonstrating the power of the human body and spirit. Chapter 3 looks specifically at the 1936 Olympic athletes and shows how their successes changed the face of American sports.

Chapter 4 explores the development of air steps in the Lindy Hop and further shows how influential the Lindy was in the United States and then in dance worldwide. Chapter 5 traces the development of jump blues. Chapter 6 examines the history of the jump shot, the fast break, and the slam dunk—three enormously popular innovations in basketball that for years were either unofficially or officially outlawed by white coaches and leagues, three advances that largely account for basketball's survival and popularity.

It is impossible to talk about the 1930s and black America without talking about Joe Louis. He made people feel proud to be black and, unlike Jack Johnson, took on a patriotic status that conferred citizenship on all African Americans. In chapter 7, as throughout the entire book, I am also interested in the thousands of fans who vicariously celebrated these victories, and I offer this fan response as a form of political expression. Since cultural critics of that day and this have suggested that popular arts do more harm than good to social and political strivings, in chapter 8 I present a theoretical argument in opposition to that claim, and I incidentally include the work of two 1930s African American dancers who were hailed as creators of high art and whose choreography had "primitive" or African origins.

In chapter 9 I tender a linguistic and historical view of the jump—as a rhetorical figure and a physical gesture—by way of explaining its importance in African and African American culture. I show how deeply rooted the jump is in African culture and history and in dance and athletic competitions throughout the African diaspora. I am also interested in the connection of the jump to the minstrel number "Jump Jim Crow," one of the most popular songs and dances of the nineteenth century, particularly since in the twentieth century "Jim Crow" became the unofficial name for countless official policies of segregation. And finally, I explore the jump in religious expression, the ways in which inward and spiritual grace takes form in outward and visible expression.

Chapter 10 summarizes the history of one of the few middle-class careers open to African Americans from the late nineteenth to the early twentieth century—that of the Pullman porter. Pullman porters traveled all over the country spreading music, dance, and news of black accomplishments to black citizens across the United States. Moreover, since the Brotherhood of Sleeping Car Porters was the only all-black union in the nation, it became the voice of black American workers. Backed by thousands of grassroots supporters willing and ready to march, the brotherhood's leader, A. Philip Randolph, persuaded two presidents to outmaneuver Congress by issuing executive orders that brought about sweeping changes in civil rights, desegregating the defense industry in 1941 and the military in 1948. Randolph himself has been vastly underappreciated as a political model for activists of the 1950s, and almost everyone has forgotten that it was Randolph who proposed and organized the 1963 March on Washington. The story of the Pullman porters reveals an African American social, cultural, and political network and emphasizes the importance of ordinary men and women in creating extraordinary social change.

Chapter 11 focuses on Duke Ellington's 1941 musical *Jump for Joy*, an African American revue that intended to put an end to Jim Crow—on stage and in American culture. The revue celebrated black culture in every possible arena, from music, dance, and comedy to clothing. It was an extravagant culmination of the cultural enthusiasm that the events of the war years helped to transform into outright political rebellion.

The Afterword places this exploration of the jump within the field of play theory, building on the writings of Albert Murray, who laid the foundation for a systematic consideration of African American expressive culture.

. . .

This book is not so much about discrimination as celebration. But, truthfully, it is about a kind of celebration against which there was much discrimination. Because in the 1930s, in the United States, if you were black, there was not supposed to be much to celebrate. And if you were black, you were supposed to know that.

And if, by chance, you were black and you happened to jump for joy, well, then, you just didn't understand. You didn't understand that you weren't supposed to feel tall and high and mighty and powerful. And if you did, then you were asking for trouble.

That's what I mean when I say that the cultural stuff is political. It's political, and powerful, and dangerous—maybe more dangerous than the innovations of inventors and the achievements of scientists and the advances of engineers and the heroism of doctors.

Because anyone can jump. Moreover, many did. And because of the many, a few decided to go forward. And because of the few, many more followed. And that's just asking for trouble.

This book is about ordinary and radical troublemakers—those who made trouble unknowingly through celebration and exuberance as well those who challenged and transformed the status quo, sometimes by marching, sometimes by fighting, sometimes by running. But sometimes simply by jumping for joy.

A history book ought not to take longer to write than the period it chronicles. Sadly, this one did. I hereby apologize and thank the people in my life who experienced firsthand the glacial pace of this undertaking: Clark Dougan of the University of Massachusetts Press, who operates with more good will and less pressure than is imaginable; Joel Dinerstein, who cares as deeply as I do about what is African in American culture; and my three oldest sons—Cyrus Tabery, Pete Caponi, and Maff Caponi. My parents, Lou and Gene Dagel, and my mother-in-law, Julia Tabery, have been steadfast advocates. Finally, I am grateful to my youngest son, Julius Ellington Tabery, for understanding that the heroes of this book are part of his cultural heritage.

Many other people and institutions helped in ways both specific and general. Jack Salzman responded to my draft of a paper for *Prospects: An Annual of American Cultural Studies* with amazement that anyone would begin an academic article by quoting Bill Russell. But he published the piece in the 1999 volume, and that got the ball rolling. I am grateful to Dwight Henderson, Daniel Gelo, and the College of Behavioral and Social Sciences at the University of Texas at San Antonio for providing a semester-long faculty research leave, during which I wrote chapters 2, 3, and 9. The Dallas Institute of Humanities and Culture included me in their Ralph Ellison/Albert Murray Literary Symposium, which allowed me to frame the afterword to this book. I also thank the Texas Committee for the Humanities, who enlisted me as a speaker and thereby allowed me to preview several chapters at libraries, colleges, and community organizations across the state. St. Michael's Episcopal Church of Austin also has invited me to speak on topics related to this book. Parishioners Sue and Tom Allen, Klaus Bichteler, Claire Bray, Elaine Diefenderfer, Doug Falls, Alice Hall, Mary Parse, Jean Perdicaris Spoor, and members of the No Agenda Prayer Group have provided a wise and loving extended family. Thanks also to my friends Angela Prescott, Ann Price, and Caren Upshaw for their good cheer and support.

For research assistance, I thank the gracious curators of the Cab Calloway Archives in the Howard Gotlieb Archival Research Center at Boston University, and the Schomburg Center for Research in Black Culture, as well as Elizabeth Falsey of the Harvard Theatre Collection, John Hasse, Ann Kuebler, and Deborra Richardson of the Smithsonian Institution's National Museum of American History, and Lauren Gurgiolo of the Harry Ransom Humanities Research Center.

Albert Murray spent hours with me on the telephone and at his home helping to bring me up to speed. I am grateful to him and to Mozelle for their hospitality and inspiration. Many other people generously shared memories and opinions with me, notably Stanley Crouch, Clarence "Big House" Gaines, Clarence Gaines Jr., Calvin Irvin, Charley Rosen, and Nevil Shed. I thank Bertram D. Ashe, Richard Crawford, Samuel A. Floyd Jr., John Gennari, Charles Keil, Guthrie P. Ramsey Jr., Timothy L. Parrish, and the late William Piersen for their insights, correspondence, and discussion on several panels at academic conferences.

I am also indebted to the two anonymous readers of the manuscript for their comments and expertise. I am deeply grateful to Carol Betsch, managing editor of the University of Massachusetts Press, and her colleague Mary Bellino, who graciously and skillfully ushered this book and its author through the many hurdles of the production process. Copy editor Amanda Heller worked wonders in clarifying and generally shaping up the manuscript.

My husband, Ron Tabery, ordered books, bought concert and theater tickets, took dance lessons, accompanied me on research trips, cleared the decks for writing, listened, read, and remains enthusiastic, or at least possesses the grace to appear so. He deserves much more than this book, and I owe him more gratitude than I can express here.

JUMP FOR JOY

CHAPTER 1:
SNEAKERS AND TUXES

Former Boston Celtics player and coach Bill Russell wrote: "People in all kinds of cultures are known to 'jump for joy' in moments of supreme happiness. Jumping is an internationally recognized expression of joy, and basketball is a sport organized around jumping. . . . It's possible for a player to jump because he's happy, but it's more likely that he's happy because he's jumping. I have heard players complain about almost every detail of the game—the rules, the size or color of the ball, the shape or temperature of the dressing room—but I've never heard anybody complain about the fact that the game requires jumping."[1]

Strangely, the game didn't always require jumping. And in many cases, it even prohibited jumping. Russell remembers playing ball in high school in the 1950s at a time when jump shots were considered showing off, and traditional coaches benched players for taking them. Just before the turn of the twentieth century, the game's inventor, James "Doc" Naismith, had envisioned a horizontal game, with the only jump being a tip-off at center court after each successful goal. But in 1937, when the National Basketball Committee did away with the center tip-off after each score, that made it a full-court game, giving rise to both the fast break and the jump shot. That same year, Kansas City bandleader William "Count" Basie recorded "One O'Clock Jump," and the word "jump" began to replace "stomp" and "shuffle" in the titles of jazz recordings. About the same time, the Lindy Hop, also called the jitterbug, started to include jumping moves called "air steps." Jump tunes, the jumping jitterbug, and jump shots all burst out of the same arenas, at a time when dance bands traveled with basketball teams, and nightspots from the Cotton Club in Harlem to the Renaissance Casino hosted pre-dance basketball games.

By the 1940s the cultural expressions and accomplishments of African Americans had become common American currency. By then, swing musicians and dancers and super-athletes defined American popular culture and, in other parts of the world, symbolized American freedom.[2] What had begun as "black" dancing and "black" music and "black" basketball became "all-American" culture. But the foundation for each of these new forms of popular culture once literally embodied blackness.

Jump music took the place of what had previously been called "race" music and evolved into jump blues, a stubbornly rhythmic and identifiably "black" offshoot of swing music. In the late 1940s, "jump" was used interchangeably with "rhythm and blues," the African American predecessor of rock and roll, which has since dominated American popular music.[3]

Changes came more slowly to basketball, where coaches exerted more control over players than any single authority could over musicians and dancers. The jump shot and fast break evolved in the late 1930s and 1940s, but they signified blackness well into the 1960s. Finally, the jump shot and fast break came to dominate the game, and though coaches resisted losing control, they had to admit the effectiveness and crowd-pleasing potential of both. The National Collegiate Athletic Association (NCAA) banned the slam dunk in 1967, but the high-flying American Basketball Association (ABA) brought it back with a slam dunk contest in 1976, and National Basketball Association (NBA) general manager George Steinbrenner transported basketball to unprecedented popularity by encouraging the fast break in his league.

The Lindy Hop represents the origin of contemporary popular dance if for no other reason than that it introduced the breakaway, a moment in the dancing when the partners release each other and dance apart. Although they continue dancing as a couple, they forsake the closed position that the waltz had introduced just before the beginning of the nineteenth century. In 1959, looking back on a career that began before the Lindy Hop, veteran dancer George Wendler sadly acknowledged that the Lindy had changed American dance forever: "I don't recall any conservative style of dancing making a hit since the Lindy revolution."[4]

Because these forms of music and dance and sport evolved and diffused so thoroughly into contemporary American popular culture, it is easy to forget how black they once were. Of their dominance in the 1930s, historian David Stowe says, "Not since the heyday of blackface minstrelsy in the decades before the Civil War had America been forced to confront so directly its indebtedness to African-American culture, to acknowledge that its culture was unmistakably formed by a racial group systematically excluded from its society."[5] And yet, despite that head-on cultural collision, the majority of Americans now, as then, have managed to ignore this particular cultural debt. The transition from African American to all-American was and is often so rapid, it is convenient to ignore our cultural ancestors.

African American music, dance, and basketball of the early twentieth century amounted to self-conscious assertions of ethnicity.[6] Coinciding with the American and European fascination with height and speed, the Lindy Hop, jump blues, and athletics of the late 1930s signified rising confidence, assertiveness, and enthusiasm, particularly among African Americans. Nothing captured the feeling of racial uplift and upward mobility more clearly than this intersection of dance, music, and sport.[7]

Marching Black

Music, sports, and dance were entertainment, but they were more than that. They were ways of expressing ideas and feelings about personal and cultural identity. As they helped to express and form a new African American consciousness, they became the foundation of a shift in the social fabric of twentieth-century America. The achievements of black Americans that most captured the public imagination—the swing music, the athletic victories, the fantastically popular new dance style—seemed to converge in one expressive gesture: the jump. In music and dance, the jump replaced an earlier, symbolic gesture, the shuffle: the slow-moving, ground-bound step of a people without hope—the physical opposite of the new jump.

Is it reading too much into such moves to give them political attributes? A rising African American politician, Adam Clayton Powell Jr., didn't think so. In 1936 the black prizefighter Joe Louis suffered a humiliating defeat in Yankee Stadium by the German boxer Max Schmeling—whom he would beat in a rematch two years later—and at about the same time, the only independent black nation in the world, Ethiopia, fell to Mussolini's Fascist forces. Powell noted the symbolic importance of Louis's career and described the political mood of African Americans in physical terms, contrasting the "sky high leap" with the despairing shuffle: "Along came the Brown Bomber, Death in the Evening, and our racial morale took a *sky high leap* that broke every record from Portland to Pasadena. Surely the new day was just around the corner. . . . Then along came the sudden fall of Addis Ababa and the Yankee Stadium fiasco and something died. Gone today is the jauntiness, the careless abandon, the spring in our stride—we're just shufflin' along."[8]

No leader of the day better understood the connection between black boxing and black power. As a boy, Adam Clayton Powell Jr. learned the meaning of powerlessness by tracing with his finger the letter "P" branded on his grandfather's back.[9] After taking over his father's enormously successful Abyssinian Baptist Church in Harlem, he marched in street demonstrations against unfair hiring practices and discrimination, such as the banning of five African American doctors from Harlem Hospital in 1931. Powell led a delegation of six thousand to City Hall, succeeding in getting the doctors rehired and in establishing an interracial staff with a Negro medical director.[10] In 1939, when the New York World's Fair Corporation placed a ban on all hiring of Negroes with the exception of domestic workers, Powell's picketers hit Thirty-fourth Street "like a blitzkrieg." "By the time they finished the picket campaign," he recalled, "scores of Negroes were employed in jobs other than as porters and maids."[11] When Powell was elected to the city council in 1942, he began his own newspaper, *People's Voice*, backed financially by Charles Buchanan, the manager of the Savoy Ballroom. The first issue appeared on February 14, 1942.

Powell's editorial agenda in *People's Voice* was clear: "better housing, an end to racial discrimination in all forms, better schools, full job opportunities in the private sector, support for Negro Business."[12] His goal was a socially relevant paper, with an emphasis on supporting the working class. Seeking to fill the vacancy left by Marcus Garvey's deportation in 1927, Powell adopted Garvey's militancy while continuing to work within mainstream politics. Powell was given to capturing his political ambitions in physical language, and through *People's Voice* he promoted "Marching Black," a bold and ingenious phrase that deliberately suggested a new direction. The word "black" itself was a distinct break from the more common "Negro," and Powell's adoption of it marked the beginning of the use of that word by African Americans as a self-conscious political statement. The social elite of the day preferred "colored," as it reflected both the varied shadings of color among African Americans and differences in their economic and social positions. The politically aware would have used the term "Afro-American."[13] Powell's new "Marching Black" suggested a physical, muscular political activism that resonated with ordinary people previously left out of elite political movements.

Powell's own Harlem was the site of one of the worst race riots of the decade, a 1935 explosion following a small-time burglary, in which more than a hundred people, mostly black, were arrested, fifty-seven civilians and seven police officers were injured, and hundreds of windows were broken. Three people died. As Howard University philosopher Alain Locke commented, "It was not the unfortunate rumors [which began the riot] but the state of mind on which they fell." [14] Immediately after the riot, Mayor Fiorello La Guardia created a commission to investigate, calling on such experts as sociologist E. Franklin Frazier, poet Countee Cullen, labor leader A. Philip Randolph, and lawyer Hubert Delany. The Mayor's Commission took its task seriously, and city officials took its findings seriously as well. As a result, several black political efforts that had previously been stalled began to move forward. Historian Cheryl Greenberg concludes, "Although in the end the fundamental problems facing Harlem persisted, the limited gains African-Americans did achieve in turn spurred political struggles on behalf of broader agendas." [15]

Powell's 1945 book *Marching Blacks* details victory after victory of ordinary people in cities across the country in the late 1930s and early 1940s. During the Great Depression in Detroit, Snow Grigsby carefully counted the number of Negroes employed in public institutions and formed the Detroit Civic Rights Committee to force the Board of Education, the Detroit Edison Company, the telephone company, and the fire department to hire Negroes. In Chicago, YMCA secretary Joe Jefferson formed the Negro Labor Relations League and in 1938 succeeded in getting former newspaper carriers hired as branch managers for the *Chicago Times* and the *Evening American*. In 1939 Cleveland workers integrated the workforce of A&P stores, movie theaters, and the Ohio Telephone Company. Pullman porter George Fuller organized voters in Savannah, while railway clerk John Wesley Dobbs registered voters in Atlanta. Fighting from his pulpit in Dallas, the Reverend Maynard Jackson formed the Negro Democrats of the South, while Sam Solomon registered voters in Miami, even though the Ku Klux Klan burned a cross on his lawn and hanged him in effigy from a lamppost. We seldom hear of these civil rights workers today, but they were there, emboldened by the victories of other, more conspicuous cultural heroes—such as the 1936 Olympians and Joe Louis, who were front-page news. Their victories provided the cultural muscle with which an activist like Powell could build his political movement.

Just as it is impossible to separate finances from politics, in 1930s and 1940s African America music, dance, and sports were vital, interconnected elements in the political atmosphere. The physicality of cultural heroes such as Joe Louis, Jesse Owens, and even dancers and bandleaders provided a background for Powell's Marching Black, a movement that had a place for ordinary people who might not personally be able to uplift the race but could still participate in the larger cause of cultural elevation and equality.

National Third Places

The historian John Hope Franklin attributes the surge of artistic activity in Harlem during the 1920s and 1930s to the newly formed sense of community, responsibility and self-confidence emanating from the "masses" who had migrated from the South to the urban North.[16] Such a "massive concentration of Black experiential energy," to quote the poet Stephen Henderson, nurtured and boosted community consciousness and expression.[17] Jumping swing tunes, dances, and high-jumping basketball games were festive expressions of black cultural unity, social rituals whose underlying purpose was, according to the novelist and jazz historian Albert Murray, "confrontation, improvisation, affirmation, celebration."[18] In dancehalls and community centers, when men, women, and children danced and listened to the music, or watched basketball games preceding dances, they were participating in the flux of community life. Music, dance, and sport flow into, out of, and within community gatherings, connecting participants to the community and to one another.

Community rituals depend on congenial sites. The sociologist Ray Oldenburg believes that communities create and sustain themselves in informal public gathering spaces, which he calls "third places," a "generic designation for a great variety of public places that host the regular, voluntary, informal, and happily anticipated gatherings of individuals beyond the realms of home and work."[19] Oldenburg has found such places to be "levelers," spaces where status distinctions are laid aside. Within third places "the charm and flavor of one's personality, irrespective of his or her station in life, is what counts." Where third places exist, even the poorest member of society has access to a richly "engaging and sustaining public life."[20] Over the course of a year, anthropologist Melvin D. Williams visited and studied several such places in the Pittsburgh neighborhood of Belmar and personally experienced their acceptance: "Everyone is welcome. . . . There is no discrimination, no ostracism, and no isolation."[21]

Although the Renaissance Casino, at 2359 Seventh Avenue, running the full block between West 137th and 138th streets, was a truly congenial community center, it was hardly an informal gathering place. In 1918 the *Real Estate*

Record and Builders' Guide announced the New Negro Social Center planned for the southeast corner of Seventh Avenue and West 138th Street, a former pasture. Norwegian architect Arne Delhi planned a roof garden, a 160-by-50-foot swimming pool, a restaurant, banquet hall, bank, dancehall, barbershop, Turkish baths, bowling alley, and billiard room. This social center did not materialize, but a smaller version appeared in Harry Creighton Ingalls's design for the Renaissance Casino. The two-story redbrick Casino, begun in 1921, housed a theater completed in 1922 and a compound including a ballroom situated above shops, stores, restaurants, and a billiard parlor, completed in 1924. The facade of the building bore a frieze of brilliant polychrome Hispano Moresque glazed tiles, and the whole of the building was covered with a canvas canopy.[22] Built by black owners on a design by a black architect, and occupied by black businessmen, the Casino truly was by, of, and for the Harlem community.

Basketball-dances quickly became a feature of the new ballroom. Bob Douglas approached fellow Caribbean immigrant William Roach, one of the owners, with a deal: practice and playing space for his club team, the Spartan Braves, in exchange for a percentage of the gate plus advertising in the form of a new team name, the New York Renaissance Big Five (they became the New York Rens in the 1925–26 season). Roach's two partners, Cleophus Charity and Joseph H. Sweeney, were also from the Caribbean. A fourth West Indian immigrant played an important part in the new venture: the sports editor of the *New York Amsterdam News*, Romeo Dougherty, a Virgin Islander, endorsed the team and its home court.

Less formal community centers evolved more spontaneously. The barbershop, for instance, provided a rent-free, service-free retreat for men in African American communities. It was "first and foremost a gathering place, a home away from home."[23] The typical black barbershop in the heart of the black hangout area had only two barber chairs, but several straight-back chairs or benches lined the walls of this all-male domain where customers and noncustomers could sit, chat, and commune with other men. In this sanctuary for male fellowship, conversation, and companionship, much of the unofficial business of the neighborhood was conducted and community ties were maintained. Business might be slow, but activity was not. Thinking back on his favorite barbershop on Central Avenue in Los Angeles, bluesman Johnny Otis wrote: "The barber shop operated as a mini-theatre. Performances every day except Sunday. The regular hanger-ons and the customers loved every minute. . . . Those who gathered for the fun were bound to place a bet or get a haircut sooner or later."[24] Barbershops also functioned as unofficial offices for musicians; in the early years of the twentieth century there were two or three barbershops in Harlem where several cabaret orchestra leaders could be found if a musician was in need of a booking. Billiard parlors would let musicians hold informal meetings in a back room.[25]

Beauty parlors served as focal points for women in the neighborhood and were a significant source of income for many black women. Madame C. J. Walker's entrepreneurship in the field of African American beauty products made her a wealthy woman. Similarly, the salons of Lucille Green financed the political activities of her husband, A. Philip Randolph, indirectly supporting the first major political victory of African Americans in the twentieth century when Randolph negotiated a fair labor contract for the Brotherhood of Sleeping Car Porters.

African American "third places" were places of contestation (of racism) as much as celebration (of race). But with regard to black–white relations in the 1930s, African American nightclubs and dancehalls functioned as national "third places," democratic islands of neutrality where ordinary social restrictions—such as segregation—were occasionally and temporarily laid aside. They were cultural playgrounds, dedicated, like all playgrounds, to something apart from everyday life, with different rules and different expectations. Exceptions were made in these exceptional places, and in them exceptional things happened. The nightclubs became home to a new, young culture, and black swing music became the new national anthem. For immigrant youth, swinging to the music was a way to leave the Old World behind and become part of modern America. For small-town youth, listening to swing music or participating in barn dances was a way to rise above the dust and pastures of their parents' towns and farms and to join the larger national youth culture.

As the 1930s drew to a close, more venues began to draw mixed audiences, and white Americans caught an eyeful and an earful of what people of color could do in music, dance, and sport on these very narrow but level playing fields. In these dancehalls performed the musicians and dancers—rug cutters, jitterbugs, Lindy Hoppers—who set the bar ever higher during the swing era.

Whether white or black, they were, in Albert Murray's words, "blues-idiom communicants" to the rest of the country.[26]

Swing Culture

The celebration of African American cultural life in a racist society is by definition subversive, but these dances and the music that fueled them were unifying. During the years culminating in World War II, swing music, of which jump was a particular variety, embodied the American melting pot. Cultural historian Joel Dinerstein claims, "African American artists integrated the speed, drive, precision, and rhythmic flow of factory work and modern cities into a nationally (and internationally) unifying cultural form: big-band swing."[27] Swing music was so effective at capturing the tempo of modernity that it became the soundtrack for American life. It was what America sounded like.

Even fans who preferred white swing artists—Benny Goodman, Glen Grey, Artie Shaw, or the Dorsey brothers—were aware of their darker counterparts. It was, after all, Duke Ellington's 1932 "It Don't Mean a Thing (If It Ain't Got That Swing)" that gave the music and the era its name. If audiences hadn't heard the black swing bands firsthand, they had heard Ellington broadcasting from the Cotton Club on the CBS and NBC radio networks. In February 1937, when Ellington played for President Roosevelt's Birthday Ball, that, too, was broadcast on radio. In 1938 Ellington melodies provided themes for thirty-seven different radio programs: "Mood Indigo" played on sixteen, "Sophisticated Lady" on twelve, and "In a Sentimental Mood" on nine.[28] Swing king Benny Goodman played to a radio audience of 2 million in 1938, three times weekly, on NBC's "Camel Caravan." Goodman's orchestra relied almost exclusively on the arrangements of black bandleader Fletcher Henderson. Of the 50 million records of all types sold in 1939, an estimated 17 million—over one-third—were swing, a style one Ellington biographer says was "launched by two [black] musicians: Fletcher Henderson and Louis Armstrong."[29]

Over the airwaves, swing music quickly became familiar to listeners who might otherwise have had little exposure to black culture. It was a small step from the music itself to the dancehalls and nightclubs where it was played—and a giant leap for American culture. Swing dances drew both white and black patrons. The Savoy Ballroom had a large white following, and white swing bands often played there. The traditionally black Apollo Theater, too, welcomed white dancers, and when Charlie Barnet brought his all-white band there, they shattered previous opening-day records.[30] While white dancehalls might not have welcomed black dancers, they certainly introduced many black bands. In the South, ballrooms separated black and white dancers with a rope across the dance floor. In tobacco warehouses and cotton barns, it was common to hold a dance for white patrons on Friday night and another for black dancers on Saturdays.[31]

The end of the swing era marked the beginning of public integration in music. In 1938, when Benny Goodman and trumpeter Harry James announced their plans to perform at Carnegie Hall with several black musicians, the news swept the country. At the highly publicized January event, Basie and James played with members of the Count Basie Orchestra. In the same concert, pianist Teddy Wilson and vibraharpist Lionel Hampton joined Goodman and drummer Gene Krupa on stage. Attendance that night was 3,900, larger than that for the New York Philharmonic, and thousands more read about it afterward.

Few Americans knew that after the 1938 Carnegie Hall concert, Goodman and his musicians, along with Ellington and many others, rushed to Harlem's Savoy Ballroom to witness a very different concert: a battle between two black orchestras, those of Chick Webb and Count Basie. A year earlier, Goodman himself had battled the Chick Webb band, surrounded by Webb's loyal Savoy audience. Webb finished with a drum solo that won a "thunderous ovation while Goodman and his drummer, Gene Krupa, just stood there shaking their heads." According to police, who feared a riot, 25,000 people tried to jam the Savoy that night, stopping traffic for blocks around.[32]

This night, both bands were black, yet they represented completely different kinds of swing music—one East, one West; one "sensational swing" and one "solid swing." Webb's band featured a medium dance tempo that the Savoy dancers loved. According to one observer, it was "fast enough for the Lindy, but relaxed enough so that a couple could Lindy to it all night if they wanted to."[33] Basie's Kansas City band had a blues-based, body- and heart-grabbing beat. At Carnegie Hall, when dancers crowded the aisles, ushers urged them to return to their seats, but the Savoy was not for bystanders. Four thousand dancers packed the hall that night, and another five thousand were turned away. Although a splendid array of musical luminaries witnessed the competition, it was the dancers who at one o'clock delivered the verdict: Basie had bested Webb. Lindy Hopper Frankie Manning recalls, "I danced harder than I ever had that night. And . . . as far as I was concerned, Basie won. It's the only time anyone ever blew Chick Webb off the bandstand." [34] Unlike the Carnegie Hall concert, where the audience sat in fixed seats and observed a performance, at the Savoy the audience *was* the performance. And the music that worked for them was Basie's driving swing—a new kind of swing and the future of American popular dance music. It was the music that dancers were calling "jump blues."

Basketball and Jazz

Historians have mentioned parallels between music and baseball—the constant touring and pressures of performing—and have noted that swing bands on tour often played pickup games. But basketball and jazz were even more closely connected. In fact, promoters often combined the two for mutual support. Both basketball and dancing were indoor forms of physical entertainment relying on expert bodies and crowds of people, and linking the two made the best use of all resources, not the least of which was hardwood flooring.

By the 1930s basketball had replaced track and baseball as the second-most-popular sport on college campuses, but professional basketball teams struggled for places to play. For a brief period in the 1930s, the professional game moved to theater stages, but most teams played on a makeshift circuit of armories, high school and college gyms, and dancehalls. Ballrooms regularly booked basketball games before dances or when no dance was scheduled. As early as 1923, the *Kansas City Call* advertised a "Basket Ball–Dance" at the Labor Temple, with music after the game by Bennie Moten's orchestra. [35] Chicago's Savoy Ballroom had its own team, the Savoy Big Five, as did New York's Renaissance Casino. Eddie Gottlieb's champion Sphas (South Philadelphia Hebrew Association) dominated the American Basketball League Championship from 1933 through 1937 and often held Saturday night "Basketball and Dance" parties at their home court, the Broadwood Hotel in Philadelphia, where the Sphas' Gil Fitch sometimes changed into a tuxedo after games to lead his band for the dance. [36] A ticket—thirty-five cents for women and sixty-five cents for men—guaranteed spectators a seat on the plush upholstery of the hotel's third-floor ballroom, from which they could look forward to

a fistfight between the Sphas' Chickie Passon and one of the opponents.[37]
Pittsburgh's Iron City Elks hosted game and dance combinations at the
Pythian Temple, with music by touring bands led by nationally known musicians such as Jimmie Lunceford or locals like Gertrude Long.[38] South Brooklyn's magnificent Prospect Hall, home of the Brooklyn Visitation, was such
a rough basketball arena that visiting teams called it the "Bucket of Blood."
The Irish fans there were known to throw bottles, trip players, burn them by
throwing lighted cigarettes at them, or stick them with hatpins (particularly
when those players were black or Jewish).[39] College games also ended with
dances. The Alabama State Hornets basketball team traveled with Erskine
Hawkins's band, the 'Bama State Collegians, a favorite on campuses across
the country.

Because few exclusively black high schools and relatively few colleges
could afford gymnasiums, black youth often played basketball at community
centers. Even in integrated schools, black students were not allowed to participate in after-school activities. The journalist and poet Frank Marshall Davis,
who grew up in Arkansas City, Kansas, recalled that the city's YMCA secretary
formed a basketball team for black youth, who were allowed to practice in the
integrated high school gym only at night.[40] Pittsburgh basketball player and
coach Cumberland "Cum" Posey wrote that during his early years of playing in
Pittsburgh, black youngsters were allowed in only one gym for two hours on
two nights a week, when "every colored boy in Allegheny county who owned
a pair of rubber soled shoes" would crowd the floor. Then in 1915 a group of
basketball enthusiasts saw potential in the Labor Temple and rented it for basketball and dances.[41] By 1936 the practice of pairing basketball and dancing at
various community centers was so common that Chester C. Washington of
the *Pittsburgh Courier* pleaded with the Center Avenue YMCA to make the following New Year's resolution: "To allow dancing (supervised) in the gym after
basketball games like most other modern Y's and Community Centers do so
that the games would pay and the young folks would get clean recreation."[42]
Posey complained that even then, the few large halls available to black players
in Pittsburgh were "not really suitable to develop exceptional talent."[43] Bad
flooring and low ceilings were not the stuff from which championship teams
were made.

In the 1930s, the nation's premier black professional basketball team,
the New York Renaissance, or "Rens," traveled almost constantly, playing

their home games in the Renaissance Casino chiefly over the Thanksgiving and Christmas holidays. The high-ceilinged ballroom was transformed into a basketball court through the addition of baskets and markers for the foul lines. On one side of the court was a musicians' bandstand, and a wooden barrier surrounded the dance floor. "All the big [dance bands] played the Renaissance—Fatha Hines, Duke Ellington, Count Basie, Ella Fitzgerald, Chick Webb's band," remembered Rens star William "Pop" Gates. "It wasn't a big floor. It was far from being a regular basketball floor."[44] Spectators sat at tables arranged in three tiers around the court, measuring sixty by thirty-five feet, and Gates recalled players "flying over that barrier into people's laps" while playing on the "very slippery floor."[45]

As the literary explosion of the Harlem Renaissance expanded outward into other forms of cultural expression, the Rens belonged to the pantheon of African American public achievers, with celebrity status equivalent to the bandleaders and musicians of the day. Black bandleaders, some of whom bore noble titles—"Duke" Ellington, "Count" Basie, "the Pres" (Lester Young)—stood for success and dignity in a world that tried to deny them both. Ralph Ellison looked up to such men in his youth and later wrote:

> They were news from the great wide world, an example and a goal; and I wish that all those who write so knowledgeably of Negro boys having no masculine figures with whom to identify would consider the long national and international career of Ellington and his band, the thousands of one-night stands played in the black communities of this nation. Where in the white community, in *any* white community, could there have been found images, examples such as these? Who were so worldly, who so elegant, who so mockingly creative? Who so skilled at their given trade and who treated the social limitations placed in their paths with greater disdain?[46]

Musicians and athletes associated with each other on and off the court. Trumpeter Rex Stewart of Duke Ellington's orchestra and his fellow musicians Ben Webster and Sid Catlett often worked out with the Rens at the Casino in the afternoons and once formed a musicians' team to play against the Rens for a benefit game.[47] Bandleader Cab Calloway was another basketball fan, and for a while the Cab Calloway Jitter-Bugs, a team composed entirely of Calloway band members, played local basketball teams when the Calloway Cotton Club Orchestra was touring. One newspaper article declared that

Calloway himself was one of "Harlem's speediest basketball hurlers." [48] Once, in 1936, the Calloway team, augmented by a group of dancers called Whitey's Lindy Hoppers, challenged and defeated a Jimmie Lunceford–led team in a charity fundraiser refereed by Jesse Owens. Spotted in the crowd of what one writer called "the largest collection of celebrities seen around these parts for a good while" were dancer Bill "Bojangles" Robinson, Rens owner Bob Douglas, and Rens star Eyrie Saitch. According to reports, Calloway dominated the game, using his patented stage yell to terrify the opposition into dropping the ball, which he then grabbed and "hi-de-hoed" down the court to the basket. [49] Bands of Count Basie, Tiny Bradshaw, and Willie Bryant all had teams that played on occasion, usually for charitable causes. [50]

The high-profile Rens and Harlem Globetrotters represented success in one of the few areas of American life where competition between the races was permitted. The Renaissance Big Five won their first game on November 3, 1923, against the Collegiate Big Five with a score of 28–22. At first they faced stiff competition at home from fellow Harlemites Commonwealth Big Five and on the road from Cumberland Posey's Loendi team in Pittsburgh. But soon these teams disbanded, leaving the all-black crown—and some of their best players—to the Renaissance. In 1926 Ape Saperstein organized the Harlem Globetrotters—originally Chicago's Savoy Big Five but then renamed by their owner so it would be clear that they were a black team. Between them the Globetrotters and the Rens commanded the sixteen best African American players in the country. In a bus called the "Old Blue Goose" the Rens traveled hundreds of thousands of miles, winning hundreds of games and losing few. [51] Between 1923 and 1949, when they quit playing, the Rens compiled a 2,318–381 record. Although no longer a competitive team, the Globetrotters continue to this day.

The American Basketball League refused to admit the Rens to membership in 1926, but when it suspended its operation in 1931, the Rens began their rise to success. They defeated the Original Celtics in 1932 and 1933 in what was billed as a championship series, and their 1932–33 record of eighty-eight consecutive wins (in eighty-six days) doubled the Celtics' record of forty-four. In 1939 the organizers of basketball's World Tournament invited both the Harlem Globetrotters and the Rens for the first time, and the Rens went on to win the championship, defeating the Oshkosh All-Stars in the final game. When the Rens finished that year with 112 wins in 119 games, the *New York*

Evening Telegram declared: "They are the champions of professional basketball in the whole world. It is time we dropped the 'colored' champions title."[52] Yet the *Pittsburgh Courier*'s Wendell Smith noted that in pre-tournament play, the Harlem Globetrotters had lost only three of their season's 136 games. "If they hadn't been paired in the same bracket with the flawless Rens," Smith fumed, "we might have two sepia teams playing for the title. . . . But, of course, they just couldn't let that happen, could they?"[53] According to the *Courier*, that year the Rens outdrew their white rivals, the Celtics, five to one, in money and in crowds.[54]

For all their popularity, as New York Rens' Eyre Saitch remembers, combining basketball and dancing was a shrewd marketing move: "We had to have a dance afterwards, or else nobody would come to the damn thing." And it worked. "If you didn't get there by seven o'clock, you didn't get in the damn door. The big game didn't start until 10 o'clock."[55] The Rens drew large crowds, usually two thousand or more. John J. O'Brien Jr., who played at the Casino with the Brooklyn Visitations, recalled: "The fans were the wealthiest black people in Harlem, dressed, believe it or not, in tuxedos. A good-looking crowd—handsome women, good-looking guys—and they loved the basketball game, but they loved to get the game over for dancing afterward."[56]

In Harlem's Renaissance Casino, Commonwealth Casino, Manhattan Casino, and many other clubs across the country, basketball players were among those dancing after games, raising the question: Who inspired whom to jump? Whether the cultural exchange flowed from musicians to dancers to basketball players, or from basketball players to dancers to musicians, all were connected to one another. College coach Clarence "Big House" Gaines said of his players in the 1940s: "Those kids were all excellent dancers. To be a good basketball player you have to have an excellent sense of rhythm and good feet. The ones with slow feet were the first you cut."[57] And Lindy dancer Frankie Manning found that playing basketball helped on the ballroom floor: "I think being an athlete helped me with dancing, particularly once we started doing air steps . . . because of the timing and the ability to anticipate or react to what was coming next."[58] In fact, "the connection is not far-fetched at all," says Albert Murray, who remembers attending dances after Tuskegee and Alabama State basketball games, as well as basketball games at clubs in Harlem.[59] In games and dances, the jump emerged as the brightest point of the social constellations Murray eloquently christened "ceremonies of affirmation."[60]

Reasons to Hope

Although the Savoy Ballroom, "home of happy feet," was the premier dancehall in the nation, cities and towns across the country held dances in "auditoriums, stadiums, armories, skating rinks, warehouses, barns, roadhouses, and open fields."[61] Into the 1940s, swing bands and then jump bands toured the country, bringing not just their sound but also themselves as examples of worldliness. Lionel Hampton recalled, "Earl Hines [another popular swing and jump bandleader] is right when he says the people in the bands were the 'first freedom riders.'"[62] As they toured throughout the South, swing bands offered what one historian has called "an urban model of freedom."[63] Exemplifying both economic and geographic mobility, big bands such as Ellington's fused African American musical traditions with modern sensibilities, structure with improvisation. Basketball, jazz, and dance were not solely urban phenomena, for new transportation and communication networks connected African Americans nationwide.

One such network was the International Brotherhood of Sleeping Car Porters. This all-black labor union provided one of the three major public victories that raised the hopes of African Americans from 1936 to 1938. By the 1920s, over twenty thousand African Americans were working as porters on railroads, making this the largest category of black labor in the United States and Canada and an important continental network. The descendants of men and women who had been transported across oceans against their will were now paid to traverse the country. As they did, they ferried music, customs, and news from city to country and back again. Operating as a reverse Underground Railroad, northern porters smuggled African American newspapers to local ministers in the South, delivering them to parishioners who otherwise would have been isolated from national events of import to black people.[64]

A. Philip Randolph helped to organize the Brotherhood to try to correct some of the injustices this group suffered. Among the worst was the workload itself: four hundred hours per month or eleven thousand miles, whichever came first. On August 25, 1937, after twelve years of bargaining and a long strike, the Pullman Company recognized the IBSCP as the official union of the porters and signed a contract with them that reduced working hours, increased wages, and gave them job security and union representation. The IBSCP became the first African American union to win a collective bargaining agreement, a highly publicized victory that resonated throughout African America.

Even before the Pullman contract raised hopes for African Americans across the country, the astounding accomplishments of black athletes at the 1936 Olympics made world news. The United States team included seventeen male and two female African Americans—ten of the men in track and field. By the end of the games, all but one of the male track and field athletes had stood on the podium. Nine men brought home a total of thirteen medals—one bronze and twelve gold and silver. Jesse Owens won an unprecedented four gold medals to become the most decorated Olympic athlete in history. And although Adolf Hitler had invited one Finnish and two German gold medalists to his box, when African American Cornelius Johnson won the high jump event, Hitler left the stadium before the playing of the American national anthem. At Berlin in 1936, with the eyes of the world upon them, nine African Americans blew Hitler's theory of white supremacy sky high. Half of the U.S. team's total score—83 of 167 points—had been earned by black athletes in track and field events. It was a national victory, but African Americans considered it a racial triumph.

Prizefighter Joe Louis also offered African Americans a new idea of what might be possible for black people in the United States. The theory of racial uplift held that equality could best be achieved through individual effort, through the example and model of outstanding individuals such as Louis. This strategy was one of accommodation, of fitting into the dominant society. By contrast, the emerging civil rights movement, led by such men as Adam Clayton Powell Jr. and A. Phillip Randolph, challenged society through an activist, interventionist strategy. Louis's victories in the 1930s merged the two approaches and made him one of the first of a new kind of race leader. Through his status as a media star, Louis presented an intriguing transition between the two opposing strategies for social equality. Photos and stories of Louis emphasized his modesty, work ethic, and determination to overcome whatever obstacles life placed in his way. But Louis became a champion by doing the impossible: nowhere else but in the boxing ring could a black man beat up a white man with impunity, much less be celebrated for it. After Louis's 1935 victory over Max Baer, Richard Wright wrote "Joe Louis Uncovers Dynamite," an essay still important today, in which Wright declared, "Joe was the consecrated essence of black triumph over white." [65]

Successful athletes are by definition winners, idealists who believe in the possibility of being the best and who strive for superiority over all others. Winning athletes reject the status quo; their quest is to break records. The real and symbolic meaning of the athletic victories of the 1930s was lost on no one: Negroes had triumphed in a world in which they otherwise had little power. Joe Louis and the African American Olympians were hard workers driven to succeed: in that sense, they were accommodationists. But these athletes rejected their place in a white-dominated society. With heroic determination, they fought and ran and jumped to places of distinction, bringing home victories of global significance.

Many African Americans who lived through the 1930s still see those victories as pivotal. Roy Wilkins, assistant secretary of the National Association for the Advancement of Colored People (NAACP) in the 1930s, said that what he remembered most about that "radical" decade were the three events that "produced faith that black people were making their way forward to equality": Jesse Owens's performance during the 1936 Olympics, Joe Louis's 1938 defeat of Max Schmeling, and "the day the Pullman Company, after a contract wrangle that had lasted more than a decade, summoned in A. Philip Randolph and the leaders of the Brotherhood of Sleeping Car Porters and said, 'Gentlemen, the Pullman Company is ready to sign.'"[66] Victories such as Owens's, Louis's, and the porters' went beyond the mere success of the moment: they marked instances of cultural equality. Black Americans saw them as such and wanted more.

Added to the hope elicited by these events was the perception that the Roosevelt administration and the Second New Deal represented the best chance yet for a better life for African Americans. During the depths of the Great Depression, when estimates of unemployment among non–farm workers ran as high as 33 percent, perhaps 50 percent of urban African Americans were without work.[67] A conference at Howard University in 1935 produced evidence that the depression and New Deal recovery policies had forced black Americans into even lower economic and social positions.[68] As Lawrence Levine writes, "For many black Americans the Depression merely intensified an unjust economic situation that had long been prevalent."[69] Or, as Roy Wilkins wrote, "It wasn't as if F.D.R. and his brain trust had worked out a program for uplifting the country's Negroes from generations of neglect and centuries of servitude."[70] Nevertheless, writing shortly after the fact, historian John Hope

Franklin noted: "President Roosevelt was not long in office before he gained a large following among Negroes. . . . [H]is fireside chats gave many a sense of belonging they had never experienced before. Negroes early regarded the relief and recovery programs which he advocated as especially beneficial to them."[71]

If African Americans benefited disproportionately less from New Deal programs than did whites, the New Deal still marked a new stage in government interest in their fortunes, thanks largely to Eleanor Roosevelt.[72] It was she who made the president aware that checks from the Agricultural Adjustment Act often went directly to white landholders rather than to the black tenant farmers and sharecroppers who needed them. The National Recovery Act sanctioned differential pay scales for black and white workers, and the Works Progress Administration (WPA) set no minimum wage for Negroes, who were paid as little as ten cents an hour for twelve-hour days. The Social Security Act contained no provisions for farmers, domestics, casual labor, or Negro workers. But with Roosevelt's 1935 executive order banning discrimination in such projects, by decade's end 300,000 black youth were involved in National Youth Administration (NYA) training programs, a quarter-million served in the Civilian Conservation Corps, and the WPA was providing earnings for 1 million black families.[73]

If Franklin Roosevelt was silent during the sentencing of the Scottsboro Boys, and if he did nothing to aid the campaign for an anti-lynching bill, at least Eleanor Roosevelt resigned from the Daughters of the American Revolution when they refused to allow Marian Anderson to sing in their auditorium. And it was Eleanor Roosevelt who placed her chair squarely in the aisle between black and white patrons in a segregated Birmingham, Alabama, auditorium.[74] She invited hundreds of African Americans to the White House and worked for many black causes across the country. According to historian Doris Kearns Goodwin, the first lady represented the idealism and humanitarian beliefs that the president could not publicly embrace in the face of a southern-dominated Congress.[75] Even W. E. B. Du Bois, who had withheld support from Roosevelt in 1932, worked for the president in the three subsequent elections, along with millions of other blacks. As Roosevelt turned to socialist measures to right the wrongs of capitalism, as he engaged African Americans at high levels in the administration of federal programs, and as Eleanor Roosevelt continued to champion the cause of minorities, African

Americans saw in the Roosevelts their greatest hope yet for improved social and economic conditions. In the 1936 presidential election, according to one black newspaper, "the Negro vote stood like a stone wall against [Republican Alfred] Landon in every one of the pivotal states, including Massachusetts, New York, Pennsylvania, New Jersey, West Virginia, Ohio, Michigan, Indiana, Illinois, Missouri and Kentucky."[76] More than one hundred African Americans served the administration in advisory or public relations positions during the 1930s, and while few policy or legislative changes resulted from their presence, the visibility of such black leaders heightened a sense of progress for the race.[77]

As international events drew the United States out of its isolation, African America's cultural victories increasingly took place on a global stage. The artistic and intellectual flowering of the Harlem Renaissance became part of a wider, more influential set of cultural performances. Jesse Owens and his teammates became international heroes, and suddenly, people who lacked civic standing in their own country became, for the rest of the world, the face of that country. Joe Louis's defeat of Max Schmeling was an American victory. African American innovations in dress, language, music, and dance seemed to capture the freshness and energy of the American spirit. For Europeans, who adored jazz and American dance, these new art forms and different ways of moving and speaking were what distinguished American culture from their own. African Americans, still systematically excluded from much of American life, looked through the lens with which the rest of the world saw the United States, and for the first time they saw their own faces looking back. With increasing velocity, their culture was defining American culture.

CHAPTER 2 : UP, UP, AND AWAY

In a 1937 article titled "What Is This Thing Called Swing?" Billy Rowe, writing for the *Pittsburgh Courier*, declared, "Swing is the blues on roller skates, the old fox trot in the heat lap of a marathon; it's dance time TNT."[1] The upbeat tempo of swing music and jump blues reflected and embodied the newer, faster tempo of urban, mechanized twentieth-century American life. Now, in the 1930s, music and dance made the superpowers of speed and defiance of gravity available to everyone. The music critic Stanley Dance compared a swing band to "an airplane taking off after roaring down a runway."[2] And jump dancers who took the horizontal sweep of swing dance to vertical tosses and leaps almost felt as if they could fly.

Trains, planes, and automobiles were elements of a nearly unfathomable change in the pace and spaces of American life. They made it possible to live differently, in different places, to get there in a different, noisier way and at a new and different speed. As such technologies became more and more a part of daily life, they occupied simultaneously more cultural space and vocabulary, because Americans needed to experience the new modes of transportation and technology in as many forms as possible just to take in what was happening in their rapidly accelerating universe. In *Swinging the Machine*, Joel Dinerstein suggests that a culture assimilates mechanical and technological changes by absorbing them physically—by putting the sounds of machines into our music, for instance, or by mimicking the movement of machines in our social dances and stage productions.[3] People literally "incorporate" change: we make it part of our bodies, our corporeality. Dinerstein makes a powerful argument for the importance of African American music and dance in helping Americans comprehend the ever-accelerating tempo of modern life.

Rail travel accelerated the pace of modern life: the railways of the late nineteenth century moved so fast that travelers spoke of "flying." But airplanes redefined high-speed travel and gave it a new dimension—upward. The history of flight is astonishingly short, and because of the rapid curve from inception to development, and also because traveling through the air was unprecedented, air travel was even more challenging to the American psyche than the train had been. American aviation began just at the turn of the twentieth century through the ingenuity of Orville and Wilbur Wright, from Dayton, Ohio. Their first experimental aircraft, launched in the summer of 1899, was a kite with a five-foot wingspan. One year and $15 worth of materials later, the Wrights had finished building their first piloted plane, a biplane with a seventeen-foot wingspan, tethered with ropes to two men on the ground. The longest glides of that first season were about one hundred yards, and those depended on a lot of help from the ground crew, who ran alongside the plane and lifted the wings when they tipped. Within a year the glider had grown to a twenty-two-foot wingspan, but the results were so dismal that Wilbur Wright predicted flight would not occur within his lifetime. Even so, Orville accepted an invitation to present his findings to the Western Society of Engineers in 1901. His modest paper, "Some Aeronautical Experiments," was widely reprinted and hailed as the new standard of design for aircraft.

Field tests, which in those days invariably resulted in a crash, were tough on pilots and planes. So the Wright brothers built a wind tunnel in their bicycle shop, and throughout the next year, with the aid of hacksaw blades and bicycle spokes, metal shears and sheets of tin, they tested various designs and gathered data for lift and drag equations. By 1903 the Wrights had dramatically increased the wing area to 510 square feet, with a wingspan of a little more than forty feet, and had added a four-cylinder, twelve-horsepower engine and a propeller. The pilot lay prone on the lower wing and steered the airplane by shifting his hips from one side to the other. The brothers tested this plane—a biplane built of spruce, ash, and unbleached muslin—in four flights on December 17, 1903, at Kill Devil Hills, about four miles from Kitty Hawk, North Carolina. The famous first flight lasted twelve seconds and traveled 120 feet. On his final flight that day Wilbur managed a distance of 852 feet while staying aloft for fifty-nine seconds. In the space of four years, two bicycle mechanics had progressed from soaring on a five-foot kite to powered flight.

Enthusiasts tested other designs based on what they had learned of the Wright brothers' experiments, while the Wrights worked on patenting theirs. Inventor Alexander Graham Bell formed the Aerial Experiment Association, and several French designs were also under development. But by 1905 the Wrights had flown as far as twenty-four miles at a stretch. No one else came close to this feat. By 1908 the two inventor-businessmen had patented their design in the United States and in several European countries, and they had contracts with the U.S. government and with a group of French investors. They began an extensive tour of Europe, demonstrating the Wright Model A and meeting with royalty and heads of state. When they returned to the United States in 1909, Wilbur made a thirty-minute flight up the Hudson River and back, a feat that 1 million New Yorkers witnessed.

A decade after the Wrights launched their first big kite, aircraft demonstrations, races, and competitions were attracting spectators by the thousands across the United States and Europe. World War I fostered the growth of the new industry, and by 1919, profits from aviation topped $14 million.[4] Images of aircraft adorned clothing, household items, postcards, even jewelry boxes. The ceiling murals in the lobby of the Chrysler Building in New York included airplanes. Artists, authors, and songwriters tried to capture the thrill of powered flight in various media. The West Indian–born aviator Hubert Julian made a name for himself as the "Black Eagle of Harlem" with a failed parachute jump in 1923 in which he narrowly escaped electrocution. Julian had hoped to be the first to fly from North America to Africa, but the trip never materialized.[5] He was perhaps the first African American to obtain a pilot's license, but soon there were others. Pilot Simon Berry flew a charter service for wealthy oilmen in Tulsa during the 1920s, only one of many commercial aviation operations in the country's new transportation field.[6]

Then, a mere twenty-four years after the first successful powered flight—a flight that lasted just a few seconds—a twenty-five-year-old airmail pilot named Charles Lindbergh flew an airplane across the Atlantic in a journey of 3,610 miles. Three teams had already crashed trying to make this flight (the two pilots in the last team had both been killed), and one team from France had disappeared altogether just two weeks previously. Two more teams were ready to take off, but one was mired in legal disputes and the other was still making repairs. Lindbergh was the only pilot to attempt to make this flight alone, hoping not only to avoid the complications of team flying but also to limit the weight of everything but fuel. Even so, Lindbergh's custom-built plane—not much more than a 2,700 pound gas tank with wings forty-six feet long and a Wright Whirlwind J-5C engine—had been so heavy with fuel when it took off from a dirt field on Long Island that it barely cleared the telephone wires at the end of the runway. Although he cruised over Nova Scotia at an altitude of ten thousand feet in icy clouds, the fog over the Atlantic Ocean was so bad that Lindbergh sometimes had to fly only ten feet above the waves, where the spray from the whitecaps helped to keep him awake. Along the way he fought numbness, hallucinations, and magnetic storms that made his instruments go haywire. Nearing the European coastline, Lindbergh was flying so close to the water that when he spotted a fishing crew, he circled several times and called out, "Which way is Ireland?" But he got no reply.

By the time he reached Paris, Lindbergh had been airborne for thirty-three and a half hours. So many headlights from automobiles circled the landing field at Le Bourget that he did not recognize it as an airfield. When he finally landed, at 10:24 P.M. Paris time, 150,000 people were standing everywhere, on top of cars, on the roofs of airport buildings, and behind a police-guarded fence that fell before them as they rushed to greet Lindbergh along with the police themselves. Someone quickly pulled off Lindbergh's helmet and placed it on the head of a hapless American reporter next to him. While the crowd joyously carried the reporter away on their shoulders, Lindbergh ran toward a waiting Renault and fled to the shelter of a nearby hangar.[7]

Lindbergh's flight connected the continents. Europe was now a hop away, and although the Wright brothers had made that flight possible, Charles Lindbergh became the first American superhero. On the day he landed in Paris, Wright Aeronautical stock closed up 5¾ points. All the boats in New York harbor blasted their horns, while Broadway matinees halted to announce the landing; people shredded telephone books and threw the confetti out the windows as pandemonium broke loose across the country. Radio stations played "The Marseillaise," and that evening orchestras opened their concerts with "The Star-Spangled Banner." Theater audiences in Berlin applauded the flight, as did those in Buenos Aires. Newspapers from Bombay to Rome editorialized on Lindberg's "marvelous feat." In London, the Sunday Express declared: "Lindbergh is no ordinary man. . . . It is difficult to imagine anything more desperately heroic than his solitary flight across the ocean."[8] France awarded Lindbergh the Cross of the Legion of Honor—the first ever accorded an American. His victory tour introduced him to European kings and ultimately to President Calvin Coolidge. More than 250,000 people waited for his arrival at Potomac Park in Washington, D.C. Four million people stood along the parade route in New York onto which two thousand tons of paper rained, a snowstorm through which few could see their hero. The United States Post

Office issued a ten-cent airmail stamp in his honor, the first U.S. stamp ever issued in honor of a living man.[9]

The outpouring of enthusiasm for Lindbergh's accomplishment manifested itself in every imaginable way, including at least two hundred songs, waltzes, fox trots, marches, and mazurkas with titles from "Lucky Lindy" and "The Lone Eagle" to "Lindy, the Bird of the Clouds," "America's Son," "Eagle of Liberty," and "That Airplane Man." After receiving more than two thousand unsolicited poems, the *New York Times* declared a moratorium on Lindbergh poetry. But months would pass before most Americans could pick up their hometown paper and not read couplets of "boy," "joy," "youth," and "truth." [10] The most popular dance of the next two decades took its name from his flight.

Why such excitement? Lindbergh democratized the air. He was every man, every woman, every youth in flight. Even more than the Wright brothers or the barnstormers of the 1910s and 1920s, Lindbergh dramatized and publicized the miracle of flight, the new possibilities of speed and altitude. Air travel began to seem a real possibility, and an ocean whose breadth had been measured in weeks could now be crossed in hours. For twentieth-century Americans, pilots such as Charles Lindbergh humanized the still unbelievable new flying machines. It wasn't just that planes were taking to the air: people were flying. And the thought of people being able to fly was still just short of miraculous.

Tall Buildings

While Lindbergh raced to be the first to cross the Atlantic in an airplane, another race to the heavens was taking place in two of America's largest cities, Chicago and New York. This race was all about height—a race to construct the tallest building in the world. Where once there were only clouds, now there were not just airplanes but skyscrapers.[11]

Clearly there are practical reasons for skyscrapers. But the impulse toward height, even in building, is not solely practical. Modern skyscrapers are part of a long human tradition of erecting tall buildings. From the Tower of Babel to those of San Gimignano and Pisa, towers signify the audacity and power of human beings. Mayan temples, Chinese pagodas, and the tiered sandstone spires of the Khmer Empire of Southeast Asia all expressed a human need to connect with the divine, to emulate the divine, and even to compete with the divine. The highest point affords the greatest view, and the greatest view is the most powerful one. Sometimes simply the suggestion of height confers power. In colonial America, rebels defied British soldiers and raised tall liberty poles in town squares. In 1850 the highest building in New York was Trinity Church; for a shilling, sightseers could get a view of the city from 284 feet. In Washington, in 1884, an obelisk honoring a president achieved the impressive height of 555 feet.

Until the mid-nineteenth century, the country's tallest buildings were dedicated to religious or political institutions. But as innovations in transportation, communication, and energy fueled migration to the cities and growth in new industries, cultural authority shifted from religious and political institutions to those of commerce. By the end of the nineteenth century, businessmen competed for the honor of constructing the tallest buildings in their fields, monuments to the gods of industry. Visiting New York in 1935, the French architect Le Corbusier looked up at the skyscrapers and noted, "The great masters of economic destiny are up there, like eagles, in the silence of their eminences." [12]

To be the best, one must rise to the top. But without elevators to take people up, skyscrapers would never have been practical. The first passenger elevator—"the great emancipator of all horizontal surfaces"—was installed in 1857 in the Haughwout Department Store in New York City, a steam-driven car that climbed the five-story building in less than a minute. [13] Designed by Elisha H. Otis, this was the first elevator to include an automatic safety device. [14] The first electric passenger elevator appeared in the Demarest Building in New York City in 1889, the first push-button controls in 1904, and by the opening of the Empire State Building in 1931, elevators were climbing at the rate of 1,200 feet per minute—more than ten times the rate of the first Otis. Elevators added to skyscrapers the element of speed. Le Corbusier marveled at express elevators that could travel sixty-five stories in forty-five seconds. Elevators in France could climb only six floors in the same amount of time. [15]

Tall buildings must not only go up, they must also stay up: William Le Baron Jenney's ten-story Home Insurance Building in Chicago, begun in 1883, was the first to use the steel-girder construction method, and the wedding of the elevator to the steel frame was the starter's gun that set off one of the most costly races in the history of humanity. Midwestern communications czar Joseph Pulitzer's goal was to conquer the East, which he did first by buying and increasing the circulation of the *World* newspaper and then by deciding to build the tallest skyscraper in the world. In 1889 he selected a site adjacent to his rival, the *Tribune*—at the time called "the Tall Tower"—and erected a structure of graduated colors of red sandstone, brick and terra cotta, rising to a golden dome compared at the time to Nebuchadnezzar's palace. Pulitzer's 309-foot World Building was now the tallest. Pulitzer stressed that there was no mortgage on this building, which he had funded from his own pocket. He placed his offices near the top of the building, emphasizing his position at the top of the hierarchy of rising floors and colors. F. W. Woolworth's dream was to build something higher than New York City's Metropolitan Tower because Metropolitan Life had once denied him a loan. It didn't make financial sense, but Woolworth didn't care. When the Woolworth Building was complete in 1913, it reached 792 feet. By the end of the 1920s, there were nearly four hundred buildings taller than twenty stories in cities all across the country. For the American writer Henry James, skyscrapers were like "youth on the run and with the prize of the race in sight."[16] A 1929 *New York Times* editorial declared, "No dream is too steep for America."[17]

Architects and owners vied with one another to soar skyward. Over two thousand daily newspapers and the brand-new NBC and CBS radio networks kept Americans across the country up to date on each new development. Bitterness between two former partners, architects William Van Alen and Craig Severance, fueled the race between the Chrysler Building and the Bank of Manhattan Building. The Chrysler Building was advertised at 925 feet, which the Bank of Manhattan, finishing first, beat by two feet. But then Van Alen added the "vertex," and the Chrysler Building topped out at 1,046 feet, making it higher than Severance's Bank of Manhattan, taller than the thousand-foot Eiffel Tower, and the tallest building in the world. But only temporarily.

By the time tenants began to move into the Chrysler tower in May 1930, a new building had begun advertising itself as the world's tallest. It was to be called the Empire State. Rising at the rate of four and one-half stories a week, the Empire State Building eventually reached 1,248 feet. Two hundred engraved invitations went out for its opening on May 1, 1931, and no one declined save Walter Chrysler. President Herbert Hoover excused himself from a cabinet meeting to press a golden telegraph key and officially light the building. At the celebratory luncheon, former governor Al Smith declared: "There may have been loftier meals on mountain tops or in airplanes but not in buildings. This is the world's record."[18] He then returned a telegram to Hoover from the "highest telegraph station in the world."[19] During the Empire State's first month of operation, 84,000 visitors paid a dollar each to mount the eighth wonder of the world.

In the Roaring Twenties, when land values soared to as much as $400 per square foot, tall buildings offered the greatest return on investment—a way to reduce land costs by increasing rentable floor areas. The maximum rate of return on skyscrapers was called their "economic height." Beyond a certain point, the elevators, steel, foundation, and utility amendments began to eat into rental income, and then the driving force was not economic height but the powerful fuel of pride. The economic climate of the 1930s changed the equation; so much floor space went unrented that the last of the giants to leap to the sky, the Empire State Building, came to be called the "Empty State Building." It was not until 1970 that the World Trade Center towers became the first to top the Empire State, but then they, too, were bested four years later by the Sears Tower in the midwestern city of Chicago.

Le Corbusier's trip to the United States, which he recorded in his book *When the Cathedrals Were White*, took place after the big skyscraper boom. The race had ended, but Le Corbusier saw its results all around him, and in his opinion, the buildings themselves were the victors. "Sky scrapers were not constructed with a wise and serious intention," he wrote. "They were applauded acrobatic feats. The skyscrapers as proclamation won."[20]

The Vertical City

Tall buildings seem to spring from densely populated areas, but seldom does scarcity of land dictate vertical growth. Quite the contrary. One often finds the tallest buildings in the center of cities with the largest urban sprawl. The modern steel-framed building originated on the Great Plains of the Midwest, in Chicago, where space was hardly the issue. Unlimited space was, in fact, the point of Chicago. In his essay "The Myth of Natural Growth," Thomas van Leeuwen concludes that rather than taking advantage of such space, skyscrapers seemed instead to demonstrate "the workings of the law of a scarcity that did not exist." While they may symbolize and physically suggest upward mobility, skyscrapers ignore horizontal mobility. The "culture of congestion" denies two historically American urges: the pioneers' claiming of space—or homesteading—and the restless urge to move on toward better horizons. Horizontal mobility is sacrificed for the physical expression of economic power in an urban equation of height with might. It is almost as if verticality and slenderness compensate for horizontal spread and volume. As one architect explained, "When the aspiring spirit has been diverted from its upward course by an obstacle it will seek immediately and indeed throughout the conflict to assert its upward tendency." [21]

By the 1930s, height alone wasn't enough. The "true skyscraper" is one in which lines "sweep unbrokenly upward," emphasizing the vertical. [22] Verticality communicated energy, if not divinity. the architect Eliel Saarinen wrote in 1923, "The vertical emphasis is more logical and purposeful for an architecture which, like the Gothic, reaches up to the heights." [23] Architect John Mead Howells applied Saarinen's theory of verticality to his 1927–29 Panhellenic Tower, only twenty-eight stories tall but a magnificent structure in which vertical spires shoot upward in brick piers or columns created by deeply recessed windows. Raymond Hood's landmark RCA Tower, built between 1931 and 1934, echoes the Panhellenic in its upward-shooting exterior. Architect and mystic Claude Bragdon, who wrote the foreword to Louis Sullivan's *Autobiography of an Idea* (1924) and edited *Kindergarten Chats* (1901), called the skyscraper a "frozen fountain," by which he meant that it was a form of underground energy erupting into the air like a geyser and caught by the architect. Art Deco skyscrapers reflected the ideal of a frozen fountain in friezes, in sculpted facades, and in actual fountains at their base or in interior rooms.

The tall building didn't just stand tall, it stood for the best strivings of humanity, the upward thrust of the human spirit. John Ruskin had encouraged giving form to a primal urge in his first lecture on architecture in 1853: "Go to now. Let us build a tower whose top may reach unto heaven." [24] Skyscrapers embodied the ambitious spirits of architect, patron, and culture. But Sullivan first stated the idea of the skyscraper as an active and inspirational force in the city: "The force and power of altitude must be in it, the glory and pride of exaltation must be in it. It must be every inch a proud and soaring thing, rising in sheer exultation." [25] The skyscraper should embody "loftiness" and should be action itself—the act of soaring, of flying, of elevation at every level of being. The skyscraper was the very essence of arrested upward motion, and the race to the skies captured in stone the American preoccupation with height and upward movement. Le Corbusier declared, "New York is a vertical city . . . a city animated by the new spirit." [26]

More often than not, skyscrapers have been built in times of economic depression: 1875, 1929, 1982. In such times they signal that neither economic nor natural forces, such as gravity, can tether the human spirit. Skyscrapers rise above the temporal and material, transcending present concerns and, given their usually hefty mortgages, demonstrating enormous faith and confidence in the future. Yet in the face of overwhelming evidence to the contrary, such faith can falter.

In 1935 Le Corbusier saw the skyscrapers of New York as evidence of a superhuman effort. "It is the first time that men have projected all their strength and labor into the sky," he wrote. [27] These buildings symbolized the same qualities we attribute to Lindbergh's flight—and to the jump: power, vitality, loftiness, confidence in the future, self-expression, pushing the limits. But there were limits all the same. A race that began with William Le Baron Jenney's Home Insurance Building in 1883 ended with a thud as the Empire State Building was opened in 1931.

Dinerstein suggests that the early 1930s marked the first technological plateau in American history, a time when "social doubt" about mechanization and technological progress outran cultural faith in the same. [28] Parallels to later decades and plateaus abound. The late 1960s saw excitement over the space program replaced with demands for social and economic reform; the 1986 *Challenger* space shuttle explosion coincided with an economic downturn, as did the shuttle *Columbia* disaster of 2003. The total destruction in 2001 of the World Trade Center's twin towers marked an even lower point in the fortunes of the country and a sharp break with the optimism of the 1990s. In each of these plateaus, cultural belief in the technology of the age dimmed as that technology appeared vulnerable, flawed, and threatening to jobs and lives.

If technology had been the reason for the high spirits and economic boom times of the 1990s, in 2001 technology was blamed for the greatest of all threats to American lives: weapons of mass destruction. As it turned out, an administration that justified going to war on the basis of technological terror had to change that justification to one of human terror. Ambivalence toward technology continued: some legislators opposed stem cell research but supported technological and medical intervention to maintain the life of Terry Schiavo, a woman in a persistent vegetative state. Americans conducted more and more of the business of daily life through the Internet but worried about privacy and identity theft. Nuclear proliferation returned, and global warming, causing the North Pole to melt and the South Pole to expand, threatened to climinate species at an alarming rate. Scientists around the world can identify and isolate a new flu strain but can do little to contain the impending pandemic.

From the miraculous to the monstrous—from the Wright brothers' first powered flight to the airborne destruction of the World Trade Center—the passage took less than a century. During that time Americans flew farther and faster and built their buildings taller than ever before. But flight is no longer the miracle it once was: for most airline passengers, it has become a dreaded ordeal. The much-lampooned 1960s slogan of the Starship Enterprise, "To boldly go where no man has gone before," morphed into the preposterous claim of Toy Story's space hero, Buzz Lightyear: "To infinity and beyond!" But when Buzz Lightyear bragged about his ability to fly beyond all horizons, his rival Woody pointed out that Lightyear could fly only when dropped. One wonders whether Woody was addressing larger cultural concerns when he said, "That's not flying—that's falling, with style."

The Power of the Body

The technological plateau of the 1930s coincided with a new fascination with the power of the human body to accomplish superhuman feats. In June 1938 an imaginary hero appeared, a man whose superhuman powers might meet the challenge of a changing environment—a Superman.[29] But unlike Charles Lindbergh, this Superman did not "fly like a bird."[30] Instead, he jumped.

Creators Jerome Siegel and Joe Shuster presented Superman as an ordinary businessman, wearing a suit. On the first page of his Action Comics debut, there was Superman, in his business suit, jumping over skyscrapers. The caption said he could "leap ⅛ mile; hurdle a twenty-story building."[31] If necessary, Superman could also handle skyscrapers under construction: in a second panel, still in his business suit, Superman stands in front of a skyscraper, holding a steel beam over his head with one hand, showing that he can "raise tremendous weights." According to a third panel, Superman could "run faster than an express train," and "nothing less than a bursting shell could penetrate his skin."[32] In this first comic book episode—which Siegel and Shuster cut and pasted together from four years of rejected, unpublished comic strips—Superman jumped through town and city, over buildings and across the chasms between them, saving women in distress and defeating criminals and corrupt government officials. Whether jumping over buildings, lifting steel girders, or speeding through the city by leaping an eighth of a mile at a time, Superman captured in literal form the powers that technological advances had figuratively given to human beings. As Charles Lindbergh spanned the Atlantic in one flight, Superman spanned the channels cut through the urban landscape, showing fans that it was still possible to be master of an environment that otherwise seemed nearly overwhelming.

Siegel and Shuster had been drawing Superman since 1933, but they were unable to sell the comic strip until Action Comics bought it in 1938. Superman was fast and he could move. He knew how to get around. To beat the bad guys, he had to work his way through what amounted to an urban jungle. And he could leap. No tall building could stand in his way as long as he could jump. Not until 1943 did Superman learn to fly.

In the mid-twentieth century Superman seemed to offer hope that human beings could keep their place in the urban universe, that the power of locomotives and the speed of all things mechanical and technological could still be controlled, and no skyscraper—"buildings of the mutant kind"—would get the better of him.[33] Superman would never get lost in the jungle of brick and mortar that had redefined the American cityscape. From 1938 until 1943 Superman was preoccupied with keeping order in the new city. And he did it by jumping.

The Real Masters of the Air

At the time, the fastest runners and the best jumpers in the world were not from the planet Krypton but from the United States. In forty-five minutes at a college track meet in 1935, Jesse Owens tied the world record for the 100-yard dash, broke the world record with a long jump of more than twenty-six feet, broke the world record in the 220-yard dash, and broke yet another world record in the 220-yard low hurdles. He went on to win four gold medals at the Olympic Games a year later, where he set new Olympic records in the

200-meter dash, long jump, and 4 x 100-meter relay. Cornelius Johnson and Dave Albritton won gold and silver medals with their spectacular high jumps. But in 1938 white readers were more likely to accept a comic book superhero with a white face than a real hero with a black one. Or perhaps those readers needed a comic superhero with a white face *because* all the best jumpers were black.

In gymnasiums, in track and field, and on dance floors, the Americans who seemed to have mastered space with their bodies—those who really could jump highest and farthest and hang in mid-air the longest—those Americans were African Americans. Jesse Owens pushed the limits of speed and height as far as any human alive—except, perhaps, for Charles Lindbergh. How else to describe Owens than to compare him to an airplane, as a reporter for the *Chicago Defender* did in June 1933: "Owens was away with the rush of an airplane, but the grace of a fawn, streaking down the runway faster and faster, until it appeared he would be forced by his own momentum to continue on into the air." As the sportswriter watched Owens take off in his long jump, he thought, "Higher than usual he was, but shooting through space faster, too."[34] Chester Washington, writing for the *Pittsburgh Courier*, said: "If ever there was a runner with rhythm, joggin' Jesse has IT. His long, muscular legs swing with the perfect tempo of a mighty baton, the pistons of a streamline train or the twin motors of a racing plane."[35]

"Fats" Jenkins, the wiry player-coach of the "Fast-Flying Rens" and a star baserunner for the Black Yankees and the Brooklyn Eagles, was too fast even for comparisons to airplanes. He was known simply as the "human skyrocket." As a basketball player, Jenkins was "the fastest man in the fastest game on earth," a "wavering streak of lightning," capable of "zigzagging his way in such a deceptive manner that he completely bewilders his opponents."[36]

The skyscraper boom went bust, and human skyscrapers took their place. When African American Gilbert Cruter set a new high jump record in March 1936, the *Pittsburgh Courier* called him the world's newest "ski scraper."[37] At the Olympics, Cornelius Johnson of Los Angeles and Dave Albritton of Ohio both broke records with high jumps, earning them the nickname "Sepia Sky-Scrapers."[38] Even boxer Joe Louis, who excelled by not leaving his feet, was compared to skyscrapers. When Louis came to New York in the spring of 1935 to fight Primo Carnera, a cartoon appeared in the *New York Post* showing Louis standing astride the skyscrapers of midtown Manhattan. The legend on his trunks reads "18 Kayos in 24 Pro Fights," while Louis knocks the tops off the Empire State and Chrysler buildings with his mighty left.[39]

If the skyscraper was power transformed to matter, then the jump was power reclaimed by humans. If twentieth-century America was about pushing the limits of speed and height, the Americans who actually and physically accomplished more in that realm than any other were black.

Duke Ellington once said that the finest black entertainers towered over others as skyscrapers did over other buildings, drawing a comparison between human and architectural aspirations.[40] The modernist architect Le Corbusier also saw in the Manhattan of 1935 a connection between architecture and music: "Manhattan is hot jazz in stone and steel." All the same, Le Corbussier said, "jazz is more advanced than the architecture. If architecture were at the point reached by jazz, it would be an incredible spectacle." He wrote, "Nothing in our European experience can be compared to it." Louis Armstrong towered above American culture. He was "mathematics, equilibrium on a tightrope."[41] The Belgian critic Robert Goffin also compared skyscrapers to jazz, declaring in 1934 that jazz required mastery of the medium but also provided "ample scope for independence and spontaneity of expression." For Goffin, artists such as Louis Armstrong, Coleman Hawkins, and Earl Hines were "surely of more importance than sky-scrapers."[42]

The Lindy Hop took Charles Lindberg's dramatic flight and spun it out endlessly over dance floors and then it, too, took to the air. Musicians, dancers, and athletes were partners in defying gravity, as they mimicked the upward thrust of the urban environment, demonstrating the power of the human body and spirit, even when dominated by technology and weighed down by fearful economic realities and social and institutional injustice.

CHAPTER 3 : THE 1936 OLYMPICS

The performances of America's black athletes at the 1936 Olympics was unprecedented in world history. No country before had taken so many black competitors to the games, and to take such a team to Berlin, home of a new social and political system built on the presumption of racial purity, was audacious on an international scale. Many believed that with this Olympic team, the United States made a statement to the world, and specifically to Hitler, about the nature of democracy and equality.

But the United States in 1936 was far from an egalitarian society. The German theologian Dietrich Bonhoeffer, later killed for his opposition to Hitler, came to New York for postgraduate work at Union Theological Seminary in 1930. In a course called Applied Theology, taught by the Christian ethics professor Reinhold Niebuhr, Bonhoeffer discovered works by African American writers Langston Hughes, Countee Cullen, James Weldon Johnson, and W. E. B. Du Bois, whose ideas deeply influenced Bonhoeffer's later thinking and writing. At the seminary, too, Bonhoeffer became friends with African American divinity student Franklin Fisher, who took Bonhoeffer to the Abyssinian Baptist Church, where Adam Clayton Powell Sr. had formed the largest Protestant congregation in the country. For six months Bonhoeffer attended services and taught Sunday school at the Harlem church, absorbing theological and musical vocabularies that he incorporated into his later writings and teaching. Bonhoeffer loved the music and the people of Harlem, and he hated the racism he found everywhere in New York. When Bonhoeffer returned to Germany, he continued to wrestle with the issue of racism, and in 1933 he became the first pastor to protest publicly—in a radio address—the rise of fascism.[1] Bonhoeffer learned about racism not in Germany but in New York, from the writings, music, and lives of black Americans.

The NAACP's Roy Wilkins writes of those years: "For black Americans, there was an unmistakable irony behind the headlines: a country that denied democracy to millions of its citizens in the South was suddenly rousing itself to defend democracy thousands of miles away across the Atlantic; a country that placidly countenanced lynch ropes and faggots for Negroes was suddenly expressing horror over the persecution of minorities in Europe; a country that abominated Nazis still winked at the Ku Klux Klan and the white master race ideology of Southern Democrats." Concluded Wilkins, "The truth was that a black person could not escape the stain of race anywhere in America."[2]

While many Americans protested Hitler's racism, black Americans were most attuned to homegrown racism. The American Olympic athletes may have returned to a heroes' welcome, but they did not experience equal opportunity or citizenship at home, the lack of which had for years limited and inhibited their performance in athletics, as well as in other areas. What accounts, then, for their suddenly stellar performance at those games? What explains the sudden rise of black athletic superiority on the American team? Why in 1936 and not before? And what did that seemingly meteoric rise mean to other African Americans?

Not until the first Penn Relay Carnival in 1895 were African Americans allowed to participate in national athletic competitions. Although the Scottish American Highland Games welcomed African Americans, and "colored" branches of the YMCA organized events as early as 1853, most athletic clubs prohibited African American members or participants. The New York Athletic Club, founded in 1868, denied entrance to African Americans and other ethnics, as did the national governing body that grew out of the Athletic Club, the Amateur Athletic Union (AAU), formed in 1888.

Track competitions, the most universally known sport and the easiest to arrange, began to surge just after World War I in 1920, when the YMCA held its first national meet and the Olympics resumed after an eight-year pause with games in Antwerp.[3] The English started to hold track competitions in the late nineteenth century, and the sport spread to the United States, Scotland, Ireland, and Finland. Through the first two decades of the twentieth century, white runners and jumpers dominated. But when the NCAA held its first championship in 1921, the National Collegiate Track and Field Championship, the first person to break the 25-foot barrier in the long jump was Harvard's Edward "Ned" Gourdin, one of the few black participants. Gourdin also won the 100-yard dash. His leap of 25 feet, 3 inches, got the attention of the *New York Telegram*, which called it "almost impossible . . . the greatest feat in track and field in a generation."[4] Gourdin won a silver medal in the same event three years later at the 1924 Olympics (and earned his law degree that same year).[5] But black athlete William DeHart Hubbard's running jump was good enough for the gold medal at Paris that year, and he became the first African American ever to earn the gold in an individual event. Hubbard then broke Gourdin's record by nearly 8 inches in 1925, lowered the 100-yard dash record to 9.6 seconds, and graduated from the University of Michigan as one of only eight African Americans in his class.

The training and resources behind such achievements as Gourdin's and Hubbard's was out of reach for most black athletes. Few black colleges offered track programs until well into the 1930s; most were struggling with scarce academic resources. Black clubs offered an outlet to some athletes, although few had time to train outside of work, and the AAU admitted no black clubs until the mid-1920s. The Colored Intercollegiate Athletic Association (CIAA), formed in 1924, offered a black alternative to the NCAA. But records set at a black college meet would not have been accepted by the AAU or the Intercollegiate Association of Amateur Athletes of America (ICAAAA).[6] Black track athletes could aim for only three major meets: the Penn Relays, the CIAA meet, and the Tuskegee Relay Carnival, begun in 1927. Not until after World War II did an athlete from a historically black college participate in the Olympic Games. The most successful black athletes were products of white colleges, where wealthy alumni built athletic facilities and government funds provided money for drill fields.

A significant exception to the generally inadequate training in track at black colleges prior to World War II was the Tuskegee track program. The first major black college track meet took place at Tuskegee in 1893. Events included running, jumping relays, weight throwing, broad jumping, wall scaling, standing broad jump, tug-of-war, and a centipede race. At Tuskegee relays were of particular importance, since they were thought to foster teamwork, group coordination, and persistence. Athletic director Cleveland Abbott initiated the first modern black college track event there on May 7, 1927, modeling his competition on the Penn Relays, but with an important exception: the Tuskegee Carnival included women—in two events in 1927 and four in 1930. In 1923 a national Council on Women's Sports had passed a resolution urging women's sports organizations to deemphasize competition, and white college varsity sports cooperated with the edict. Even the Olympics had included women only since 1928. Abbot bucked the trend, hired Amelia C. Roberts as women's track coach, and built a track team that swept the AAU

TABLE 3.1. Women's African American AAU Winners through 1945

High Jump

1939	Alice Coachman	Tuskegee	5' 2"
1940	Alice Coachman	Tuskegee	4' 11"
1941	Alice Coachman	Tuskegee	5' 2¾"
1942	Alice Coachman	Tuskegee	4' 8"
1943	Alice Coachman	Tuskegee	5' 0"
1944	Alice Coachman	Tuskegee	5' 1⅝"
1945	Alice Coachman	Tuskegee	5' 0"

Long Jump

1935	Etta Tate	(Unattached)	16' 6"
1936	Mable Smith	Tuskegee	18' 0"
1937	Lula Hymes	Tuskegee	17' 8½"
1938	Lula Hymes	Tuskegee	17' 2"

Compiled from Arthur R. Ashe Jr., *A Hard Road to Glory: A History of the African-American Athlete*, 1919–1945, vol. 2 (New York: Warner Books, 1988), 449.

National in 1937. Tuskegee athletes won the AAU long jump events three years in a row, from 1936 through 1938, and won fourteen team titles between 1937 and 1950. One athlete—Alice Coachman—won the high jump every year from 1939 through 1948, when she won the Olympic gold medal. (See table 3.1.)

African American men who wanted to star in track events had better luck at white colleges than at black ones. Gourdin's 1921 long jump collegiate record was set at Harvard, not at a black institution. From 1921 to 1924, during his first three years at the University of Michigan, William DeHart Hubbard was so successful in the long jump that Michigan had to lengthen the jumping pit. He was also an impressive sprinter and could have been an asset to the football team had the coach allowed African Americans on the squad.

The phenomenal performances of these and other black athletes at white colleges explains why the AAU decided to move the 1927 national meet to Lincoln, Nebraska, when New Orleans officials refused to accept black athletes. In football, baseball, or basketball, white athletes could have filled in for African Americans, who would have been left at home. But in track and field, many predominantly white schools had begun to depend on black athletes, particularly in the jumping events.

"Mercury in Motion": Jesse Owens

When James Cleveland "Jesse" Owens enrolled at Ohio State University in 1933, the *Chicago Defender* and other black newspapers criticized his choice, editorializing against institutions that discriminated against black students. "Why help advertise an institution that majors in prejudice?" asked the *Chicago Defender*.[7] But Owens wanted to be close to his family and his high school coach. Black athletes were not spared institutional prejudice, nor were they given scholarships: Owens worked his way through college as a freight elevator operator, in the rear of the State Office Building, far from public view. Because black students were not allowed to live on campus, Owens lived not with his teammates but in a boardinghouse about a quarter of a mile off campus. Yet his track performances admitted no barriers: in one day at the National Intercollegiates in Ann Arbor, Michigan, in 1935, Owens set three world records and tied a fourth. Many people knowledgeable about track and field still consider this the most remarkable single day in the history of the sport.

Owens's feats dominated the black press, which could not invent enough superlatives to describe his abilities. In one article for the *Pittsburgh Courier*, following Owens's stunning performance at the (integrated) Penn Relays in May 1936, Chester Washington called Owens "the bounding Buckeye bullet," "phenomenal," "the great Buckeye blizzard," "Mercury in motion," "a perfect symphony in racing rhythm" with "torpedo-like speed," the "streaking spearhead of speed" who "combined the speed of an express train with the grace of a faun." And being fast wasn't enough: Owens was also "universally liked," "tall and clean-cut with plenty of personality." He was "the most popular man . . . on the field." Even Harvey Wallender, the University of Texas (white) tornado, called Owens "as fine a fellow as anyone would want to meet" and invited Owens to visit his father's large ranch in Texas, a state known for extremes of racial prejudice.[8]

Such phenomenal performance from so likable and modest an athlete as Owens posed problems for the white press, which couldn't dismiss him as a jungle killer the way it did boxers Jack Johnson and Joe Louis. The *New York Times* offered a speculative article on whether and why blacks were better suited to running and jumping events. For decades African Americans had been dismissed as lacking the necessary work ethic and moral fiber to compete in such events. Now they found their deeds explained away through comparisons to animals.

Yet these accomplishments represented a cultural advance for African Americans as they poked more holes in the theory of total white superiority. In New York's black newspaper *Amsterdam News*, Roi Ottley wrote: "The Negro has lifted himself to a dominating position in track and field. The Negro is not only keeping pace, but he is frankly surpassing the efforts of his white brothers."[9] An editor for the *Cleveland Call and Post*, Jesse Owens's hometown paper, wrote: "The Negro youth has been starved for their own heroes a mighty long time. Everything they have seen glorified in the past has been white. They have heard of Babe Ruth, Jack Dempsey, etc. But deep down in their little hearts, they have gone to bed and reflected that, after all, these fellows are white. A hero of their own flesh and blood, they have lacked."[10] Until now. George Schuyler wrote in the *Pittsburgh Courier*, "brown young men are the greatest runners and jumpers in the world. These young men have had training. They have had a chance. With ability and training and opportunity, they have topped the world."[11] Schuyler wondered what African Americans in other fields might accomplish, given comparable training and opportunity.

Qualifying for the Olympic team in April 1936, Owens set another world record in the 100-yard dash, breaking his old record by one-tenth of a second (at 9.3 seconds). In the final Olympic tryouts at Randall's Island in July, Owens set a world record in the 200-meter event, at 21 seconds. Other African American Olympians included sprinters Ralph Metcalfe—joint 100 meter world record holder and favored to win the sprint events—and Matthew "Mack" Robinson, Jackie Robinson's brother. High jumpers Dave Albritton and Cornelius Johnson, Archie Williams and James Luvalle in the 400 meters, "Long" John Woodruff in the 800 meters, Fritz Pollard Jr. in the 110-meter hurdles, and long jumper John Brooks also made the team. Louise Stokes and Tidye Pickett were on the women's team (in 1932, both were pulled from the team and replaced with white runners). Never had African America been so well represented at the Olympics. Black newspapers heralded the news on their front pages: "Race Stars Dominate U.S. Olympic Team."[12]

TABLE 3.2. Men's African American NCAA Winners through 1945 (Jump Events Only)

High Jump			
1936	Mel Walker	Ohio State	6′ 6 1/8″
	Dave Albritton	Ohio State	
1937	Gil Cruter	Colorado	6′ 6 1/4″
	Dave Albritton	Ohio State	
1938	Gil Cruter	Colorado	6′ 8 3/4″
	Dave Albritton	Ohio State	
1942	Adam Berry	Southern U.	6′ 7 3/4″
Long Jump			
1923	DeHart Hubbard	Michigan	25′ 2″
1925	DeHart Hubbard	Michigan	25′ 10 7/8″
1929	Ed Gordon	Iowa	24′ 8 1/2″
1930	Ed Gordon	Iowa	25′
1931	Ed Gordon	Iowa	24′ 11 3/8″
1933	John Brooks	Chicago	24′ 4 3/4″
1935	Jesse Owens	Ohio State	26′ 1 3/8″
1936	Jesse Owens	Ohio State	25′ 10 7/8″
1937	Kermit King	Pittsburgh	25′ 3 1/4″
1938	William Lacefield	UCLA	25′ 1 1/8″
1940	Jackie Robinson	UCLA	24′ 10 1/4″

Compiled from Ashe, *A Hard Road to Glory*, vol. 2, 452.

The Berlin Games

African American medalists at the 1924 Olympics had numbered only three; at the 1932 event there were four African Americans on the team, three of whom brought home five medals among them: Thomas "Eddie" Tolan Jr. became the first African American to win a gold medal in a sprint event, narrowly beating his black teammate Ralph Metcalfe, who finished second, and setting a world record. Tolan also set the Olympic record in the 200-meter event, in which Metcalfe placed third, and Edward "Ed" Gordon won the gold in the long jump. Some newspapers suggested that these victories could be a dangerous trend. "Colored Boys Sports Threat: Athletic Prominence Grows

Year after Year," warned the *Los Angeles Times*.[13] By 1933 Elmer A. Carter was able to write in *Opportunity*: "That the Negro was deficient in the qualities of which athletic champions are made was long one of the accepted shibboleths of the American people. That rare combination—stamina, skill, and courage—it was commonly believed were seldom found under a black skin. Like many other myths concerning the Negro, this myth is being exploded, not by theory, nor argument, but by performance."[14] The black athletes in Berlin—ten men and two women in track and field, five boxers, and two weightlifters—represented a fourfold increase over the number of blacks who had participated in the 1932 Olympics.[15] The *Amsterdam News* celebrated the team, writing, "Those who mourn the defeat of Joe Louis at the hands of the determined German, Max Schmeling, can find not only solace, but also genuine pride and appreciation in the results of the Olympic selections."[16]

The 1936 Olympics offered an international platform for testing the truth about white superiority and black inferiority. Appointed chancellor of Germany in January 1933, Adolf Hitler almost immediately began the *Judenrein* (clean of Jews) campaign, opening the first concentration camp at Dachau in March. The Amateur Athletic Union passed a resolution stating that the United States would not participate in the 1936 Olympic Games, already scheduled for Berlin, if the present trend continued. But the president of the American Olympic Committee, Avery Brundage, opposed the protest and privately minimized the importance of the "Jew-Nazi altercation." Brundage agreed to visit Germany in 1934, and returned proclaiming that the Jewish issue was minor compared to the momentousness of the Olympic Games. "Certain Jews must now understand that they cannot use these Games as a weapon in their boycott against the Nazis," said Brundage.[17]

The NAACP and a few newspapers supported the boycott. Walter White sent a telegram to the AAU at its December 1935 convention saying that participating would "place approval upon the German government's deplorable persecution of racial and religious groups."[18] But most believed that a shutdown of the Olympics would deprive African Americans of the chance to perform at a world-class event. The black press decried the nationalism that permeated the 1936 Olympics; the *Courier* complained about "propaganda hurled at foreign newsmen, according to the New York Times; swastikas hung where no flag was ever hung before." The *Courier* declared such efforts "an excuse for expressing tyranny in new forms."[19] But the black press also pointed out the hypocrisy of such concerns over discrimination abroad when American blacks experienced racial segregation daily in a country where even the president failed to support an anti-lynching bill, and athletes lived and played under apartheid. When the boycott resolution failed by two and a half votes, the black press celebrated. And when the official Nazi newspaper, *Völkischer Beobachter*, editorialized that Negroes should be excluded from the games, the stage was set for an international showdown.

As Hitler continued to exploit the event, the 1936 Olympics—the first of the modern games to be fully organized by government authorities—became more than games.[20] It was Germany in 1936 that inaugurated the ritual of relaying the torch from Greece, in order to establish Germany as the protector of the ideals of Western civilization.[21] The harder Hitler tried to use the Olympics to endorse the ascendance of Nazi power, the more significant became any defeat of Hitler's athletes. And the Olympics, which ideally served to bring nations together, were now a peaceful enactment of war. Suddenly African American athletes became the quintessential Americans, more American than Negro, as Americans cheered for their representatives in the undeclared war against Nazism.

The Berlin games shattered previous performance results by African Americans. The United States had the second-largest team, with 312 members. Of those, only nineteen were black, but they captured the attention of Berliners and others at the games even before the games began. Jesse Owens was recognized everywhere: women slipped notes under his door at night proposing marriage, and there was no shortage of dancing partners, as even married men asked him to dance with their wives.[22] Competition began on August 2, and late that day Cornelius Johnson won the high jump, David Albritton came in second, and Owens tied a world record in his qualifying run for the 100-meter race with a time of 10.3 seconds. On the third day of August, Owens finished first and Ralph Metcalfe second in the 100-meter race. On August 4, John Woodruff won a gold medal in the 800 meters, and Owens beat Lutz Long of Germany in the long jump event, setting a new Olympic record at 26 feet, 5 ¼ inches. Owens's third gold medal came on August 5, when he ran a world record 200-meter race in 20.7 seconds, beating his teammate Mack Robinson, and besting Eddie Tolan's 1932 Olympic record by a full five-tenths of a second. Two days later Archie Williams won the 400-meter race to bring the U.S. individual gold medal count to six—all won by African Americans.

In all, thirteen medals went to nine of the ten male track and field competitors, including eight gold medals—one-third of the U.S. total of twenty-four. Gold and silver medals went to African Americans in the high jump, gold in the long jump, gold and silver in the 110 meter, gold and silver in the 200 meter, gold and a bronze in the 400 meter, gold in the 800 meter, two golds in the 400-meter relay, and a bronze in the 110-meter hurdles. Bantamweight boxer Jack Wilson brought home a silver medal, bringing the African Americans' medal total to fourteen. By the end of the event, black athletes, who represented slightly less than one-eighteenth of the team, accounted for one-quarter of all U.S. medals—half the gold medals and nearly half the U.S. team's total score (70 of 187 points). Jesse Owens brought home a stunning four gold medals.[23] (See table 3.3.)

Owens said that winning the 100-meter race was the greatest thrill of his life, partly because of the huge ovation he received. *Courier* editor Robert L. Vann wrote that the spectacle was the greatest event of its kind he had ever seen: "Sunday, I witnessed 110,000 people cheer two Negro athletes, because they were supreme in their field. . . . And the . . . wonder of wonders[,] . . . I saw Herr Adolph [*sic*] Hitler, salute this lad. I looked on with a heart which beat proudly as the lad who was crowned king of the 100-meters event got an ovation the likes of which I have never heard before."[24] From Berlin, Owens cabled home this heartfelt message: "I am proud that I am an American. . . . Maybe more people will now realize that the Negro is trying to do his full part as an American citizen."[25]

Radio announcers did their part to fulfill Owens's dream of full citizenship, making no distinction between the white and the dark Americans on the Olympic team. But white newspaper writers unfailingly identified athletes as Negroes, quoted them in dialect, and explained their astonishing successes through some of the same qualities that had previously been used to define their inferiority as a race. Grantland Rice wrote, for syndication, "Easily, almost lazily, and minus any show of extra effort, they have turned sport's greatest spectacle into the 'black parade of 1936.'" Sprinting and jumping were described as natural skills in which Negro athletes excelled. A writer for *Newsweek* said, "Owens runs as easily as Bill (Bojangles) Robinson tap dances," and John Kieran wrote for the *New York Times*, "Apparently it takes time to work up endurance, but speed comes by nature."[26]

Black writers saw it differently. There was no need to draw on jungle metaphors when swing era, machine age icons were closer at hand. In a piece titled
"A Runner with Rhythm," *Pittsburgh Courier* columnist Chester Washington
compared Owens to train pistons and airplane motors.[27] Other black reporters
called him a "perfect piece of running machinery."[28] High jumpers were compared to skyscrapers. Or if one wanted to leave the urban landscape in search
of metaphors, one could look to the skies: Owens was called the "Cleveland
comet."

The American public claimed the athletes as its own. Overall, the U.S.
team's performance represented a shocking low in America's Olympic participation. It was the first time since the 1908 games that the U.S. team had
not brought home more medals, including more gold medals, than any other
country. So the victories of Owens and his teammates became even more important and were widely held up as proof of the superiority of the American
democratic society. These successes became the nation's answer to the rest
of the world that in the United States, the Negro could become part of mainstream society. In another time, the performance of the black athletes might
not have garnered so much publicity. But in 1936, in view of the overwhelming desire to defeat Hitler and the underwhelming performance of all but the
African American athletes, black Americans emerged as all-American heroes.
Even if for a short time and in appearance only, Americans united in celebration of the accomplishments of fellow (black) Americans. And with the exception of the 1938 Joe Louis–Max Schmeling rematch, no event of the 1930s so
captured the attention of the black press and African Americans as the 1936
Olympics.

Public acclaim for the black Olympic athletes was enormous and demon-
strable, and of those athletes, quadruple gold medal winner Jesse Owens was
the best known. No athlete in the history of the Olympics had won four gold
medals. Owens came home to a huge celebration in New York, where people
literally threw money at his feet. "For a time, at least," wrote Owens later in
one of his memoirs, "I was the most famous person in the entire world."[29] Yet the
Amateur Athletic Union's James E. Sullivan Award for outstanding amateur
achievement during 1936 went not to Owens but to decathlon champion Glenn
Morris, an immodest rogue who had celebrated his gold medal by ripping
open Leni Riefenstahl's blouse and kissing her breasts in the middle of the

TABLE 3.3. 1936 African American Olympians

1936	Cornelius Johnson	Gold	High Jump	6' 8"
1936	David Albritton	Silver	High Jump	6' 6¾"
1936	Jesse Owens	Gold	100 Meters	10.3
1936	Ralph Metcalfe	Silver	100 Meters	10.4
1936	Jesse Owens	Gold	200 Meters	20.7
1936	Mack Robinson	Silver	200 Meters	21.1
1936	Jesse Owens	Gold	Long Jump	26' 5½"
1936	Jesse Owens	Gold	400M Relay [1]	39.8
1936	Ralph Metcalfe	Gold	400M Relay	39.8
1936	Archie Williams	Gold	400 Meters	46.5
1936	James Luvalle	Bronze	400 Meters	46.8
1936	John Woodruff	Gold	800 Meters	1:52.9
1936	Fritz Pollard Jr.	Bronze	110-Meter Hurdles	14.4
1936	Jack Wilson	Silver	Bantamweight boxing	

Compiled from Ashe, *A Hard Road to Glory*, vol. 2, 453.

1. White teammates on the gold medal 400-meter relay team were Frank Wykoff and Foy Draper.

Olympic stadium.[30] Many believed that Owens should have won the award the previous year, too, on the basis of his record-breaking performance at Ann Arbor. But the Sullivan Award had never gone to a black athlete, and not even Owens's spectacular performances two years running could challenge that precedent. Still, Owens was named the Associated Press Athlete of the Year, receiving fifty-three first-place votes from sixty-nine sportswriters, defeating not only Glenn Morris but also Joe DiMaggio, Dizzy Dean, England's world tennis champion Fred Perry, and boxers Joe Louis and Max Schmeling.

The 1936 Olympics created a watershed in track and field performances among African American athletes, particularly upwardly mobile college students. No other sport save boxing was so open to black athletes. Major league baseball had not allowed black players since 1889. Some college conferences barred black athletes in basketball, and professional opportunities for basketball players were limited. Professional football banned black athletes from 1934 through 1946. Consequently, after the Olympics many black athletes concentrated on track, hoping to emulate the great Jesse Owens. The fact that all of the black athletes in 1936 came from predominantly white universities underscored the need for better facilities and training at black colleges, where, lacking the luxury of running tracks, starting blocks, hurdles, or uniforms, athletes trained on hard-packed grass fields—and continued to do so for decades beyond the 1930s.[31]

The achievements of Jesse Owens alone may never be matched. He tied the world record in the 100-meter dash and set new Olympic records in the long jump and 200-meter sprint. His opening run of the 400-meter relay pushed his team toward new world and Olympic records in that event. Each of these records lasted more than two decades—into the 1950s—and it was 1960 before anyone broke his long jump record.

Most stunning of all, Owens had accomplished these feats without starting blocks, wearing heavy, soggy leather shoes on an uneven, messy cinder track. In the rain.

A New Generation

The numbers of African Americans who became NCAA competition winners soared in the 1930s and reversed the racial balance of track and field competitions for the rest of the century. African Americans excelled in athletic jumping events in the 1930s in unprecedented fashion. By 1939 no white person other than Superman had high jumped beyond 6 feet, 9 inches, while four black athletes had done so: Cornelius Johnson, Dave Albritton, Ed Burke, and Melvin Walker. And by the end of 1945, most major track and field records were held by African Americans and had been set in the 1930s. (See tables 3.2 and 3.4.)

Sociologists and historians have studied the effects of the Great Migration of African Americans to urban areas from the standpoints of shifts in rural-urban population density as well as changes in character and complexion of cities. Much has been made of the so-called social ills that resulted. Ralph Ellison called such studies the "fakelore" of African American pathology. What is to be made of such astounding gains in athletic performance by African Americans during this period of shifting population? Clearly, something had changed, and it is doubtful that training or equipment alone can explain the improved performances. Rather, we might conclude that the concentration of black cultural and experiential energy coalesced in a new generation that became convinced of its right and ability to succeed in areas where whites

TABLE 3.4. American Records Held by African Americans at the End of 1945

MEN'S RECORDS

60 Yards

Ralph Metcalfe	6.1	March 11, 1933
Jesse Owens	6.1	March 9, 1935
Herbert Thompson	6.1	February 4, 1939
Bill Carter	6.1	March 15, 1941
Barney Ewell	6.1	February 7, 1942
Herbert Thompson	6.1	March 14, 1942
Herbert Thompson	6.1	March 27, 1943
Edward Conwell	6.1	February 26, 1944
Edward Conwell	6.1	March 9, 1946

100 Yards

Jesse Owens	9.4	May 25, 1935

220 Yards

Jesse Owens	20.3	May 25, 1935

800 Yards

John Woodruff	1:47:7	March 14, 1940

1,000 Yards

John Borican	2:08:8	March 11, 1939

220-Yard Hurdles

Harrison Dillard	22.5	June 8, 1944

Running High Jump

Mel Walker	6' 9¾"	March 20, 1937

Running Broad Jump

Jesse Owens	26' 8½"	May 25, 1935

WOMEN'S RECORDS

50-Yard Run

Elizabeth Robinson	5.8	July 27, 1929

50-Meter Run

Alice Coachman	6.4	July 14, 1944

100-Yard Dash

Jean Lane   10.9   May 29, 1940

220-Yard Run

Elizabeth Robinson   25.1   June 20, 1931

Running Broad Jump

Lula Mae Hymes   18' 1½"   September 3, 1939

400-Meter Relay

Tuskegee Institute   49.3   July 13, 1940

Compiled from Ashe, A Hard Road to Glory, vol. 2, 450.

---

had dominated. Quite possibly the generation that came of age in the mid- to late 1930s had no more or less ability that those that preceded it; what those athletes possessed in contrast to their predecessors was confidence in their abilities, optimism about the future, and reasonable hopes for success. In the 1930s the weight of cultural conviction finally overcame historical precedent.

The blessings of these victories were definitely mixed. One stereotype gave way to another: that of the weak and incompetent idler was replaced by that of the animal-like survivor—or worse, predator. In 1941 Dean Cromwell, head coach of the 1936 U.S. Olympic team, reflected on the phenomenal success of African American athletes in Berlin. "The Negro excels in the events he does because he is closer to the primitive than the white man," he wrote in *Championship Technique in Track and Field*. "It was not long ago that his ability to sprint and jump was a life-and-death matter to him in the jungle. His muscles are pliable, and his easy-going disposition is a valuable aid to the mental and physical relaxation that a runner and jumper must have."[32] A black former sprinter from the 1920 British Olympic team, Harry F. V. Edward, worried: "For years it has been said the Negroes can sing and dance. From now on we will hear the platitude that all Negroes can run and jump."[33]

It takes some historical diligence to grasp the notion that for countless African Americans, this new stereotype represented a significant step forward. However theorists and racists twisted the evidence, it could no longer be said that African Americans were inferior in every way. Damaging stereotypes and truisms persisted, but the one about African Americans being too lazy, slow, or physically inferior to compete with white athletes would be heard less and less frequently.

And for countless African Americans, the accumulation of public victory upon public victory created an aggregate cultural permission to achieve, excel, and express in other public arenas.

CHAPTER 4 : THE LINDY HOP TAKES TO THE AIR

One of the earliest descriptions of the Lindy Hop appears in Carl Van Vechten's novel *Parties: Scenes from Contemporary New York Life*. In the 1930 novel Van Vechten states that the "first official appearance" of the Lindy Hop was at the Negro Marathon staged at the Manhattan Casino in 1928. Van Vechten, an active socialite and keen cultural observer, claims that by 1929 "it was possible to observe an entire ball-room filled with couples devoting themselves to its celebration."[1] Van Vechten's colorful narrative is full of the hyperbole of the era: "The Lindy Hop consists in a certain dislocation of the rhythm of the fox-trot, followed by leaps and quivers, hops and jumps, eccentric flinging about of arms and legs, and contortions of the torso. . . . After the fundamental steps of the dance have been published, the performers may consider themselves at liberty to improvise, embroidering the traditional measures with startling variations, as a coloratura singer of the early nineteenth century would endow the score of a Bellini opera with roulades, runs, and shakes."[2] Exaggeration or not, this passage tells us a lot about the Lindy in 1929: it contained hops and jumps, it was centered in the lower body and it invited improvisation.

The earliest recorded image of the Lindy is of George "Shorty" Snowden and Pauline Morse dancing in the 1929 Paramount film *After Seben*. Their Lindy—filmed in 1928—was a modified Charleston with a slight breakaway step, giving them a little room and time to improvise. According to dancer Frankie Manning, the Lindy was born when two popular dances merged: the Charleston and the breakaway. Both couples and individual dancers performed Charleston steps, but the breakaway was always a partner dance. The breakaway included a narrow separation between the couple, then a brief release of the hands. Gradually, in response to the rhythm of swing music, the breakaway became wider, lasted longer, and led to more improvisation, and to the dance that was called the Lindy.[3]

The Lindy was a couples' dance, like most European social dance. But as in other African-derived dances, the emphasis was on couples dancing apart.

dancers, who helped to propel the music. Saxophonist and arranger Eddie Barefield played with the swing bands of Bennie Moten, Fletcher Henderson, Cab Calloway, and Don Redman, and also supplied arrangements for orchestras such as those of Calloway, Glenn Miller, Goodman, and Jimmy Dorsey. He recalled: "When you went to a dance you could hear the feet on the dance floor. Everybody was beating in time, it was one of those things, you could hear the patting of the feet right along with the music. And this made a lot of the momentum of the swing more predominant."[11] Duke Ellington said: "It's a kick to play for people who really jump and swing. . . . You start playing, the dancers start dancing, and they have such a great beat you just hang on."[12] Lunceford drummer Jimmy Crawford remembered, "In ballrooms, where there's dancing like I was raised on, when everybody is giving to the beat, and just moving, and the house is bouncing—that inspires you to play."[13] Bandleader Andy Kirk made his name in Kansas City, but he played in dancehalls all over the South and Southwest, where dancers let him know just how they wanted him to play: "A group [of dancers] always would come around the bandstand and request something. 'Play so-and-so,' they'd say, so I'd say, 'Where do you want it, Man?' . . . And they'd pat off the tempo they wanted."[14] Dicky Wells, who played at the Savoy, claimed that "the Lindy Hoppers there made you watch your P's and Q's. The dancers would come and tell you if you didn't play. They made the guys play, and they'd stand in front patting their hands until you got the right tempo."[15] Crawford also took his cue from dancers: "If I didn't look at the dancers' feet as well as the music, I couldn't make those transitions right."[16] Rex Stewart, of the Ellington orchestra, wrote in his memoir: "Dancing/singing and/or playing an instrument in the same environment created a healthy rapport between these arts and forged an unbreakable chain of reflected creativity. We were all in show biz together."[17]

Swing music and the Lindy Hop evolved simultaneously, each reinforcing and encouraging developments in the other, particularly with regard to the characteristic swing 4/4 beat, although, of course, not all swing music followed this rule of thumb. The Jimmie Lunceford orchestra, for instance, one of the most popular dance bands, was known for a medium-tempo two-beat pulse so distinctive it was called the "Lunceford Two-Beat." Even so, in the Lindy, dancers move constantly in time to four, with either a step and a bounce or a step and a rock-step (a shifting of weight from the forward foot to the backward foot and then a return to the front). There are both six-beat and eight-beat versions of the Lindy, although some instructors and scholars will argue that the Lindy is an eight-beat dance while the Jitterbug is a quicker, six-beat dance: step-bounce, step-bounce, rock-step.[18] Both are subsets of the Swing genre. Like the breakaway, the Lindy is danced in place, but dancers swing out into larger patterns, in response to the more expansive rhythms of the music, in other words, in response to its "swing."

In trying to define swing—something like trying to "eff" the ineffable—the jazz historian and composer Gunther Schuller suggested that swing is both subjective—a felt experience—and technical, "the ability to maintain a perfect equilibrium between the 'horizontal' and 'vertical' relationships of musical sound."[19] The horizontal elements of music, that is the melody, riff, or theme, are what move it forward in time. But at any one moment in a musical composition or performance, there is a particular harmony happening on a particular beat. The harmonic and rhythmic elements of music are what Schuller refers to as "vertical." Music that swings has a steady, driving beat, but it is not metronomic. It doesn't march, or thump, or jerk. It moves forward smoothly, but with endless subtle variations of attack and release of the notes that give it a felt, internal rhythmic swing.

The Lindy, too, had to swing to match the music, and in keeping with Schuller's idea of equilibrium between the horizontal and vertical, the Lindy's evolution seemed contrived to keep those two dimensions in balance. One of the Lindy's most inventive dancers, Frankie Manning, is responsible for at least two major innovations, one of which expanded the dance horizontally and the other vertically. Manning says he began to change his dancing about 1934, to "imitate the new sound" of swing, stretching his movements out to match the music. Manning recalls: "I found that I could . . . use my body to express what I was hearing in the music, which was changing over from a more up-and-down rhythm of the '20s to this real smooth type of swing. . . . Soon, I was dancing almost horizontal to the ground. . . . Folks started to say, 'Man, you look like you're flying!' And I said to myself, *Yeah, that's exactly the way I want to look. Like I'm flying!*"[20] The Lindy is essentially a horizontal dance that over the course of its development swung out into broader and broader spaces, until finally the only place to go was up. The result, and Manning's next innovation, was air steps.

While swing music evolved simultaneously in several different venues, the home of the Lindy Hop was the Savoy Ballroom. Not that it was the only ballroom in Harlem. Dancers could choose among the Renaissance Casino, the Alhambra Ballroom, the Dunbar Ballroom, the Audubon Ballroom, the Rockland Palace, the Golden Gate, and others. But dancing was specialized, and dancers moved from one venue to the next depending on what kind of dance they preferred or on their skill level. Frankie Manning remembers, "The Alhambra was like elementary school; the Renaissance was like high school; and the Savoy . . . was like going to college." [21] Most of all, the Savoy was where you danced the Lindy. Manning writes: "When you walked into the Renaissance or the Alhambra, you might see some people dancing the Lindy, but others would be doing a foxtrot or two-step. At the Savoy, it seemed as if everyone was doing the Lindy hop." [22] Manning was a dance club regular, frequenting the Cat's Corner at the Savoy, where he often won the Saturday night dance contests.

From the time of its March 12, 1926, opening, the Savoy attracted patrons of all colors and classes and from all neighborhoods. It was a dancehall for Harlem locals, an uptown waterhole for socialites, a tourist attraction, and a recreational opportunity for blue-collar workers. And the Savoy was truly integrated. Many clubs and ballrooms in Harlem hired African American entertainers but refused to admit black customers. The Savoy welcomed black and white alike: it was probably the only place in New York where black and white patrons could dance with each other. [23] Movies, newsreels, and popular magazines featured dancing at the Savoy, and Times Square sightseeing buses put the Savoy on their New York night-life tours. Lindy Hopper Norma Miller recalls in her memoirs visits by screen stars Marlene Dietrich, Greta Garbo, Lana Turner, and director Orson Welles. But celebrity took a backseat to dancing. Manning remembered one night at the Savoy: "Somebody came over and said, 'Hey man, Clark Gable just walked in the house.' Somebody else said, 'Oh, yeah, can he dance?' " [24] Between 1926 and 1940, 10 million visitors were said to have walked through its doors—700,000 each year. Perhaps some people went to the Savoy to watch, but they stayed to dance, and the spring-loaded dance floor was replaced every three years out of respect for their needs.

The Savoy was luxurious but affordable and respectable; it did not sell alcohol during Prohibition. The *New York Age* described the Savoy in a March 6, 1926, article, saying:

There is no amusement place uptown to compare with the new Savoy. When one enters the building he finds himself in a spacious lobby set off by a marble staircase and cut glass chandelier. The hall itself is decorated in a color scheme of orange and blue. One half of the floor is heavily carpeted. There are tables, settees, etc., where guests may rest between the dances or watch those on the floor. A soda fountain is at one end of the hall. . . . The dance floor is about 200 feet long and about 50 feet wide. It is made of the best quality maple flooring, polished to the highest degree. Two bandstands and a disappearing stage are in the rear. Above are vari-colored spot lights. . . .[25]

The Savoy spanned the block of Lenox Avenue from 140th Street to 141st, and the dance floor occupied half that space. Railings divided the floor from the tables and chairs.[26] With two bandstands, bands could alternate playing, so the music and dancing were continuous. According to Dicky Wells, bands that failed to please the dancers didn't last at the Savoy: "If you didn't swing, you weren't there long."[27] Manning recalls: "That was life, Baby. Just to hear them bands and that beat pulsating through the ballroom and you'd see dancing feet and everybody on the floor seemed to be moving. At times the music got so terrific, it looked like the floor was dancing, going up and down."[28]

The dancers were going up and down, too. Shorty Snowden, who was much smaller than his partner Big Bea, often executed what was called a "jump turn," in which he jumped high enough for his arm to clear her head as he spun her around in an over-the-head turn. Other dancers, such as Manning, copied the jump turn, and it became a standard Lindy move. But it was just a preview of the air steps that would follow.[29]

Manning remembers conceiving and learning the first air step he recalls anyone performing, one that he Frieda Washington executed during a competition at the Savoy Ballroom early in 1936, a moment that introduced a new phase in Lindy Hopping.[30] Snowden, dancing professionally at another club, had challenged the amateur Savoy dancers to a contest. As Manning began preparing for the competition, he thought of a step that might compete, a variation of one of Snowden's own favorite moves. At the end of their act, Snowden and Big Bea turned their backs to each other, Big Bea would pick Shorty up and then carry him offstage on her back. Manning's idea was to complete the move: pick Washington up on his back and have her continue over his head with a back somersault onto the floor.

Manning and Washington, his next-door neighbor, began practicing in his apartment, with a mattress nearby to cushion the frequent falls. One day, Manning says, his mother walked by and saw the two of them lying on the mattress after another unsuccessful attempt. They tried to explain that they were working on a dance step, but his mother didn't buy it. "What kind of step do you need to do on a mattress?" she asked.[31] The trick, Manning said, wasn't going up but coming down: what they had to get right was the landing. It had to be on the beat. "We worked on it every single day," he recalled, "till we got it down to a point where I could bring her over every single time in time with the music."[32] The night of the competition the Chick Webb band was playing, and when Shorty Snowden finished his routine, Webb asked Manning what tune he wanted. Manning chose a "real swingy tune" called "Down South Camp Meeting," dictating the tempo to Webb with a few snaps of his fingers. The band started and, Manning says, "I flung that girl so far across the floor that we almost took up the whole ballroom! This was one time when we *really* danced to the music, and it seemed like the band was catching everything that we were doing." When it came close to the end of the song, Manning asked Washington whether she was ready for the step, and she said, " 'Yeah, let's go for it.' . . . I swung her out and did a jump turn over her head while Chick said, 'SHUUMMP!' Then I jumped so we were back to back and flipped her. While she was going over, he played 'CHI-CHI-CHI-CHI-CHI-CHI-CHOOO.' And when she hit the floor right on the beat . . . 'BOOMP!'" Webb crashed down on his drums just as Washington's feet hit. "The Savoy Ballroom just exploded," Manning says, and the contest was called, then and there. "No one cared about the contest no more."[33]

From that point on, it was a high-flying, high-jumping dance, and the music continued to change right along with it.[34] Manning called that move "over-the-back," an "air step," not an "aerial," because he wanted to distinguish it from the graceful lifts of ballroom dancing. "In the Lindy hop, you *throw* the girl in time with the music," says Manning, who believed "they should *always* be done with the music." Manning chronicles the development of several other air steps: his own over-the-shoulder, George Greenidge's side flip, the handspring-front-flip, the handspring-down-the-back, and something he called "ace-in-the-hole," invented out of necessity when his partner began to fall and he bent forward to let her slide down his back and then reached through his legs to pull her forward.[35] Manning says most dancers at the Savoy reserved the air steps for contests, although they occasionally crept into social dancing.[36] But it is clear that the air step became a feature of the Lindy that dancers had to include if they wanted to be truly competitive.

"Frankie represented everything that was best in Lindy Hop dancing," said Norma Miller, another of the Savoy dancers. "He could execute, swing, lift a girl effortlessly, and never miss a beat."[37] While Manning claims credit for introducing the first air step, he is equally forthright in stating that dancers freely exchanged steps and copied each other. "Back in the early '30s, there weren't any dance schools that would even teach the Lindy because they didn't accept it as a dance. . . . So the only way we could learn was by exchanging steps."[38] But according to Miller, *"It was Frankie's dancing that most dancers wanted to imitate."*[39] Through imitation, the dance spread and advanced. And not just in Harlem, where it originated, but all over the world.

Manning and Washington danced for Whitey's Lindy Hoppers, dedicated amateur dancers handpicked from the Savoy Ballroom dance floor and encouraged by former prizefighter and Savoy bouncer Herbert "Whitey" White, a sharp dresser with a streak of white down the middle of his hair, whitened with shoe polish on special occasions. One of Harlem's original dancing waiters (at Baron Wilkins's club and Small's Paradise), White had trained other waiters to dance.[40] But for the Lindy Hoppers, White operated more as a booking agent than choreographer. Using his Harlem connections, Whitey monopolized show business jobs for Lindy Hoppers for nearly a half-dozen years, and their technical innovations spread throughout the country via feature-length films such as MGM's *A Day at the Races* (1937), Republic Pictures' *Manhattan Merry-Go-Round* (1937), RKO's *Radio City Revels* (1938), MC Pictures' *Keep Punching* (1939; later released as the short *Jittering Jitterbugs*, 1943), Universal's *Hellzapoppin* (1941), and MGM's *Cabin in the Sky* (1943). They reached audiences through newsreels and through the "soundies" (the music videos of the day, short musical clips played on machines called Panorams) *Air Mail Special* (1941), *Hot Chocolate* (also known as *Cottontail*) (1941), *Outline of Jitterbug History* (1942), and *Sugar Hill Masquerade* (1942). Whitey's Lindy Hoppers even appeared on Broadway in *The Hot Mikado* (1939), and *Swingin' the Dream* (1939).[41]

Whitey's Lindy Hoppers also spread their dancing through personal appearances. In New York, they appeared in shows at the Alhambra Theatre, Roxy Theatre, Apollo Theater, Small's Paradise, Cotton Club, and Radio City Music Hall. They toured Atlantic City, the Catskills, and the Poconos. As Manning invented new steps for himself and his partner, he turned to coordinating other members of Whitey's Lindy Hoppers into ensemble dancers. Miller remembers, "It was with Frankie that Whitey began the first of the ensemble dancing that moved the Lindy Hop from a dance in a ballroom to a slick professional act that became a show stopper in theaters around the country."[42] The dancers regularly traveled to the Lincoln Theatre in Philadelphia, the Royal Theatre in Baltimore, and the Howard Theatre in Washington, D.C. They played the Moulin Rouge in Paris and the Palladium in London, and they performed for King George VI and Queen Elizabeth in 1937. They toured New Zealand and Australia in 1939 and got stranded in Rio de Janeiro in 1941 by the outbreak of World War II. They danced with Ethel Waters, Billie Holiday, Bill "Bogangles" Robinson, Cab Calloway, and Duke Ellington. As their audiences learned and absorbed their steps, Whitey's dancers took their craft to new levels of innovation and experimentation, and what had originally been an amateur group of fun-loving teens became a professional corps of dancers, highly choreographed, more often than not by the inventive Manning, who also was also rehearsal director. Although there were several teams of dancers under Whitey's name, the top dancers usually included Norma Miller and Leon James, Willamae and Billy Ricker, and Ella Gibson and George Greenidge, along with Frankie Manning, whose favorite partner was Ann Johnson.

Some African American leaders were dismayed by the kind of athletic abandon Whitey's Lindy Hoppers seemed to specialize in. But it was ingenuity and devotion to craft carried them forward, not careless enthusiasm. They believed in the integrity of their work, and in Whitey's dictum: "This is a black art form, and a great part of American culture."[43] In conscious defiance of all criticism, the dancers continued to develop their steps. The 1937 film *A Day at the Races* put this dancing on film, marking the first screen appearance for Whitey's Lindy Hoppers. It also introduced air steps to a national audience. In ninety seconds of performance, each of four couples manages to present a solo turn; in all but one of the solos, the partners separate for independent dancing; and all but one couple perform at least one air step. Spectacular moves include dancer Norma Miller's somersault over Leon James's back (an over-the-back step), Ella Gibson's back flip over George Greenidge's shoulder (a side flip) and an ensemble finale move called "doing the horses," in which two women "ride" one man by wrapping their legs around his waist as he walks out. The dancing is so physically demanding and athletic that by the end of the minute-and-a-half segment, all the dancers are dripping with sweat. The distinctive performance of eight young African Americans in *A Day at the Races* caught the attention of the black press: one reviewer for the *Amsterdam News* referred to it as "A Day at the (Negro) Races."[44] This was contemporary social dance at its most ambitious—spectacular, muscular, and vigorous—and it had come straight from the Savoy Ballroom, from talented young people dancing. When the Lindy Hoppers returned to Hollywood a year later to film *Radio City Revels*, Fred Astaire dropped by the set to observe. "I wish I could dance like that," he said as he watched them rehearse.[45]

Over the years, Whitey's Lindy Hoppers also dominated the nation's largest dance competition, the annual Harvest Moon Ball. Sponsored by the *New York Daily News*, the first ball was to have been held on August 15, 1935, in Central Park. But when 150,000 people showed up, organizers, fearing they could not control such a crowd, cancelled the contest and rescheduled it for Madison Square Garden two weeks later. A charity event, with all profits going to the News Welfare Association to pay for summer vacations for underprivileged children, the ball was the kind of multiracial event that few cultural forms other than swing music could have inspired. Two bands were to supply two different kinds of music for two different kinds of dancing: a white society band (Abe Lyman) for the ballroom competition and a swing band (Fletcher Henderson) for the Lindy Hop. The Lindy Hoppers, who were dressed in sneakers and skirts, admired the evening dresses and dinner jackets of the ballroom dancers, but the crowd cheered the loudest for the Lindy Hoppers. They were the only contestants in the competition who were not white, and they entered the competition in style: "holding our partner's hand and laughing, skipping, jumping, cutting little steps, and carrying on."[46]

At the Savoy Ballroom competitions, audience response determined the winner. But here at the Harvest Moon Ball there would be judges—also all white. Norma Miller was dumbstruck: "We'd never heard of dancing to rules. We couldn't be away from our partners and had to have our feet on the floor. And the crowd didn't decide the winner—they had all white judges and a point system!"[47] Apparently the rules eliminated what would soon become the Lindy Hop's most distinctive characteristics: the breakaway and the jump.

Ignoring the rules, Leon James and Edith Mathews took first place, Maggie McMillan and Frankie Manning came in second, and Norma Miller and Billy Ricker were third. Savoy Ballroom dancers had won the top three places that year, and African American dancers won the Lindy competition every subsequent year till 1950, except for 1943, when, after a summer race riot, Mayor La Guardia virtually banned African Americans from the contest. And, Manning says, after 1937 the Lindy Hoppers were allowed to do "whatever they wanted at the Harvest Moon Ball." [48] In 1940 *Daily News* reporter William Murtha described a fervid event: "They call it dancing, but it included everything from the old-fashioned airplane spin to something that looked like a baseball slide, preceded by a cartwheel." By 1942 Murtha was reporting that "in the name of rhythm . . . [dancers] tossed each other around in a screaming array of shagging, pecking, big appling, Lindy hopping and any miscellaneous gyrations you care to mention. The crowd howled and all but fell out of the balconies as the jitterbugs did their stuff." [49]

Such athleticism and enthusiasm were often unwelcome. Couples who tried to dance at the first Benny Goodman concert sponsored by the Chicago Rhythm Club were booed off the floor, and at Goodman's first Carnegie Hall concert, dancers were barred from the aisles. In a display of wishful or prescriptive journalism, *Metronome* reported in 1939 that "the vast majority of dancers stop dancing when real swing bands begin their swing numbers. . . . [T]he real fans are beginning to realize that swing is appreciated more by those who listen and watch than the ones who attempt to dance to its music." [50] And in fact, many sophisticated white New York clubs, catering to an older clientele, provided no room for dancing whatsoever in an effort to keep the riffraff away. But African American and young swing audiences expected to dance. When Benny Goodman and Count Basie gave a joint concert for six thousand at Madison Square Garden in 1938, accommodations were made for dancers. [51] At the Savoy, dancing continued apace, and dancers and musicians inspired each other to ever greater heights. "The bands seemed to be swinging faster every night," said one Savoy dancer, "and all the best dancers could follow them, in new and different ways." [52]

Meanwhile, many professional dance instructors continued to boycott the step. At their 1939 convention the Dancing Masters of America attacked the jitterbug and other "*jumping dances* . . . such as the 'Shag,' 'Big Apple,' and other athletic steps." The president of the association emphasized that the jitterbug had "no place in the instruction program," and the group as a whole issued a manifesto "consigning the jitterbug to oblivion."[53]

Professional dance instructors may have deplored the Lindy, but dancers and critics were more enthusiastic. In later years dance critic John Martin wrote about the cultural transmission of black dances to white dancers, which he saw happening at the Savoy: "The white jitterbug is oftener than not uncouth to look at, though he may be having a wonderful time and dancing skillfully, but his Negro original is quite another matter. His movements are never so exaggerated that they lack control, and there is an unmistakable dignity. . . . There is a remarkable amount of improvisation . . . mixed in with . . . Lindy Hop figures. Of all the ballroom dancing these prying eyes have seen, this is unquestionably the finest."[54] White dancers who wanted to learn the latest steps traveled to the Savoy in New York or to black clubs in other cities. Record producer Jerry Wexler often snuck into the Savoy when he was a teenager to watch the "undulating, lindy-hopping dancers" and try his own dancing out. "That took guts," says Wexler. "Most of the patrons, perhaps 80%, were black, meaning that the quality of dance was exceedingly high."[55] Ernie Smith, who became an important collector of dance on film, remembers the irresistible attraction of the early 1940s dances in Hill City, the African American section of Pittsburgh. As a youngster, Smith would "sneak over to Hill City and study the dancers from the balcony of the ballroom. I found what I'd been missing." Smith imported the Hill City versions to his high school prom, "shocking and impressing" his friends, who immediately tried to copy him.[56]

White America also received formal introductions to the Lindy. In 1937 three prominent African American dancers organized a "Negro Dance Evening," which began with African dances, proceeded to slave dancing, continued with contemporary social dances such as the Lindy Hop and truckin', and ended with modern concert dance. Presented at the Kaufmann Auditorium of the Ninety-second Street Young Men's Hebrew Association, New York's most prominent new venue for white modern dancers, the program claimed African roots not just for the African American dances but for "dancing in the Americas today."[57]

In 1938 a Carnival of Swing featuring twenty-five bands introduced the Lindy on Randall's Island in New York City at that year's biggest jazz concert. *Life* magazine photographs confirm the *New York Times'* description of the audience: "Young and old, rich and poor. They were all races, all colors, all walks of life."[58] The 1938 newsreel "Jitterbugs Jive at Swingeroo" transmitted news of the concert and details of the dance to the nation.

Although the New York World's Fair, "The World of Tomorrow," featured Whitey's Lindy Hoppers, it was not easy to find them. As fairgoer and *New Yorker* chronicler E. B. White reported: "Gaiety is not the keynote in Tomorrow. I finally found it at the tag end of a chilly evening, far along in the Amusement Area, in a tent with some colored folks. There was laughing and shouting there."[59] White had stumbled onto the Savoy pavilion, the only large African American concession at the fair, featuring all-Negro personnel, musicians, and dancers, including many of Whitey's Lindy Hoppers, dancing in ten to twelve shows a day, plus informal dancing outside the tent. At the Savoy's inauguration, Erskine Hawkins played for the Lindy Hoppers, "breaking in the sod."[60] The pavilion was hugely popular with white youth, and when a Lindy Hop contest was held there on May 21, 1939, a *New York Times* reporter noted that the white kids, all from Long Island, "had all the enthusiasm of Harlemites and just about their skill." The jitterbugs, said the reporter, "made everybody forget everything else."[61] But the Savoy pavilion remained open only until August of 1939. Despite being one of the few Amusement Area exhibits that turned a profit, the Savoy had to close down after producer Michael Todd stole White's dancers, nearly all the Lindy Hoppers at the concession, to perform in a modified version of his Broadway show *Hot Mikado* at the fair.[62] A swing version of the Gilbert and Sullivan operetta, *Hot Mikado* was billed as "the loudest, craziest, hottest and most brilliantly organized jam session of this cockeyed jazz age."[63] The *New York Daily News* said that *Hot Mikado* stood "absolutely unrivaled among all the colored shows of our time."[64] Clearly part of the appeal was the Lindy Hoppers, for the *New York Mirror* promised that the show would "have the local jitterbugs shagging in the aisles."[65] Although there were problems between the younger Lindy Hoppers and the great Bill "Bojangles" Robinson during rehearsals, by the time the show opened the Lindy Hoppers had become so popular that Robinson proclaimed at a backstage party, "Nobody had better mess with me or the Lindy Hoppers—*they* take care of the first act and I take care of the second."[66]

Swingin' the Dream (1939) was another jazz adaptation of a classic theatrical work, in this case Shakespeare's *Midsummer Night's Dream*. The setting was New Orleans in 1890, and the duke of Athens had become the governor of Louisiana. Clarinetist Benny Goodman led a sextet that included vibraharpist Lionel Hampton, pianist Fletcher Henderson, and guitarist Charlie Christian. Louis Armstrong played the role of Bottom. The Lindy Hoppers performed in three numbers: as backup to the Dandridge Sisters singing "Swingin' A Dream," a production number with chorus girls, and a Lindy Hop routine danced to "Jumpin' at the Woodside," in which they dressed as wood fairies. Photos of the Broadway production show Whitey's Lindy Hoppers jumping several feet off the ground as they entertain Titania (Maxine Sullivan).

The Lindy would survive and spread. More than seventy years later, American popular dance continues to evolve in the direction in which the Lindy sent it. And the Lindy itself thrives as a distinct form as well as in variations such as the West Coast swing (an eight-count Lindy danced in a straight track) and East Coast swing (a circular, six-count Lindy, or jitterbug), the "shag" of the Carolinas, the St. Louis imperial style, and the Dallas push and Houston whip. The swing dance revival continues among Americans from adolescent to senescent.

On this point dance critics agree: it was the air steps that propelled the Lindy to nationwide fame.[67] When the Lindy went airborne, it projected the energy not just of the young African American jitterbuggers but of the future itself. The beauty of the Lindy was in the way it allowed dancers to stylize, authorizing each version with innovation and personality. By endowing their dancing with personal style, Lindy dancers managed to keep from being simply faces in the crowd.

Yet the faces of the style's originators faded into invisibility. The Savoy Lindy Hop teams dominated public presentations of the Lindy, from their fourteen championships at Madison Square Garden's Harvest Moon Ball to film, stage, and the 1939 World's Fair. Nevertheless, when *Life* magazine published an issue on American dance forms, Leon James and Willamae Ricker, pictured demonstrating the Lindy's swing-out, were identified only as "Harlem Negroes."[68] James and Ricker made it to the pages of *Life* again in 1943, when the magazine published several pictures of them demonstrating aerial steps—but not on the cover, where two white dancers represented the globally popular American dance.[69] Professional dance teachers who had formed a unified front against the dance in the 1930s organized to teach the "Lindy/jitterbug," and white jitterbugs began to appear in movies. During the war, American servicemen danced the Lindy all over the world. Whitey's Lindy

Hoppers disbanded when many of their members were drafted, including Frankie Manning, who joined Betty Grable on stage in the Philippines for one memorable USO performance. By that time the Lindy was no longer considered black vernacular dance but rather served as a symbol of America itself. It was just as Carl Van Vechten had predicted in 1930: "Nearly all the dancing now to be seen in our musical shows is of Negro origin, but both critics and public are so ignorant of this fact that the production of a new Negro revue is an excuse for the revival of the hoary old lament that it is a pity the Negro can't create anything for himself, that he is obliged to imitate the white man's revues. This, in brief, has been the history of the Cake-Walk, the Bunny Hug, the Turkey Trot, the Charleston, and the Black Bottom. It will probably be the history of the Lindy Hop." [70]

In Frankie Manning's memories of that time, sports and dance and celebration all merge together, and he saw no reason for them not to, then or now. "Nowadays, you see athletes dancing when they make a touchdown or a basket. That's exactly what I used to do after I'd made a couple of points on the basketball court. The coach would yell, 'Manning, you're not on the dance floor now!' I'd say, 'Okay, Coach,' and dance on down the court." [71] Like the jump shot of the 1950s, the slam dunk of the 1960s, and the end zone celebration of the 1990s, the "jumping dances" and air steps of the 1930s were a recognizably African American form of exuberance. *Life* magazine, writing about the Lindy, stated, "Negroes were its creators and principal exponents, and Arthur Murray would no more have taught the Lindy Hop than Rachmaninoff would have given lessons in boogie-woogie." [72] Which is not to say that Arthur Murray *couldn't* have taught the Lindy Hop. Just that he wouldn't. Declaring war on swing dance was a small skirmish in the longer, ongoing war of "cultural segregation," determined to maintain distinctions of race and class. [73] The replication of this impulse in nearly every form of cultural expression—from music, to dance, to boxing, to basketball—only emphasizes its systematic (if not institutional) pervasiveness in American society. Air steps were both the jump shot and the slam dunk that drove dancers, like athletes, to ever greater displays of virtuosity while enraging those trying to maintain social control.

It is not enough to say that these physical gestures threatened white America because they spoke of blackness, or because, as I show in chapter 8, they spoke of Africa. These physical gestures—air steps, the jump shot, the slam dunk—speak of individual pride in a context that, according to the rules of the day, ought not to allow for such an emotion. Unwritten rules forbade the jump shot, just as more recently the slam dunk and the end zone celebration were outlawed in outdated rules that, as Joel Dinerstein suggests, were really applying penalties to the "illegal use of black culture." [74] William Carlos Williams once wrote that his black neighbors in Paterson, New Jersey, had "poise in a world where they have no authority." [75] Black people in 1930s America had no authority. And yet they jumped. They jumped to the heavens. At the Olympics they jumped higher than any other people on earth. They jumped as if they were jumping for joy. What right had they to express such joy? And to express it so powerfully? It was as if they refused to acknowledge centuries of oppression, as if they did not carry the burden of the ages. As if they considered themselves the equal of anyone.

CHAPTER 5 :
THE JOINT IS JUMPING

The new social dances of the 1920s led to a nationwide demand for dancing and dance music. Bands that had previously specialized in ragtime or country-fiddle dance music, in brass band music, or even in supplying music for minstrel or carnival shows began to include jazz in their repertoire. Traveling territory bands brought dance music to small towns but also provided jobs and experience to young musicians and served as nomadic conservatories, where musicians could develop skills in playing, arranging, and in the business of music. In *The Swing Era*, Schuller asserts that "virtually all jazz orchestras were at one time territory orchestras, at least of territory origin."[1] Many of the orchestras that contributed to a national swing style began as regional bands with highly individual styles. Schuller reminds us that Jimmie Lunceford began in Nashville and Memphis with a group called the Chickasaw Syncopators, Chick Webb came from Baltimore, Duke Ellington from Washington. And the Count Basie Orchestra, of course, operated out of Kansas City.

During the first wave of urban blues, from 1925 to 1942, big bands of eight pieces and larger toured the South and Southwest playing the blues in arranged form. Schuller describes traveling bluesmen from Texas, Arkansas, and Oklahoma who were among the best-known and most influential of all blues musicians, particularly in the Southwest, where blues somehow broke through social and economic barriers into a middle-class and urban world: "Southwestern orchestras quickly adopted the form and used it more consistently than bands anywhere else . . . out of this earthier, deeper feeling in the music developed a way of playing jazz which was eventually to supercede the New Orleans, Chicago, and New York styles."[2] In recordings from these years, Schuller says, there is "a spirit and musical feeling which was at once radically new and thoroughly indigenous to the Southwest. The difference is clearly the blues."[3] In addition to the blues tradition, the Southwest bands drew heavily from the rocking boogie-woogie piano style that Schuller says was "spreading like wildfire throughout the Southwest."[4] Jesse Stone's Blues Serenaders, the

Dallas-based Alphonse Trent band, Walter Page's Oklahoma City Blue Devils, and the bands of Terrence Holder, Andy Kirk, George Lee, San Antonio's Troy Floyd, and Oliver Cobb flourished and competed for audiences (often in face-to-face confrontations) in an area reaching as far north as Chicago, west to Denver, east to Memphis, and as far south as San Antonio.

Strategically placed in the middle of this landscape, Kansas City became a mecca for such bands, because its political boss, Tom Pendergast, maintained a wide-open entertainment district that defied the laws of Prohibition. Musicians who played the clubs and casinos of Kansas City from the late 1920s until Pendergast's death in 1938 fused jazz and blues styles so tightly that few distinguished between them. One of the strongest of these bands was that of Bennie Moten, whose pianist, Count Basie, had been stolen from Walter Page in 1929, after a battle with Page's band. With a recording contract from Victor, Moten acquired a national reputation and became the undisputed ruler of the "territory" bands, although the group had to fight to stay on top: one battle in 1931 involved no fewer than six different bands.[5] Moten's band, according to Schuller, accomplished a "rhythmic revolution," completing the transition from the earlier "stiffly vertical" beat of New Orleans–style jazz to the swinging, horizontal ensemble work of the rhythm section: piano, guitar, drums, and bass.[6] When Moten died in 1935, Count Basie took over. The Kansas City style of the Count Basie Orchestra marked the culmination of the Southwest blues style, but it also marked an important step in the evolution of swing. And it may very well have been the origin of the jump style that defined the high-energy music and dance that emerged in the late 1930s.

Like his swing counterpart Duke Ellington, Basie was a pianist. But unlike Ellington, who composed and orchestrated lush harmonies for his featured melodic soloists, Basie let his rhythm section fuel the rest of the band. While rhythm guitarist Freddie Green and drummer Jo Jones laid down a driving rhythmic pattern, Walter Page played melodic bass lines, more often than not a "walking bass," notes that climbed and descended the pitches of the blues scale or outlined chords. The walking bass was a musical gesture common first in boogie-woogie piano music, then in Kansas City swing, and finally it became the signature bass line of jazz in the thirties and forties.[7] The remainder of the band played short, furious riffs, often one section, perhaps the saxes, against another—the brass. On top of these pulsing patterns, soloists would improvise. Basie, at the piano, filled in with sparsely placed melodic figures, accenting but never competing with the soloist. The band often alternated riff choruses with solos, using the choruses as background for solos, or alternating between solos and the entire band in a call-response arrangement.

"One O'Clock Jump" was such a tune, conceived at the Reno Club in Kansas City sometime around 1935 or 1936. According to the Basie band's Buster Smith: "We were fooling around at the club and Basie was playing along in F. That was his favorite key. He hollered to me that he was going to switch to D Flat and for me to 'set' something. I started playing that opening reed riff [from "Six or Seven Times"] on alto. Lips Page jumped in with the trumpet part without any trouble and Dan Minor thought up the trombone part. That was it—a 'head.'"[8] Through group collaboration, building on a melodic fragment from the 1920s, the band had just come up with the head for one of the most influential jazz pieces of all time (a "head" is the standard opening version of the piece, on which subsequent improvised verses will build). One devoted listener to the Reno Club radio broadcasts was John Hammond, who assisted the band in securing a recording contract. Basie took the group to Chicago, then New York, and on July 7, 1937, the Count Basie Orchestra recorded "One O'Clock Jump" for Decca. It immediately became a hit and the swing bands scooped it up. By 1940, "One O'Clock Jump" had been recorded at least a dozen times.[9] Basie continued recording in his own inimitable style, with one jump tune after another. The Basie band alone recorded "Do You Wanna Jump, Children" (1938), "Jumpin' at the Woodside" (1938), "Jump For Me" (1939), "The Apple Jump" (1939), "Hollywood Jump" (1939), "Love Jumped Out" (1940), and "Jump the Blues Away" (1941). Basie's 1939 "Lester Leaps In" may not be a jump tune exactly, but it, too, reflects the new upbeat mood of the late 1930s, a mood that was officially called "jump" on July 7, 1937.

It is impossible to number the jump tunes of the 1930s and 1940s. But it is possible to count the number of recordings that use the word "jump" in their title. The definitive catalogue of recordings for this period is Brian Rust's *Jazz Records, 1897–1942*. This slim but comprehensive volume includes at least 135 record titles with the word "jump" in them, and all but eleven were recorded between 1937 and 1942.[10] (See table 5.1.) That list doesn't include the many titles with synonyms for jump, such as "hop" and "leap." And clearly it doesn't include the countless legitimate jump tunes that don't use the word "jump" in their titles. It is impossible to brush away this sudden mountainous accumulation of jump tunes. But what does it mean?

Clearly, after 1937 "jump" has something to do with dancing. But not before 1937. Up until then, the word "jump" had more to do with children's play, athleticism, or simply joy itself. Other words were used to describe vernacular dance. The hit black musical *Shuffle Along*, which opened off-Broadway on May 21, 1921, institutionalized the word "shuffle" as a generic term for African American, or jazz, dance.[11] "Stomp," a similarly generic term for vernacular dance, appeared in the titles of many dance tunes of the 1920s and early 1930s, as did "shuffle," "wobble," and "truckin'."[12] As for definitions, Count Basie said: "I really don't know how you would define stomp in strict musical terms. But it was a real thing. What I would say is if you were on the first floor, and the dance hall was upstairs, that was what you would hear, that steady *rump, rump, rump, rump* in that medium tempo. It was never fast."[13]

Bennie Moten's Kansas City band recorded ten or so stomps, shuffles, and wobbles between 1924 and 1932, and between 1926 and 1938 Duke Ellington recorded about a dozen stomp or shuffle tunes.[14] Basie played both stomps and jumps and didn't differentiate much between the two, except to say that jumps were a little "snappier." Albert Murray, an expert on jazz and coauthor of Basie's memoirs, notes that stomps and jumps were indistinguishable in performance. "The dance steps are different, of course," writes Murray, "but even so one can jump to a stomp and swing; stomp to a jump and swing; or swing to a jump and a stomp."[15] Even more significant, then, is the change in nomenclature from the downward "stomp" to the upward "jump," reflecting not simply a new style of music but a public naming and claiming of an increasingly "upbeat" attitude.

Jump tunes were fast-paced swing blues built on riff choruses.[16] Early jump music relied on a hard-driving 4/4 meter that placed equal emphasis on all four beats, although jump blues of the 1940s tended to collapse to a peppy 2/4 feel, emphasizing the backbeat, which is also called the upbeat. Often, but not always, jump tunes featured the Kansas City walking bass. Musicians often talk about "jumping" on the bass, so perhaps the "jump" designation was also related to the prominence of the bass line in such tunes. By the late 1930s, jump tunes were the specialty of small rhythm bands that "made the customers want to jump and dance."[17]

"Jumping" meant having a good time. One of the most famous jump tunes was Basie's "Jumpin' at the Woodside." When in New York, the Count Basie band members lived at a Harlem hotel called the Woodside, where many of New York's, and the nation's, elite African American artists often stayed—and partied. "Talk about jumping at the Woodside," Basie wrote laconically. "That was our thing." But jumping wasn't simply having a good time, as Basie explained. It was rapidly becoming a new trend in music and dance, one that Basie had helped to shape: "It was at the Woodside that I began to feel, and I mean really get a deep feeling, about the difference that fate had made in my life." [18] Dancer Manning writes, "By early 1937, some of us were turning into Basie-ites. To me, Basie swung more than any band out there." [19]

Basie's "One O'Clock Jump" quickly became the signal to dancehall patrons that the evening was coming to an end and they'd better get their dancing done before the joint closed. In the words of Dizzy Gillespie: "You know a dance is from nine to one. One o'clock means getting outta there. So when one o'clock jumped, you played that." [20] Drummer Jo Jones remembered playing the tune at the Apollo: "We used to do a thing every Thursday night at the Apollo when we closed. The theater's packed, but there are two seats set aside for Sid Catlett and his wife. I used to throw the sticks to Sidney and a man would put a light on him and BOOM—he'd catch it. Then, BOOM, he'd throw the stick back to me and we'd go into 'One O'Clock Jump.' Don't ask me. Ask the people that were there." [21]

One can't avoid the obvious connection between the word "jump" and one of the most distinctive characteristics of jump tunes: their "upbeat" nature. "Basie was always stomping down like this," Albert Murray told me, lightly stamping the floor with his heel. "But Hamp [Lionel Hampton, sometimes called the "Jump King"] always counted up like this," said Murray with quick upward jerks of his right hand, index finger making a circle with his thumb. [22] Through 1937 Hampton continued to call jump tunes "stomps," recording "Stomp," "Stompology," "China Stomp," "Drum Stomp," and "Piano Stomp" for Victor that year. But soon after, Hampton recorded "Down Home Jump" (1938) and "The Jumpin' Jive" (1939), and in the 1940s he carried jump tunes to their next stage, jump blues. [23]

Very few of the larger bands—Basie's was one—survived the many threats to the existence of touring groups in the 1940s. World War II put many musicians into military service. Gasoline shortages made touring difficult, and shellac shortages cut down on record production. A recording industry strike only exacerbated an already difficult situation. Major record labels focused on big-selling white artists but "very few blacks." [24] With slightly different instrumentation—featuring a blues singer, electric guitar, saxophone solos, and an even stronger emphasis on rhythm and blues—small groups continued to tour, playing a unique combination of swing and jump music.

By the mid-1940s, jump had become a "stylistic sanctuary for African-Americans and many whites" who would not play bebop or sweet music for popular vocalists. Bands led by Cab Calloway, Lionel Hampton, Erskine Hawkins, Charlie Barnet, Tiny Bradshaw, Lucky Millinder, Bill Doggett, Roy Eldridge, and Earl Bostic employed a small army of former swing musicians. [25] As white dance music became increasingly, in Schuller's words, "insipid," and bebop combos played more and more esoteric music, rhythm and blues provided a "musical haven" for many black musicians and their audiences. [26] Charlie Barnet's 1939 "Jump Session," "Swing Street Strut," and "Midweek Function" demonstrate the transition from swing to jump, and Tiny Bradshaw's 1944 "Straighten Up and Fly Right" and his "Bradshaw Bounce" are typical of what he always called his "bounce" pieces. In 1943, Roy Eldridge recorded "Minor Jive" and "Jump through the Window," both in the small-group jump style. [27]

One of the most successful of these small bands was that of Louis Jordan. Born and raised in Brinkley, Arkansas, about sixty miles from Memphis, Jordan came from a family of entertainers: his father was the bandleader for the Rabbit Foot Minstrels. Jordan was primarily a jazz musician early in his career, and played with Chick Webb until the bandleader's death in 1938, when Jordan formed his own, smaller group, one that, according to producer Jerry Wexler, married "the harmonic sophistication of jazz with the folk wit of the blues." [28] Jordan's Tympany Four, which thereafter was called the Tympany Five, regardless of the number of members, made its debut at the Elks Rendezvous, close to the Savoy Ballroom, on August 4, 1938. An announcement in the *Amsterdam News* in New York on October 15 of that year identified the group in print as a "Jump Band." [29] With a lead vocalist, rhythm section, and one or two horns, jump blues bands such as Jordan's scored several million-copy hits in the 1940s, despite segregation policies that ruled radio. Jordan himself recorded the crossover number-one single "G.I. Jive/Is You Is Or Is You Ain't My Baby," as well as at least twelve other songs on national charts.

On the varying forms of black artists' charts, Jordan and his Tympany Five spent a total of 113 weeks in the number-one position, with eighteen songs hitting number one and fifty-four placing in the top ten.

A saxophonist, Jordan also toured with Earl Hines and Billy Eckstine in the early 1940s. Other members of Eckstine's *Blue Ribbon Salute* shows included Dizzy Gillespie, Art Blakey, and Charlie Parker, musicians who reshaped swing jazz into bebop, a fine art. But Jordan wanted to "entertain." "These guys, except Dizzy, who's the master, the king, really wanted to play mostly for themselves," he recalled, "and I still wanted to play for the people. I just like to sing my blues and swing." [30]

Because musicians such as Lionel Hampton and Louis Jordan were well known to older generations and to mainstream listeners, they helped bring their audiences into a new era of popular music. Both led jump bands that recorded many hits, records that were formative and that reflected the cultural shift from jazz to rhythm and blues as the popular music of the day. In 1942 the *Billboard* chart for black records was known as the "Harlem Hit Parade," a category that changed in 1945 to "Race Records." But by 1949 that same chart—on which Louis Jordan appeared more often than any other artist, a fact that remains true to this day—was called "Rhythm and Blues." For jazz saxophonist Sonny Rollins, Jordan was "like a bridge between the blues and jazz. I just loved him." Tenor saxophonist Eddie Johnson, who played with Jordan, said "Louis Jordan was rocking and rolling when the Rolling Stones, the Beatles and Elvis Presley thought the only rock was in a baby's rocking chair." Chuck Berry, whom many musicians declare the father of rock and roll, says he learned everything from listening to Louis Jordan, a statement made all the more believable by the parallels in their lyrics and the similarity of Berry's guitar style to that of Jordan's guitarist, Carl Hogan. To blues-funk artist James Brown, Jordan's music was equally pivotal. "He was *Everything*," said Brown. [31] Not just Jordan but his countless jump blues imitators pointed the way and laid the paving for rhythm and blues, and from there for rock and roll.

Jerry Wexler has similar thoughts about Lionel Hampton: "Hamp was prerock, preroll, one of the sure-enough daddies of the Big Beat. Hamp was hip." [32] Hampton thought the same. In 1953, returning from Europe, he was surprised to hear "this new thing called rock 'n' roll. I found it was something we'd been playing for quite a while." To Hampton's ear, the backbeat was familiar: "I played that a long time ago. There isn't too much new under the sun. . . . We had that eight-beat thing going, what they used to call boogie woogie."[33] They also called it jump.

Jump/rhythm and blues bandleader Johnny Otis has his own memories of when bebop and jump blues musicians parted company. "The evolving R&B concept required straight 4/4, afterbeat, and steady shuffle rhythms," he said. "Highly technical and fancy modern jazz drummers were usually unsuited to the new music. In fact, it was difficult to get the average bebop-schooled drummer to lay down a steady pulse beat. The frills, bombs, and embellishments got in the way of the straight-ahead rhythm patterns that were the foundation for jump blues."[34] A drummer himself, Otis learned from listening to swing drummers like Jesse Price (who played for Count Basie, Harlan Leonard, and Slim Gaillard), Gus Johnson (who played for Count Basie and Earl Hines), and Jimmy Crawford, Jimmie Lunceford's "great rhythm master."[35] Otis played drums for Harlan Leonard's Kansas City Rockets in the early 1940s, formed the sixteen-piece house band at the Club Alabam, and in 1948 opened the Barrelhouse Club in Watts, the first nightspot in the world to offer rhythm and blues music exclusively.[36] He then formed the Johnny Otis Show, which had fifteen Top 40 rhythm and blues hits between 1950 and 1952. Composer and performer of "Willie and the Hand Jive," Otis made swing rhythms jump and then made the transition through rhythm and blues to rock and roll.

The popularity of "Hand Jive" surged again in the 1978 as it was introduced to a new generation in the musical film *Grease*. There the song provides the backdrop to one of the most frenzied—and whitest—Lindy Hops ever seen. The music and dance of the movie's rebellious teens is so contagious that even the adults begin performing the movements to the hand jive, and dancing the jitterbug. Based on dances invented in the 1930s, set in 1959 small-town America, premiered on stage in 1971, filmed in 1978, revived in 1994 and then again in 2007, through its trajectory *Grease* demonstrates as well as any cultural artifact the longevity and appeal of jump music and dance.

Much has been made of bebop as political statement and of bebop musicians as the intellectual leaders of their generation, creating a new musical vocabulary and approach that was a reproach to white swing musicians. Yet jump was the more pervasive cultural statement, as it remained the one consistently danceable offspring of the swing era. Bebop's danceable sibling, jump is the missing link between swing music and rock and roll.

TABLE 5.1. Record Titles Including the Word "Jump"

Artist	Record title	Date recorded	Catalog no.
Van Alexander and His Orch.	The Jumpin' Jive (Jim-Jam-Jump)	6/21/39	Bluebird B-10330
Andrews Sisters	The Jumping Jive (Jim-Jam-Jump)	9/15/39	Decca 2756
George Auld and His Orch.	Juke Box Jump	1/1/40	Varsity 8159
Mildred Bailey and Her Orch.	Jump, Jump's Here	7/28/38	Brunswick 8202
Charlie Barnet and His Orch.	Jump Session	2/24/39	Bluebird B-10172
Charlie Barnet and His Orch.	The Last Jump (A Jump to End All Jumps)	7/17/39	Bluebird B-10389
Charlie Barnet and His Orch.	Jump-Jump's Here	11/5/38	Thesaurus 605
Charlie Barnet and His Orch.	Do You Want to Jump Children	11/5/38	Thesaurus 605
Count Basie and His Orch.	One O'Clock Jump	7/7/37	Decca 1363
Count Basie and His Orch.	One O'Clock Jump	11/3/37	Collectors' CC-9
Count Basie and His Orch.	One O'Clock Jump	7/9/38	Collectors' CC-9
Count Basie and His Orch.	One O'Clock Jump	12/23/38	Vanguard VRS-8523
Count Basie and His Orch.	One O'Clock Jump	2/20/40	JSC AA-652
Count Basie and His Orch.	One O'Clock Jump	1/21/42	OK 6634
Count Basie and His Orch.	Jumpin' at the Woodside	8/22/38	Decca 2212
Count Basie and His Orch.	Do You Wanna Jump, Children	11/9/38	Decca 2224
Count Basie and His Orch.	Jump for Me	3/20/39	Vocalion 4886
Count Basie and His Orch.	The Apple Jump	11/6/39	Okeh 5862
Count Basie and His Orch.	Hollywood Jump	11/7/39	Columbia 35338
Count Basie and His Orch.	Love Jumped Out	11/19/40	Okeh 5963
Count Basie and His Orch.	Jump the Blues Away	1/28/41	Okeh 6157
Sidney Bechet and His New Orleans Feetwarmers	One O'Clock Jump	2/5/40	Victor 27204
Fred Boehler and His Band	Fred's Jump	11/5/40	Columbia ZZ-1006
Larry Breese and His Orch.	The Jumpin' Jive	Sept. 1939	Ammor 101
Brown and Terry's Jazzola Boys	Jump Steady Blues	Sept. 1921	Okeh 8021
Les Brown and His Orch.	Jumpin' Jive	8/15/39	Thesaurus 691
Merritt Brunies and His Friars Inn Orch.	Up Jumped the Devil	Sept. 1924	Auto (unnumbered)
Merritt Brunies and His Friars Inn Orch.	Up Jumped the Devil	11/14/25	Retrieval FJ-124
Merritt Brunies and His Friars Inn Orch.	Up Jumped the Devil	3/12/26	OK 40618
Sonny Burke and His Orch.	Jumpin' Salty	10/9/40	Okeh 5989

Artist	Record title	Date recorded	Catalog no.
Erskine Butterfield and His Blues Boy	Jumpin' in a Juleep Joint	7/23/42	Decca 4400
Cab Calloway and His Orch.	Do You Wanna Jump Children	10/27/38	Vocalion 4477
Cab Calloway and His Orch.	(Hep-Hep!) The Jumpin' Jive	7/17/39	Vocalion/OK 5005
Eddie Carroll	One O'Clock Jump	10/10/38	Parlophone R-2579
Bob Chester and His Orch.	The Octave Jump	3/4/40	Bluebird B-10649
Larry Clinton and His Orch.	Jump Joe	10/8/40	Bluebird B-10961
Alix Combelle and His Swing Band	Jumpin' at the Woodside	2/20/40	Swing 93
Eddie Condon and His Windy City Seven	Carnegie Jump	1/17/38	Commodore 1500
Al Cooper and His Savoy Sultans	Jump Steady	7/29/38	Decca 7499
Al Cooper and His Savoy Sultans	Jumpin' at the Savoy	5/24/39	Decca 2526
Al Cooper and His Savoy Sultans	We'd Rather Jump Than Swing	5/24/39	Decca 2526
Al Cooper and His Savoy Sultans	Jumpin' the Blues	10/16/39	Decca 2930
Al Cooper and His Savoy Sultans	Sophisticated Jump	3/29/40	Decca 3274
Al Cooper and His Savoy Sultans	Second Balcony Jump	2/28/41	Decca 8545
Rosetta Crawford	My Man Jumped Salty On Me	2/1/39	Decca 7567
Bob Crosby's Bob Cats	Big Foot Jump	3/14/38	Decca 2108
Devonshire Restaurant Dance Band	Up Jumped the Devil	12/10/26	Zonophone 2856
Al Donahue and His Orch.	The Blue Jump	9/11/40	Okeh 5828
Al Donahue and His Orch.	Jumpin' at the Juke Box	2/18/41	Okeh 6136
Jimmy Dorsey and His Orch.	The Jumpin' Jive (Jim Jam Jump)	7/14/39	Decca 2612
Duke Ellington and His Famous Orch.	Jumpin' Punkins	2/15/41	Victor LPV-517; 27356
Duke Ellington and His Famous Orch.	Jumpin' Punkins	2/15/41	Caracol CAR 422
Duke Ellington and His Famous Orch.	Jumpin' Punkins	9/17/41	
Duke Ellington and His Famous Orch.	Jump for Joy	7/2/41	Victor 27517
Seger Ellis and His Orch.	Jitterbug's Jump	1/19/40	Okeh 6051
Leonard Feather's All-Star Jam Band	Men Of Harlem (Tempo di Jump)	4/20/39	Decca 18118
Slim Gaillard (Slim and Slam)	Jump Session	8/17/38	Vocalion 4346
Slim Gaillard and His Flat Foot Floogie Boys	Broadway Jump	8/2/40	Okeh 5792
Slim Gaillard and His Flat Foot Floogie Boys	Palm Springs Jump	4/4/42	CBS AL-33566
Nat Gonella and His Georgians	One O'Clock Jump	5/2/39	Parlophone F-1436

(continued on next page)

Artist	Record title	Date recorded	Catalog no.
Nat Gonella and His Georgians	(Hep! Hep!) The Jumping Jive	8/14/40	Columbia FB-2492
Benny Goodman and His Orch.	One O'Clock Jump	1/16/38	Columbia B-1701
Benny Goodman and His Orch.	One O'Clock Jump	2/16/38	Victor 25792
Benny Goodman and His Orch.	Jumpin' at the Woodside	8/10/39	Columbia 35210
Benny Goodman and His Orch.	One O'Clock Jump	10/6/39	Polygon 6007
Jimmy Gordon and His VipVop Band	(Roll 'Em Dorothy) Let 'Em Jump For Joy	9/29/39	Decca 7794
Lionel Hampton and His Orch.	Down Home Jump	10/11/38	Victor 26114
Lionel Hampton and His Orch.	The Jumpin' Jive	6/13/39	Victor 26304
Erskine Hawkins and His Orch.	Do You Wanna Jump Children	10/20/38	Bluebird B-10019
Erskine Hawkins and His Orch.	Jumpin' in a Julep Joint	8/8/41	Bluebird B-11547
Horace Henderson and His Orch.	Swingin' and Jumpin'	5/8/40	Vocalion 5606
Woody Herman and His Orch.	Jumpin' Blues	7/18/39	Decca 2664
Woody Herman and His Orch.	The Rhumba Jumps	12/13/39	Decca 2939
Woody Herman and His Orch.	Jukin' (Ski Jump)	4/18/40	Decca 3272
Milt Herth (Quartet)	Jump Jump's Here	11/30/38	Decca 2277
Earl Hines and His Orch.	Up Jumped the Devil	4/3/41	Bluebird B-11237
Earl Hines and His Orch.	Up Jumped the Devil	6/17/41	Alamac QSR-2418
Earl Hines and His Orch.	The Father Jumps	10/28/41	Bluebird B-11535
Earl Hines and His Orch.	Second Balcony Jump	3/19/41	Bluebird B-11567
Earl Hines and His Orch.	Jumpin' Up and Down	6/17/41	Alamac QSR-2418
Johnny Hodges and His Orch.	The Jeep Is Jumpin'	8/24/38	Parliament R-3225
Johnny Hodges and His Orch.	My Heart Jumped over the Moon	6/2/39	Vocalion/Okeh 5330
Johnny Hodges and His Orch.	The Rabbit's Jump	9/1/39	Vocalion/Okeh 5100
Saxi Holtsworth's Harmony Hounds	Hop, Skip, and Jump	Dec. 1920	Emerson 10307
Bob Howard and His Orch.	Hop Skip Jump	10/12/36	Decca 983
Will Hudson and His Orch.	Start Jumpin'	12/5/40	Decca 3579
Harry James and His Orch.	One O'Clock Jump	1/5/38	Brunswick 8055
Harry James and His Orch.	One O'Clock Jump	1/5/38	Col 36232
Harry James and His Orch.	Two O'Clock Jump	3/6/39	Brunswick 8337
Harry James and His Orch.	Cross Country Jump	11/8/39	Columbia 35531
Harry James and His Orch.	Jump Town	7/22/42	Columbia 36683
Pete Johnson	Let 'Em Jump	4/16/39	Solo Art 12005
Pete Johnson	Boogie Woogie Jump	5/7/41	Victor LEJ-1
John Kirby and His Orch.	Jumpin' in the Pump Room	4/22/40	Okeh 5661

Artist	Record title	Date recorded	Catalog no.
Andy Kirk and His Twelve Clouds of Joy	Jump Jack Jump	10/24/38	Decca 2226
Gene Krupa and His Orch.	Do You Wanna Jump, Children	12/12/38	Brunswick 8289
Gene Krupa and His Orch.	The Rumba Jumps	1/3/40	Columbia 35366
Brian Lawrance and His Lansdown House Quartet	Jump on the Wagon	6/14/35	Decca F5592
Harlan Leonard and His Rockets	Hairy Joe Jump	1/11/40	Bluebird B-10625
Harlan Leonard and His Rockets	Society Steps Out (Rachmaninoff Jumps)	11/13/40	RCA PM43263
Jimmie Lunceford and His Orch.	It's Time to Jump and Shout	1/5/40	Vocalion-Okeh 5430
Wingy Mannone and His Orch.	Jumpy Nerves	4/26/39	Bluebird B-10289
Joe Marsala and His Delta Four	Three O'Clock Jump	4/4/40	General 3001
Jay McShann and His Orch.	The Jumpin' Blues	7/2/42	Decca 4418
Jay McShann and His Orch.	One O'Clock Jump	2/7/42	AFRS 71
Jay McShann and His Orch.	One O'Clock Jump	2/14/42	AFRS 72
Jay McShann Quartet	So You Won't Jump	11/18/41	Decca 8607
Metronome All-Star Band	One O'Clock Jump	1/16/41	Victor 27314
Lucky Millinder and His Orch.	Apollo Jump	9/5/41	Decca 18529
Frank Newton and His Café Society Orch.	Frankie's Jump	4/12/39	Vocalion 4821
Jimmie Noone and His Orch.	The Blues Jumped a Rabbit	1/15/36	Decca 18439
Red Norvo and His Orch.	Jump Jump's Here	7/28/38	Brunswick 8202
Hot Lips Page	Jumpin'	4/27/38	Bluebird B-7583
(Tony) Parenti's Liberty Syncopators	Up Jumped the Devil	4/12/26	Columbia 836-D
Danny Polo and His Swing Stars	Montparnasse Jump	1/30/39	Decca F-6989
Sam Price and His Texas Bluesicians	Jumpin' the Boogie	12/6/40	Decca 8515
Don Redman and His Orch.	Jump Session	3/23/39	Victor 26206
Jan Savitt and His Top Hatters	It's Time to Jump and Shout	2/4/40	Decca 3185
Gene Sedric and His Honey Bears	The Joint Is Jumpin'	11/23/38	Vocalion 4576
Artie Shaw	Everything Is Jumpin'	10/20/39	Victor LPT-6000
George Shearing	Jump for Joy	4/23/41	Decca F-915
The Six Swingers	Jumpin' Jive	3/28/40	Columbia FB-2431
Sousa's Band (Will Marion Cook)	Jump Back, Honey	4/13/00	Berliner 01208
Mugsy Spanier	Two O'Clock Jump	6/1/42	Decca 4336

(continued on next page)

Artist	Record title	Date recorded	Catalog no.
Rex Stewart and His Feetwarmers	Montmartre (Django's Jump)	4/5/39	Swing 56
Tampa Red	The Jitter Jump	11/27/40	Bluebird B-8744
Jack Teagarden	Big T Jumps	1/23/40	IAJRC 5
Three Bits of Rhythm	Bronzeville Jump	5/13/41	Decca 8553
Skeets Tolbert and His Gentlemen of Swing	The Stuff's Out (It Jumped Just a Minute Ago)	7/5/39	Decca 7630
Skeets Tolbert and His Gentlemen of Swing	Jumpin' Jack	3/12/40	Decca 7791
Skeets Tolbert and His Gentlemen of Swing	Jumpin' Like Mad	10/2/40	Decca 8528
Skeets Tolbert and His Gentlemen of Swing	Jumpin' in the Numbers	5/22/41	Decca 8565
Big Joe Turner with Willie The Lion Smith	Jumpin' Down Blues	11/26/40	Decca 7827
Fats Waller	The Joint Is Jumpin'	12/11/38	(on LP)
Fats Wallerand His Orch.	Up Jumped You with Love	7/13/42	Bluebird 30–0814
Fats Waller and His Rhythm	The Joint Is Jumpin'	10/7/37	Victor 25689
Fats Waller and His Rhythm	The Joint Is Jumpin'	12/11/38	FW-AR
Fats Waller and His Rhythm	The Joint Is Jumpin'	11/7/40	Film Short/RFW2
Fats Waller and His Rhythm	Buck Jumpin'	10/1/41	Bluebird B-11324
Ethel Waters	At the New Jump Steady Ball	3/21/21	Cardinal 2036
Ethel Waters	At the New Jump Steady Ball	July 1922	BS 14128
Chick Webb and His Orch.	One O'Clock Jump	1/9/39	Polydor 423248
Chick Webb and His Orch.	One O'Clock Jump	2/10/39	Polydor 236524
Doc Wheeler and His Sunset Orch.	Keep Jumpin'	3/30/42	Bluebird B-11559
Paul Whiteman and His Orch.	The General Jumped at Dawn	May 1942	Capitol 101
Teddy Wilson and His Orch.	Jumpin' for Joy	6/28/39	Brunswick 8438
Teddy Wilson and His Orch.	Jumpin' on the Blacks and Whites	9/12/39	Columbia 35232

Compiled from information in Brian Rust, *Jazz Records, 1897–1942* (1969; reprint, Chigwell, Essex: Storyville Publishers, 1975).

CHAPTER 6 : "THAT'S NOT BASKETBALL" : FAST BREAKS, JUMP SHOTS, AND SLAM DUNKS

Basketball originated under city conditions—at a YMCA in Springfield, Massachusetts. It quickly became a game for all kinds of people and was played all over the United States—in small towns, in barnyards, on Indian reservations. Gymnasiums, schoolyards, and playgrounds put up hoops, and if they didn't, players could make their own by nailing a tire rim or a basket to a post or a tree. Dedicated players who didn't have a ball would make one by stuffing a sock with rags and dribbling it in the air. Old ball covers could be re-sewn and stuffed with sawdust.

In urban areas, newly arrived immigrants quickly adopted the sport, and many teams before World War II reflected ethnic origins. The Original Celtics,[1] Olson's Terrible Swedes, and the Buffalo Germans were among the great teams of the 1920s and 1930s. Eddie Gottlieb's South Philadelphia Hebrew All Stars was the most notable all-Jewish team at a time when Jews dominated the sport: estimates are that half of all players in the American Basketball League in the 1930s were Jewish.[2] The Sphas' jerseys bore the team name spelled in Hebrew letters: Samach, Pey, Hey, and Aleph, along with the Magen David— the Jewish star. The back of each jersey proclaimed "Hebrews."[3] The Israelite House of David might sound like another outstanding Jewish team, but these players, who wore long hair and beards in emulation of Jesus, belonged to a Christian commune from Michigan. A team of Chinese players, the Hong Wah Q'ues, barnstormed the Midwest for one season. Pittsburgh's Loendi Big Five, the Harlem Globetrotters, and the New York Renaissance were outstanding African American teams. The Swedes' owner, C. M. Olson, also sponsored a famous women's team. Olson's wife owned several beauty parlors, and one night the entire team dyed their hair red. From that point on, they were the Red Heads. The Red Heads toured for forty years, beginning in 1935, when they claimed a victory rate of 50 percent against the men's teams they played.

For some years industries sponsored teams; among the best were the Akron Firestones (later the Akron Firestone Non-Skids), Akron Goodyear Wingfoots, Fort Wayne General Electrics, and Indianapolis U.S. Tires. Players on these teams were company employees, paid to work, not to play, but hired for their basketball skills. Some businesses sponsored teams but turned over operations to a basketball expert, while other businessmen ran their own teams. Frank Kautsky, owner of two grocery stores in Indianapolis, owned and managed the Indianapolis Kautskys, whom he paid in cash after each game—an unusually generous $25 per game, more if he was "particularly pleased."[4] There were also independents, such as the Buffalo Bisons and the Pittsburgh Young Men's Hebrew Association. Few of these teams paid well, and the work was seasonal, so professional athletes in the 1930s often played for more than one team, sometimes on the same day.

Barnstorming teams traveled throughout the country, concentrating on games in the Midwest and West, where attendance was often ten times that of games on the East Coast. But without television to broadcast nationally, and without the possibility of cross-country air travel, basketball remained a local game between teams that played with their own particular regional style. College ball was more popular than professional ball; its styles of play developed according to where coaches recruited their players. With no game tapes, no travel budget, and limited transportation systems, coaches had to operate by word of mouth. Relying on informal networks of former players, family members, and fellow coaches, college coaches recruited from areas that specialized in the style or skill they particularly needed. Coaches in Kansas and other midwestern states emphasized a fundamental passing game and physical conditioning, while New Yorkers went for set shots from the perimeter. Since professional teams often recruited local players, hoping to capture loyal college audiences, pro team play was heavily weighted toward local styles.

Basketball has changed a great deal since its invention by a Canadian in 1891. Working for a YMCA training institution in Springfield, Massachusetts, James "Doc" Naismith was charged with finding a form of indoor exercise for a group of men so rough-and-tumble he called them his "incorrigibles." Naismith considered all the sports he knew, but none seemed exactly right. Although he loved rugby, it was out of the question, because its brutal nature went against the Christian principles he was trying to instill in his men. Playing soccer, the men broke windows in the gym and knocked all the dumbbells off the racks on the walls. Indoor lacrosse was a complete disaster, resulting in cuts and bruises on hands and faces. Musing on his efforts, Naismith wrote:

"I realized that any attempt to change the known games would necessarily result in failure. It was evident that a new principle was necessary."[5]

Naismith's overriding ethos was muscular Christianity: he wanted to develop a game of finesse, one that emphasized skill over strength and speed while discouraging roughness. Naismith's ideal was a game in which both teams would occupy the same space at all times but without physical contact. His first brainstorm was to do away with running. If a player couldn't run with the ball, he thought, "we don't have to tackle; and if we don't have to tackle, the roughness will be eliminated."[6] Instead, players would move the ball by passing it. Naismith next decided that a center tip-off would be more elegant than struggling for possession as in English rugby. One player would deflect the ball to his teammates after each goal. But Naismith's true inspiration was the basket itself. Naismith believed that an elevated goal, parallel to the floor, would remove the need for force: "If the goal were horizontal instead of vertical, the players would be compelled to throw the ball in an arc: and force, which made for roughness, would be of no value."[7] Naismith went looking for boxes, eighteen inches square. The YMCA building superintendent found him a couple of peach baskets. At either end of the lower rail of the running track that formed a balcony above the gym floor, Naismith nailed the baskets up—each about ten feet off the ground. To make the game even more skillful, he required that the ball stay in the basket in order to count as a goal. For years, goaltenders would spend the game standing on a ladder next to the basket to remove the ball. Then people began experimenting with nets and a chain to turn the net inside out. It was two decades before someone thought to remove the bottom of the basket.

From the first day, Naismith's game was a hit, and almost immediately the YMCA began to draw an audience. A group of local teachers asked Naismith whether he thought girls could play the game. He saw no reason why not, and quickly the group organized the first girls' basketball team. Naismith's training school students took the game to their hometown YMCAs over the Christmas break, and boys who played it at the YMCAs took basketball to their high schools. Other athletic clubs adopted the game, as did churches and settlement houses. Basketball was hugely popular on Indian reservations and was played at the 1892 Sioux conference at Big Stone Lake, South Dakota. Military and naval organizations took it up. The first college games were held

to play in this tournament. McLendon became the first African American to coach white professionals, the Cleveland Pipers, an integrated team that defeated the 1960 American Olympic team—a team that included such players as Oscar Robertson and Jerry West. McLendon coached the Pipers to victory in the Eastern Division of the American Basketball League in 1962. In 1966, at Cleveland State, McLendon became the first African American head coach of a predominately white university, leading them to their best record in the school's history in 1969. He coached the U.S. Olympic team in 1968, and was the first black coach in the American Basketball Association, coaching the Denver Rockets in 1969.

McLendon grew up in Kansas, a state known for one-hand set shots and strenuous training programs. Playing at Kansas City Junior College, McLendon, a small player, was assigned to outrun his opponent and score from a long-pass assist. Playing always from the pre-1937 center jump line, he was working on a half-court version of a running game. Says McLendon, "I would not have made it by any other system."[15] At the University of Kansas, reviewing fundamental basketball philosophy with James Naismith, McLendon found justification for his own evolving ideas. Naismith strongly believed that one should play the ball, not the man—meaning that the team with the ball had an obligation to get to the basket, and the team without the ball had an obligation to gain possession of the ball.[16] After working with Naismith and with the legendary coach Forrest "Phog" Allen, McLendon saw no reason why his team couldn't move to the basket as soon as they had retrieved the ball after a score. He called this move the "fast break."

As a coach, McLendon devoted himself to developing the full court fast break, "a system in which the coach who has relatively poor material can still think of success."[17] Coaching teams that lacked height and were often untrained in defensive fundamentals, McLendon discovered that the best defense was a good offense: if you can't defend against your opponents, then you must outscore them. McLendon wrote more about the strategies of fast break basketball than anyone else, documenting, categorizing, and analyzing countless strategies for setting up and executing the fast break. Behind all the fundamentals, tactics, and drills for mastering the move, the philosophy is relatively simple: the team must execute "swift movement down-court *each* time it gains possession of the ball."[18] Defying the urban legend that the fast break is the bailiwick of hotshots, McLendon coached team-oriented basket-ball, pointing out that he won the CIAA tourney in 1946 with a group of play-ers so individually forgettable that not one was named to the all-conference team. Four of his "mighty mites" that year were between five-foot-four and five-foot-seven, three of them starters, and yet as a team, they made the fast break the winning strategy of the tournament.[19]

McLendon also coached in what is widely regarded as the first integrated game in the South. In 1944, when his North Carolina Eagles were 19–1 in the CIAA, McLendon played against the Duke Medical School team, a group of ex-ceptional players from around the country enrolled in an accelerated wartime medical program. Duke players walked into the gym with their jackets over their heads so no one could see that they were white. As the game got under way, one of McLendon's Eagles, Aubrey Stanley, experienced an epiphany: "Suddenly, it occurred to me that these weren't supermen. They were just men. And we could beat them."[20] Interviewed years later, men on both sides remembered the outcome: Eagles 88, Duke Medical School 44. They also re-membered the way the Eagles played—the high-speed fast break, fancy pass-ing, reverse pivots and steals: it was the future of basketball.[21]

Clarence "Big House" Gaines (1923–2005) was another powerhouse coach. After coaching at Winston-Salem State from 1946 to 1993, he retired with 828 victories. He was named CIAA Coach of the Year in 1949, the year he gave up coaching both football and basketball to concentrate solely on basketball.[22] In 1967 his basketball players won the Division II championship. Gaines credits McLendon with changing the way everyone played ball by turn-ing a "somewhat mild passing game" into a running game. To compete with McLendon's teams, coaches had to include more running and conditioning and had to train their teams to defend on the run. Gaines began encourag-ing the fast break at Winston-Salem after seeing what McLendon's Eagles could do with it—specifically after his team lost a game to McLendon, 119–95. Gaines decided not only that the fast break was the way to go but also that he needed players who could quickly adapt to the fast break offense. The players who came to him from the South, from southern Illinois, or from the Midwest played what he called the traditional style, "with the emphasis on waiting until everyone was in position, then passing to the open shooter, who would take aim at the basket with one of his selection of shots."[23] Gaines, now a convert to the fast break, started traveling to New York to look for players who had developed their own fast break style on the playgrounds and in the high schools of Harlem by exploiting the court and their skills to the fullest.

Coach Calvin "Cal" Irvin of North Carolina A&T also attributed the rise of fast break basketball to the innovations and improvisations of African American players and coaches after the 1937 rules change. An all-around athlete, Irvin played baseball in the Negro Leagues for the Newark Eagles in 1946 and the Raleigh Grays in 1947 and received his graduate degree from Columbia University in 1948. In 1954 Irvin went to North Carolina A&T, where he stayed for eighteen seasons. "What we were playing in the Afro-American colleges," he recalled in 1996, "that's the kind of basketball they're playing now. . . . It was a fast-paced basketball. We didn't have the slow-down, holding the ball. We didn't need the thirty-five-second clock; we never held on to it that long. It was not exactly run and gun, but it had a lot of run and gun in it. . . . What we called 'Our Basketball' is the basketball you are playing today." [24] Clarence Gaines concurred: "I feel confident in saying that what is accepted as standard basketball today at both the college and professional levels was introduced into the game by John McLendon." [25]

McLendon's fast break philosophy was more than an idea or a style: at North Carolina he developed a clear strategy with several points of inception, with specific roles for the outlet passer (a defensive rebounder—a center or forward), the outlet pass receiver (guard), the alternate pass receiver (guard), the third man (one of the three defensive rebounders, charged with filling the third lane), and the trailers (the remaining two rebounders), as well as a disciplined defense. McLendon insisted on a rigorous training program and conditioning so that if necessary, his starting players could play the entire game without substitutes. But then, when opposing teams had adjusted to the fast-paced game, McLendon's teams could switch to a delay offense—a strategy often attributed to North Carolina's Dean Smith, but one that McLendon adopted as early as 1940. McLendon offered a clinic for coaches in Colorado in 1970 to explain his delay or "two-in-a-corner" offense—a clinic that Dean Smith attended, after which he spent several hours talking with McLendon, getting more advice on a strategy he would later call "four corners." "I always say they took my two corners and made it a victim of inflation," said McLendon. [26]

Perhaps most important in the fast break offense was a mastery of fundamentals, because players had to be able to make decisions on their own, on the fly. Gaines remembered, "I always believed my job was to condition the players in preseason and during practices, remind them of the fundamentals of the game, and then permit them to play the game as it developed."[27] The fast break offense depended on players who could "read the flow of the game and make adjustments," and who had the ability to improvise—the same kind of improvisation demanded by jazz or the Lindy Hop, when musicians took off on solo flights or partners briefly broke away from each other to improvise solo steps.[28] Improvisation depends on mastery of the moves, whether they are chord changes or set plays. Improvisation is not the same as free play; it requires complete control and expertise. True, other sports allow players to improvise, or to create a personal style of play. But basketball depends on fluid interaction among a group of players whose roles are interchangeable, any one of whom may score at any moment, and any one of whom may showcase a personal style or "trademark" in the process of scoring. In its speed, sudden shifts and changes, and small group interaction, no other sport so closely resembles the flow and flair of jazz and jazz dance. "Basketball is a situation game; a reaction game," according to Gaines. "You can't call 'Play Number One.' You have to learn to adjust and adapt to the defense. Most of the kids didn't have the movements, the rhythm, to innovate."[29]

If the fast break offense depended on players' ability to improvise and innovate, it depended even more on the coach's willingness to trust his players and to give them the freedom necessary to make decisions on their own. The fast break offense evolved among black players who quickly learned to exploit the running game made possible by the elimination of the center jump. But the coaches who encouraged, developed, and exploited the fast break were those who were willing to share the responsibility for team decisions with the players.

The fast break was so effective that teams playing against it had to learn it quickly or else suffer the kind of humiliating defeat that made a believer out of Gaines. After McLendon introduced it in 1940, the fast break quietly but quickly became the dominant offense of the CIAA, and simultaneously of great playground athletes, for the same reason: the fast break won games. But white colleges did not play in the CIAA or against historically black colleges, so white teams did not have to adapt to it or adopt it. The fast break remained a "black style." Although the National Association of Intercollegiate

Basketball (subsequently the National Association of Intercollegiate Athletics, or NAIA) allowed African American players in 1948, not until 1952 did the tournament admit black colleges, and even then there was a separate district for them (District 29), from which one college would be selected to play in the general tournament. Even this token gesture of inclusion made a difference: the first District 29 college to compete in 1953, Tennessee A&I, was met at the NAIA tournament with cheers of welcome. The NAIA subsequently eliminated District 29 and included the black colleges in regional districts. Four years later, McLendon's fast-breaking Tennessee State began its three-year winning streak at the NAIA, the first time that any team—white or black—won three consecutive national titles.

Ironically, because the principles of improvisation and stylization are fundamental to an African American aesthetic, the fast break—which depends so much on improvisation at the highest level—was miscategorized as a *racial* style. White coaches who used elements of the fast break were said to be adopting a particular offense, while black coaches who used it were seen as reverting to type.[30] When African American teams used the fast break, it was derided as "run and gun," "blow and go," more of a style statement than a strategy.

There was, of course, a distinctive black style, and in part this style evolved as a way of staying out of trouble: an African American team that beat a white team could not afford to resort to the "roughness and holding that was the trademark of the American League."[31] Sportswriters of the 1930s singled out the New York Renaissance, the "Rens," for avoiding "anything resembling dirty basketball" by focusing on "speed, elusiveness and incredible marksmanship."[32] They relied on "flashy work," passing described as "dazzling," shooting that was "uncanny," and a "magic pattern of speed and deception."[33] In the 1920s and 1930s the Rens excelled at passing, which they preferred to dribbling, because it was the fastest way to move the ball. "The Rens' specialty was blinding speed and passing," writes Frank Davis. "So swiftly did they whip the ball from one player to another that often competing athletes quit and, placing hands on hips, watched as if they were spectators."[34] Indeed, one game made the sports columns in 1939 when, with a one-point lead over the Boston Celtics, the Rens passed the ball for six minutes and one second until the game ended. "The sphere never touched the floor in all that time," one writer noted, "despite the [Celtics'] frantic efforts to get it and the fans gave the Rens one of the greatest ovations they ever received."[35] The Rens played with "breathtaking precision," according to UCLA coaching legend John Wooden. "To this day," said Wooden in an interview in 2003, "I've never seen more beautiful team play than the New York Rens." In 1963 the entire 1933 Rens team was inducted into the Naismith Memorial Basketball Hall of fame.[36]

The Harlem Globetrotters, too, relied on splendid ball-handling skills to outmaneuver their opponents, and owner Abe Saperstein recruited players who had already perfected their ball-handling prowess. Among them was Marques Haynes (b. 1926), the first Globetrotter player elected to the Hall of Fame. Haynes was a standout ball player long before he joined the Globetrotters, leading his Sand Springs, Oklahoma, high school to a national championship in 1941 and Langston University (1942–1946) to a 112–3 record, including a fifty-nine-game winning streak. Haynes led the Harlem Globetrotters to a serious defeat of the George Mikan–led Minneapolis Lakers in Chicago Stadium in 1948, confusing opposing players with his dribbling innovations.

The style of the Negro teams of the 1920s and 1930s is certainly one of the forerunners of the basketball perfected at Negro colleges in the 1940s. But the fast break is equally important, and it has deep roots in basketball's family tree. James Naismith believed in the fundamental importance of getting the ball to the basket. Working directly with James Naismith, his protégé John McLendon took that idea and ran with it. He brought it to the Negro colleges, whose players, more than any others in the country, can proudly claim that their fast break offense may be traced directly to the inventor of basketball, Dr. James Naismith.

The Jump Shot: White Men Can Jump

The fast break, jump shot, and fancy ball-handling were so strongly associated with black players that they were branded "Negro basketball" for several decades. After graduating mid-year, Bill Russell played on a post–high school all-star team in the early spring of 1952 coached by a maverick named Brick Swegle, who let his players play what Russell remembers being called "Negro basketball," even though there were only two black players on the team. The white players had the time of their lives. Opposing coaches either complained that the tactics were "not cricket," an interesting Eurocentric metaphor, or vowed that the team that lived by the jump shot would die by the jump shot.

One coach considered the move so doomed to fail that he refused to let his players defend against it. Russell's team won that game 144 to 41. Russell himself pioneered a defensive jump for shot-blocking when he entered the NBA in 1956.[37] Even so, when white historians and athletes search their memories for the players and coaches who might have pioneered these moves, the ones they recall are white. The most often mentioned jump shooter of the 1930s was Stanford's all-American Angelo "Hank" Luisetti, who was taking unorthodox one-handed shots as early as 1936. Luisetti was revolutionary because he shot on the run and occasionally from a "soft" jump, rising all of two inches off the floor. Robert Peterson, a sports historian with perspective, objects to categorizing this as a jump shot, maintaining that in a true jump shot "the player springs high and releases the ball at the apex of his jump."[38] Still, something was unusual about Luisetti's one-handed shots—and effective, too. Luisetti alone scored 15 points when Stanford defeated Long Island University at Madison Square Garden in December 1936—in a game whose final score was 45–31. The next morning, the New York Times proclaimed: "It seemed Luisetti could do nothing wrong. . . . Some of his shots would have been deemed foolhardy if attempted by anybody else, but with Luisetti shooting, these were accepted by the enchanted crowd."[39] Nat Holman, known as "Mr. Basketball," a former Original Celtic and coach at City College of New York, was not among the spellbound. "That's not basketball," he complained. "If my boys ever shot one-handed, I'd quit coaching."[40]

The one-hand shot was mentioned as early as 1922, in Walter E. Meanwell's book The Science of Basketball. A physical education professor at the University of Wisconsin, Meanwell was also the varsity basketball coach for twenty years, winning four Big Ten titles, and his book became the bible of basketball. When Meanwell first published The Science of Basketball, the standard shot was one he identified as the "Two-Hand, Underhand Loop Shot." The "Overhand Loop Shot" was also popular but less common. The book offered a short discussion of another technique, the "One-Hand Push Shot." The shot began from a standing position, but Meanwell suggested that the player should jump toward the basket while executing it. Similarly, a text by Phog Allen identified a "push arch shot," which depended on a hop, and Craig Ruby's "two-hand shoulder shot" also included a little jump.[41]

Isolated players experimented with jumping on the one-handed shot. Bob Many may have used the shot in the YMCA and in industrial leagues in the 1920s before entering Lehigh University in 1926. Ben M. Horwech wrote about Many in the Bayonne, New Jersey, *Evening News*: "With the suddenness of a deer, he leaps up, and, as he jumps, up go his hands that hold the coveted pellet. And, as his hands go up with the ball, generally a goal is made from the field." [42] In *Big Leagues*, Stephen R. Fox mentions John "Jump Shot" Cooper (b. 1912), a player from western Kentucky who, in three years of varsity ball at the University of Missouri in the early 1930s, never saw anybody other than himself shoot a jumper.[43] Neither did Glenn Roberts (1912–1980), from western Virginia, who used the jump shot at Emory and Henry College and on the Dayton and Akron Firestone teams in the late 1930s.

But after the nationally covered 1937 game between Long Island University and Stanford, several players from different parts of the country went against fashion and began experimenting with a one-handed shot. Inventive high school players were often discouraged by coaches from trying the shot, but many seem to have developed the jump to a new level while playing in games between and among various branches of the military during World War II. It is likely that in the service players found more freedom to work with the shot, so that by the time they brought it back onto college courts in the late 1940s, they had moved beyond early awkward attempts to a point where college coaches could recognize the value of the jump shot. Even though high school coaches continued to discourage it, by the early 1950s a few players were using the jumper on professional courts. Players who used the jump shot were almost without exception among the highest scorers in any arena in which they played.

Belus Smawley (1918–2003) developed his two-hand spiral jump shot at North Carolina's Appalachian State College in the late 1930s before taking it to the navy teams for which he coached and played. Smawley played for the Basketball Association of America's St. Louis Bombers starting in 1946, before moving to Syracuse in 1950 and then Baltimore, where he played until 1952. Wyoming's Kenny Sailors (b. 1922) "dazzled" Madison Square Garden audiences in the 1943 National Invitation Tournament (NIT) championship.[44] Sportswriters called Sailors's jump shot an innovation from the West that East Coast teams would have to copy if they wanted to stay competitive. Sailors, who had developed the shot in clear disobedience of the First Commandment of basketball—shoot with two hands—and in flagrant disregard of the Second—thou shalt stay on the floor—simply called it "my shot." [45] After serving with the Marine Corps, Sailors returned to Wyoming in 1945 and then to the Garden. *Life* magazine published a photo of Sailors jumping to shoot, and suddenly the jump shot was national news. During his five years of professional ball, Sailors was consistently among the league's leading scorers.

"Jumping Jim" Pollard, the "Kangaroo Kid" (1922–1993), led Stanford to an NCAA championship in 1942, played for the Coast Guard until 1946, and then returned to win five championships with the Minneapolis Lakers (1949, 1950, and 1952–54). Bud Palmer (b. 1921) is said to have "pioneered" the jump shot in the East while playing for Princeton in the late 1940s.[46]

"Jumping Joe" Fulks (1921–1976) was a six-foot-five self-described hillbilly who played for Murray State Teachers College in western Kentucky. Sports historians claim he was the first to exploit the shot to the fullest. Fulks was said to have revolutionized basketball with his jump shot, which he first shot two-handed. Gradually he switched to a one-handed jumper. Fulks captivated crowds in 1946 with his "turnaround jumpers" for the Washington Capitols. In 1949 *Sporting News* called Joe Fulks the greatest basketball player in the country—the same year it named Paul Arizin college player of the year. Fulks scored 63 points against the Indianapolis Jets (February 10, 1949), a single-game record that lasted a decade until Elgin Baylor's 64 points (November 8, 1959) surpassed that mark. (In 1960, Baylor scored 71 points, a new record until Wilt Chamberlain scored 78 points in a 1961 Lakers–76ers game; Baylor scored 63 points in the same game.)

By the time "Pitchin' Paul" Arizin (1928–2006) was leading the league in scoring as a second-year player with the Philadelphia Warriors in 1952, only a few other white players had mastered the jump shot—the shot with which he was making basketball history. Historians hail Arizin as a trailblazer for having "burst into the league in 1950 with a repertoire that included a daring new weapon—the jump shot." Born in South Philadelphia in 1918, Arizin was cut from his high school team in the mid-1940s but took to playing wherever he could because he loved the game. Many of his intramural, church, and independent league teams played in low-ceilinged dancehalls, and Arizin developed a "spectacular low-trajectory jump shot" almost by accident.[47] "The floors were so slippery," Arizin said, "when I tried to hook, my feet would go out from under me, so I jumped. I was always a good jumper. My feet weren't on the floor, so I didn't have to worry about slipping. The more I did it, the better I became. Before I knew it, practically all my shots were jump shots." [48] During the 1951–52 season, Arizin claimed the newly formed National Basketball Association's scoring title with 25.4 points per game.

"Jumpin' Johnny" Adams (1917–1979) played at the University of Arkansas in the late 1930s, where his coach, Glen Rose, ran a revolutionary full-court offense to take his players to the 1941 NCAA tournament. Playing against Wyoming, whose Kenny Sailors had his own jump shot, Adams led Arkansas to a fourteen-point victory on the strength of eleven baskets, all but two of which were jump shots. Adams had developed the shot on his own, with no instruction from Rose other than to experiment with what he had already begun. Had he been playing for a coach other than the iconoclastic Rose, Adams might never have perfected the shot.

Some players seem to have happened onto the jump shot as a result of skills developed in another sport. Champion ski jumper Myer "Whitey" Skoog (b. 1926) had a jump shot, but his Brainerd, Minnesota, high school coaches wouldn't let him use it. After high school Skoog played ball during service with the navy until he enrolled in the University of Minnesota, graduating in 1951. Although his coach there wanted him to quit competitive ski jumping, he worked with Skoog on his jump shot. By the time Skoog signed with the Minneapolis Lakers, he had developed what the Lakers' George Mikan called "the greatest jump shot [he] ever saw." [49]

At five-foot-nine, "Jumpin' John" (Gonzales) Burton (b. 1926) discovered the jump shot while trying to leap above the taller players standing between him and the basket. Burton's coach, Benny Neff, at Lowell High School in San Francisco, discouraged the shot, but Burton used it in recreational leagues and took it into the army in 1944. When he returned to play for San Francisco State College in 1946, he brought his high-scoring jumper with him and became the first SFSC player ever to score more than a thousand points. Newspapers described the new shot as a "jump, over-the-head push shot." [50]

For white jump shooters, the chief ingredients for success seem to have been either early isolation or a coach who didn't interfere with experimentation, followed by the opportunity to perfect the shot during a few years of military service. By the time these players returned to college or to the professional leagues after the war, their shots had become so powerful that they were tough to beat.

Invisible Men Can Jump, Too

The jump shot was an anomaly on the courts where white players dominated, which makes its path there easier to trace. Almost without exception, white players who shot one-handed with a jump were called "Jumping" Somebody. Nobody playing for black teams bears that nickname. And it is not because no one was jumping on those teams. Quite the opposite. But in a land where red hair abounds, no one is called "Carrot-top." High jumping had been an element of black basketball from the early days. The jump was part of the developing and culturally distinct "Negro style" of play, and black newspapers are full of reports of African American teams that defeated their opponents by "outjumping" them.[51] Although professional teams played "a more deliberate and set style of game than college quintets," reports of professional games often mention the heights achieved by their players. Photos accompanying a *Pittsburgh Courier* article published in April 1939 show "Pop" Gates as he "soars skyward over the outstretched hands of Oshkosh guards" to score.[52] But, as we will see, the jump shot itself evolved so seamlessly along with high jumping and the fast break that it is difficult to know when it became a separate, exciting element. And because the jump shot was an evolving move, ways of describing it evolved, too. When observers spoke of players running, jumping, and shooting with one hand, they did not specify whether the shot was one that might be considered a classic jump shot or a one-handed shot from the run: such categories did not yet exist.

If the black press underreported a distinctive "black style" because it was the dominant style of their world, the white press didn't report it at all. Few white sportswriters traveled to the schoolyards and playgrounds of black inner city neighborhoods. Few caught the action at black college games. Outside the Negro press, the scores of such games would be mentioned on the one page devoted to "Activities within the Colored Community," and there would be little room for details. Few white people were aware of what was happening in the black community in general. Sportswriter Leonard Koppett was a child living one block away from Yankee Stadium in the 1930s, where Negro League baseball games were played. "Clearly I knew," he recalls, "because every Sunday when the Yankees were away, there would be twenty to twenty-five thousand black people coming to the game, [then] leaving the game. But with not a word about it in the sports pages I was reading. With no one saying anything about it, it never even occurred to me to go."[53]

With spotty reporting from the weekly black press and no reporting on white sports pages, there remains very little historical record of the way black ballplayers actually played the game. For instance, Cumberland Posey (1890–1946), who founded Pittsburgh's Loendi Big Five in 1912 after playing ball for Penn State and Duquesne, employed an up-tempo offense that later developed into the fast break. Posey, who often reported on sports and basketball for the *Pittsburgh Courier*, wrote about a 1918 game against the Jewish Original Coffey Club in which he scored the winning basket with "a one hand shot through the nets."[54] Was it a dunk? Or was it a one-handed shot similar to Hank Luisetti's? Was it a jump shot? We can't know.

There were countless black players in all-black college games across the country about whom we know almost nothing. The black players who shone on mainly white college teams have fared better historically. In Arthur Ashe's comprehensive history of African Americans in sports, the roster of black players on white college basketball teams begins in 1904, including eight before 1918, the most notable of whom are Cumberland Posey and actor-singer Paul Robeson, who played for Rutgers from 1915 to 1918. The list of black players at white colleges from 1920 to 1946 numbers twenty-four, including William "Dolly" King, Frank "Doc" Kelker, and Jackie Robinson (at UCLA from 1939 to 1941). Ashe called these players "stars," and we must assume that they were or they would not have been playing. There is an equally impressive list of black players on predominantly white teams at the professional level—as many as seventy-three between 1902 and 1950. There are no lists of outstanding athletes at traditionally black colleges.

William "Dolly" King (1916–1969), a three-sport letterman from Brooklyn's Alexander Hamilton High, began playing for the Long Island University Blackbirds in 1937.[55] That year King became the first black player in the national Amateur Athletic Union (AAU) tournament. Two years later, on November 29, 1939, he achieved the distinction of playing the full sixty minutes of a football game against Catholic University *and* an entire forty-minute basketball game at Madison Square Garden. He was the leading scorer in each game.[56] In his history of black basketball Ashe named Dolly King as one of the leading contributors to a developing and distinctive "black style," one that featured "speed, uncommon jumping ability, and innovative passing skills" but was "frequently at odds with white coaches' philosophies of the late 1940s."[57] King was developing this style as early as 1937. Did it include jump shots?

Frank "Doc" Kelker (1913–2003) played for Western Reserve beginning in 1937. Like Jackie Robinson and Dolly King, Kelker was a star athlete in football and basketball. Writers in the *Pittsburgh Courier* said Kelker shot baskets the same way he bagged passes on the football field, "leaping high above his opponents and throwing the ball far from danger." [58] Few football players throw a ball with two hands, so clearly Kelker shot one-handed. Could this be considered a jump shot? My guess is probably so. Photos of Kelker in the black press show him several feet off the floor as headlines proclaim, "Kelker Outjumps Opponent." [59] Kelker, described as a center who "jumps and slaps the oval into the netting," was also fast and delighted fans by tipping the ball to a teammate from the center line, dashing under the basket, taking a pass, and "bagging" a basket, a half-court version of the full-court fast break. [60] After college, Kelker formed a professional team, dubbed Kelker's Log Cabin Big Five, playing out of Cleveland. [61]

Davage "Dave" Minor (1922–1998) was a track and field star at Froebel High School in Indiana, where he set a state high jump record in 1940 that stood for sixteen years. Minor took his jumping skills onto the court with him, experimenting with running one-hand shots as a freshman, and soon launching "leaping, one-handed flings . . . bordering on the supernatural." [62] In *The Origins of the Jump Shot*, John Cristgau leaves no doubt that Minor was one of the early masters of the jump shot. In 1941 Minor took his integrated Froebel High School basketball team to the state championship. Recruited by the Harlem Globetrotters, Minor instead went into the army, where he played, then graduated from UCLA and played on the black professional Oakland Bittners until he signed with Baltimore in 1951.

By contrast, Clarence Gaines, who played ball in Paducah, Kentucky, in the 1930s, didn't recall anyone playing with a jump shot at that time. The two-hand set shot ruled. He also spent summers in Newark, New Jersey, with an uncle who was a sports fan and took him to many Negro League baseball and basketball games. But Gaines remembered the Globetrotters and the New York Renaissance as "slick ball-handling teams" whose players often shot one-handed. The Rens believed in a "zero dribble" offense, preferring the quick pass upcourt. Gaines believed that before the rise of fast break basketball, even one-handed shooters were more likely using a "one-hand push shot." [63]

Gaines credits McLendon for introducing the fast break to black colleges, where Gaines coached, and where he saw and coached players using the jump shot at least a decade earlier than their counterparts at white institutions. As fast break basketball came into its own, so did the jump shot. Fast break players figured they could throw while running, and throwing with one hand was more efficient. Soon, players took that technique and developed it as an independent move. "It's just a quick release of the ball, that's all," Gaines said.[64] He recalled that "in fast break basketball, players would run, jump, and throw at the same time." The one-handed shot and the jump evolved along with the fast break style of play. "You don't throw a ball with two hands in any other sport. Shooting with one hand is a natural reaction. If a player's got good hands and good skills and he's running, he's not going to stop and use two hands. The jump just came along with it."[65] The one-handed shot, taken on the run, soon evolved into the classic jumper.

What is most important to remember is that the fast break style was in-stitutionalized in black colleges where it was the norm, not the exception. If the jump shot evolved along with the fast break—and there is every reason to believe that it did—it, too, became institutionalized, a standard part of the way African American players approached the game. While there were many white players who mastered the jump shot early on, they stand out among the majority of holdouts who continued to associate that shot with African American players and with a black cultural style.

Some white ballplayers freely admit to having been influenced by the black style, the fast break, or the jump shot. Bob Davies (1920–1990), who played for Seton Hall beginning in 1941, recalled his early exposure to basketball in his hometown of Harrisburg, Pennsylvania, during the 1930s. Davies de-scribes a team on which the style of the black players caught his attention. They were fast, they were good ball handlers, and they took jump shots. Says Davies: "When I was a kid I couldn't afford to pay to see the high school team, so we would look through a crack in the door. The only thing I could see was the foul-lane area and the basket at the other end of the court. I'd see these great black players *jump in the air*, throw the ball, hit somebody with a pass, or *shoot the ball*, and I guess that stuck in my mind. I think that's what helped me to become a playmaker."[66] Bob Davies became one of the best ball handlers of the game; his name and deeds are recorded in every basketball chronicle, where more often than not he is called the "father of the behind-the-back dribble," the "original showtime guard," and the player who "brought a sense of style" to the game."[67] Davies himself attributed his success not to any of his coaches but to the "great black players" he watched through that crack in the gym door. He describes not one but several players jumping and shooting. But those players are lost to history. They created the style that transformed the game, but they remain nameless. They are among the many invisible men of basketball.

"Pistol" Pete Maravich (1947–1988) also learned his style from watching black players, at the urging of his father, Clemson coach Press Maravich. Press knew where the future of basketball lay, and he urged his son to learn as much as he could from the players on the other side of town. African American players from Magic Johnson to Isiah Thomas still call Maravich the game's "greatest showman." They mean it as a compliment, which is not what white sportswriters meant when they called him a showboat or a hot dog. "Maravich was turned into a freak by his father," claims Boston sportswriter Bob Ryan, mainly because he was a white player with exceptional and, in his day, African American ball-handling skills.[68] Maravich's scoring ability was indeed freakish, and to this day he holds nearly every NCAA scoring record, including most career points (3,667), highest career average (44.2 points per game), most field goals made (1,387), most field goals attempted (3,166), and most career 50-point games (28), all before the advent of the three-point shot.[69] The techniques Maravich perfected far exceeded mere showmanship.

Innovative white players such as Maravich, Davies, Bob Cousy, and the "jumpers" already cited did not "steal" their style from the black players they observed, although they readily admit to having copied it from the black players they admired. We should not forget that the moves that such courageous, pioneering players used continued to be considered "black" for at least a decade after they had been incorporated into the repertoire of many white players. All evidence suggests that audiences appreciated this new emphasis on style, speed, and elevation long before white coaches were willing to relinquish the slow, deliberate, ground-bound game they hoped to continue to control. It was precisely the speed, showiness, and innovation of the African American style that simultaneously thrilled audiences and disturbed traditionalists, who continued to draw a line between "showing off" and winning.

We forget how late the jump shot became standard in basketball. When Bill Russell was playing high school ball, from 1948 to 1952, jumping was still new to the game. As Russell describes it, the standard offensive strategy was

Joe Louis and Jesse Owens: Superstars. World heavyweight champion Joe Louis and Olympic gold-medalist Jesse Owens were celebrities for white and black Americans alike. Both men wear double-breasted suits, silk ties and handkerchiefs, and Louis's powerful fist sports rings and a heavy watch. Harry Ransom Humanities Research Center, University of Texas at Austin.

S. H. Kress & Co. 5-10-25 Cent Store, 125th Street, Harlem. On March 19, 1935, a young African American man was accused of shoplifting a knife from this store. False rumors that the police beat the youth ignited a riot, but the fuel was the historical fact that Kress, like many white-owned Harlem businesses, refused to employ African Americans. Harry Ransom Humanities Research Center, University of Texas at Austin.

Harlemites march on Lenox Avenue in support of Ethiopia, August 1935. Italy's invasion of Ethiopia caused outrage among people of African descent worldwide. Ethiopia, a black Zion, stood as a symbol of black sovereignty and pride. Harry Ransom Humanities Research Center, University of Texas at Austin.

Charles Lindbergh emerges into crowd in Croyden, England, 1927. Lindbergh had to circle the airport twice when a crowd of 150,000 stormed the airfield at Croyden, just outside London, as the aviator arrived for a reception at Buckingham Palace with King George V, Queen Mary, and their granddaughter, baby Princess Elizabeth. Lindbergh was returning to New York following his successful transatlantic flight to Le Bourget, France. Harry Ransom Humanities Research Center, University of Texas at Austin.

Hubert Fauntleroy Julian, the Black Eagle of Harlem, 1939. Julian attempted to fly from New York to Africa in 1924 in his plane *Ethiopia I* but crashed into the Atlantic. His successful 1929 transatlantic flight earned him the nickname "The Black Lindbergh," and his 1930 flight to Ethiopia garnered the rank of colonel from Emperor Haile Selassie. Copyright by Morgan and Marvin Smith, Photographs and Prints Division, Schomburg Center for Research in Black Culture, The New York Public Library, Astor, Lenox and Tilden Foundations. Courtesy of Monica Smith.

(*opposite top*) Jesse Owens, "The Buckeye Bullet," in a practice heat in 1935. On May 25, 1935, at the Big Ten meet in Ann Arbor, Michigan, Owens set world records in the 220 yards and 200 meters, 220-yard and 200-meter low hurdles, and tied the world record at 100 yards. His long jump mark of 26′ 8 1/2″ stood until 1960. Harry Ransom Humanities Research Center, University of Texas at Austin.

(*opposite bottom*) Jesse Owens practices the broad jump on board SS *Manhattan* at sea, en route to Berlin, July 26, 1936. Photograph by Joe Caneva. AP Photo.

(*above*) Jesse Owens in the 200-meter run in Berlin's Olympiastadion, August 14, 1936. Owens won with an Olympic record of 20.7 seconds. AP Photo.

Lindy Hoppers perform an over-the-shoulder air step at the Savoy Ballroom in 1938 as black and white patrons watch in amazement. Copyright by Morgan and Marvin Smith, Photographs and Prints Division, Schomburg Center for Research in Black Culture, The New York Public Library, Astor, Lenox and Tilden Foundations. Courtesy of Monica Smith.

Whitey's Lindy Hoppers (identified as "Jitterbugs") entertain Titania in this 1940 Broadway production of *Swingin' the Dream*. From photographs taken at the dress rehearsal by Roland Harvey. The Harvard Theatre Collection, Houghton Library.

Whitey's Lindy Hoppers kicking up dust at the New York World's Fair, 1939, with Herbert White standing, bouncing on his toes behind them. Copyright by Morgan and Marvin Smith, Photographs and Prints Division, Schomburg Center for Research in Black Culture, The New York Public Library, Astor, Lenox and Tilden Foundations. Courtesy of Monica Smith.

10 Days Only *Special* 60c

THE PRESS CLUB PRESENTS ITS THIRD

JUMP - SESSION

—— WITH ——

COUNT BASIE

And His
Swing Orchestra

Direct from

"Famous Door"

and Concert in Carnegie Hall,
New York City.

Bringing to You . . .

"America's Swing Sensation" that turned Broadway Jitterbugs Topsy-Turvy Over Nite.

"DO YOU WANNA JUMP, CHILDREN"

"STOP BEATIN' ROUND THE MULBERRY BUSH"

Featuring HELEN HUMES and JAMES RUSHING, VOCALISTS

TOMLINSON HALL

INDIANAPOLIS, IND.

Tues. Nite, Feb. 14 - 9 til?

ADVANCE TICKETS 85c - AT THE DOOR $1.10

TICKETS ON SALE AT
Recorder — Penish Tavern — Joe Mitchell's — Cotton Club — Walker Drug Store
Maxey's Pharmacy — Bruce's Pharmacy — Izsaks Tavern — Leisure Hour

Jump King Louis Jordan on the saxophone leads his original Tympany Five: Courtney Williams (trumpet), Clarence Johnson (piano), Walter Martin (drums and tympani), Charlie Drayton (bass, not shown), Lem Johnson (tenor sax, not shown). Copyright by Morgan and Marvin Smith, Photographs and Prints Division, Schomburg Center for Research in Black Culture, The New York Public Library, Astor, Lenox and Tilden Foundations. Courtesy of Monica Smith.

(opposite) "Jump Session." Count Basie and His Swing Orchestra advertisement for appearance at Tomlinson Hall, Indianapolis. Photographs and Prints Division, Schomburg Center for Research in Black Culture, The New York Public Library, Astor, Lenox and Tilden Foundations.

The all–African American Joe Louis team. Louis with manager Julian Black, trainer Jack Blackburn, and manager John Roxborough, 1936. Harry Ransom Humanities Research Center, University of Texas at Austin.

Joe Louis, World Heavyweight Champion, shakes hands with Max Schmeling in August 1938, two months after Louis defeated the German in a fight that lasted only two minutes and four seconds. Louis's subservient pose belies his championship status. Harry Ransom Humanities Research Center, University of Texas at Austin.

Pearl Primus on stage in a production that ran for five weeks at the Princess Theater, London in 1950. AP Photo.

Dancer Pearl Primus, known for her leaping ability, in a publicity photo from the early 1940s. Harry Ransom Humanities Research Center, University of Texas at Austin.

Katherine Dunham dances with zoot-suited partner, Haitian Roger Ohardieno in a 1943 production of *Barrelhouse*. Dunham choreographed this signature piece, also known as *Barrelhouse Blues and Florida Swamp Shimmy*, in 1938. Although the dance originated in a social dance known as the Florida Gulf Coast Shimmy, Dunham recalled first hearing the music "Barrelhouse Shimmy" in a Chicago barbecue shack. Dunham explained that the duet was about "a beat old woman who goes to a dance to recapture a moment of her lost youth." AP Photo.

Members of the Brotherhood of Sleeping Car Porters meet in St. Louis, Missouri, in 1942. The Ladies' Auxilliary of the Brotherhood included maids for the Pullman Company and wives of porters. Photographs and Prints Division, Schomburg Center for Research in Black Culture, The New York Public Library, Astor, Lenox and Tilden Foundations.

(opposite) A. Philip Randolph, president of the Brotherhood of Sleeping Car Porters, speaking in the 1930s. Randolph's legacy includes persuading Presidents Roosevelt and Truman to issue executive orders that desegregated the defense industry (1941), the armed forces, and the federal government (1948), as well as organizing the 1963 March on Washington. Copyright by Morgan and Marvin Smith, Photographs and Prints Division, Schomburg Center for Research in Black Culture, The New York Public Library, Astor, Lenox and Tilden Foundations. Courtesy of Monica Smith.

PROGRAM

ACT I.

1. SUN-TANNED TENTH OF THE NATION
Lyrics by Paul Webster   Music by Hal Borne and Otis Rene
First Drummer . . . . LeRoy Antoine
Second Drummer . . . . Edward Short
Third Drummer . . . . Sonny Greer
Duke Ellington at the Piano
Ivy Anderson, Dorothy Dandridge, Herb Jeffries, Roy Glenn,
Rockets, Hi-Hatters, Choir, Ensemble.

2. AL GUSTER
"*Stomp Caprice*"   *Music by Mercer Ellington*

3. BROWN-SKINNED GAL IN THE CALICO GOWN
Lyrics by Paul Webster   Music by Duke Ellington
The Boy . . . . Herb Jeffries
The Girl . . . . Dorothy Dandridge
Ca'ico Girls — Artie Brandon, Lucille Battle, Avanelle Harris,
Doris Ake, Myrtle Fortune, Suzette Johnson.
Dance by . . . . The Hi-Hatters

4. HUMAN INTEREST
By Hal Fimberg
Charlie . . . . Pot
Smithers . . . . Roy Glenn
Baltimore . . . . Skillet
Ohio . . . . Pan
Old Man . . . . Wonderful Smith

5. BLI-BLIP
Lyrics by Sid Kuller   Music by Duke Ellington
Girl . . . . Marie Bryant
Boy . . . . Paul White

6. I GOT IT BAD AND THAT AIN'T GOOD
Lyrics by Paul Webster   Music by Duke Ellington
Ivy . . . . Ivy Anderson
A Friend . . . . Alice Key

7. WONDERFUL SMITH

8. CINDY WITH THE TWO LEFT FEET
Lyrics by Paul Webster   Music by Hal Borne
Schoolboy . . . . Paul White
Cindy . . . . Dorothy Dandridge
First Sister . . . . Avanelle Harris
Second Sister . . . . Lucille Battle
Fairy Godmother . . . . Evelyn Burwell
Prince Charming . . . . Al Guster
Jitterbugs—Rockets, Hi-Hatters, Artie Brandon, Myrtle Fortune,
Millie Monroe.

9. POT, PAN AND SKILLET
"*Bugle Break*"—*Subtle Slough   Music by Duke Ellington*

10. FLAME INDIGO
Garbo
Lyrics by Paul Webster   Music by Duke Ellington

11. MAD SCENE FROM WOOLWORTH'S
Langston Hughes and Charles Leonard
Cornelia . . . . Ivy Anderson
Woman . . . . Avanelle Harris
First Salesgirl . . . . Suzette Johnson
Second Salesgirl . . . . Alice Key
Manager . . . . Al Guster
Passerby . . . . Wonderful Smith

12. SHHHH! HE'S ON THE BEAT!
By Sid Kuller and Hal Fimberg   Music by Duke Ellington
Proprietor . . . . Roy Glenn
Waitress . . . . Marie Bryant
Bartender . . . . Wonderful Smith
First Couple . . . . { Hyacinth Cotten
                                                                  { Andrew Jackson
Seocnd Couple . . . . { Artie Brandon
                                                                  { Henry Roberts
Third Couple . . . . { Clarence Landry
                                                                  { Udell Johnson
Fourth Couple . . . . { Avanelle Harris
                                                                  { Pot
Cop . . . . Pan

13. I'VE GOT A PASSPORT FROM GEORGIA
Lyrics by Paul Webster and Ray Golden   Music by Hal Borne
The Traveler . . . . Paul White

14. GARBO AND HEPBURN
By Sid Kuller
Garbo . . . . Garbo
Hepburn . . . . Marie Bryant

15. THE EMPEROR'S BONES
Lyrics by Paul Webster   Music by Otis Rene
The Guide . . . . Roy Glenn
Tourists—Artie Brandon, Louise Franklin, Patsy Hunter, Edward
Short, Lawrence Harris.
Hi-Hatters and Rockets.

16. CYMBAL SOCKIN' SAM
Lyrics by Sidney Miller   Music by Mickey Rooney
The Girl . . . . Dorothy Dandridge
Sam . . . . Sonny Greer

17. UNCLE TOM'S CABIN IS A DRIVE-IN NOW
Uncle Tom . . . . Roy Glenn
Aunt Jemima . . . . Evelyn Burwell
Waitress . . . . Ivy Anderson
Second Waitress . . . . Marie Bryant
Pot, Pan and Skillet, Hi-Hatters, Rockets, Ensemble.

ACT II.

1. JUMP FOR JOY
Lyrics by Sid Kuller & Paul Webster   Music by Duke Ellington
Singer, Herb Jeffries, Choir, Rockets, Hi-Hatters, Ensemble.

2. VIGNETTES
By Sid Kuller
By Sid Kuller
First Couple . . . . { Dorothy Dandridge
                                                                { Herb Jeffries
Second Couple . . . . { Marie Bryant
                                                                { Udell Johnson

3. OLD-FASHIONED WALTZ
Lyrics by Sid Kuller   Music by Duke Ellington
Singer . . . . Herb Jeffries
Couples: The Hi-Hatters, Suzette Johnson, Millie Monroe, Ava-
nelle Harris.

4. WE AIM TO PLEASE
By Hal Fimberg and Sid Kuller
Laughin' Andy . . . . Roy Glenn
Ever Joyous . . . . Paul White
Customer . . . . Skillet
"Smilin' Franky" . . . . Al Guster

5. IF LIFE WERE ALL PEACHES AND CREAM
Lyrics by Paul Webster   Music by Hal-Borne
First Couple . . . . { Dorothy Dandridge
                                                                { Herb Jeffries
Second Couple . . . . { Marie Bryant
                                                                { Paul White

6. RENT PARTY
By Sid Kuller
Hostess . . . . Ivy Anderson
The Duke . . . . Duke Ellington
Sonny Greer, Ray Nance, Ben Webster, Joe Nanton, Jimmy Blan-
ton, Rex Stewart, Roy Glenn, Henry Roberts, Suzette John-
son and Ensemble.
Concerto for Clinkers . . . . Music by Duke Ellington

7. THE FINISHED SYMPHONY
By Richard Weil
Tiger . . . . Roy Glenn
Rough-house . . . . Pan

8. CHOCOLATE SHAKE
Lyrics by Paul Webster   Music by Duke Ellington
Bartender . . . . Paul White
Boy . . . . Al Guster
Girl . . . . Ivy Anderson
Cigarette Girl . . . . Marie Bryant
Rockets, Hi-Hatters, Ensemble.

9. HICKORY STICK
Lyrics by Paul Webster   Music by Hal Borne
Singer . . . . Dorothy Dandridge
Dancer . . . . Pete Nugent

10. RESIGNED TO LIVING
By Hal Fimberg
Gertrude . . . . Suzette Johnson
Noel . . . . Al Guster
First Caller . . . . Herb Jeffries
Second Caller . . . . Henry Roberts
Man . . . . Wonderful Smith

11. NOTHIN'
Lyrics by Sid Kuller and Ray Golden *Music by Hal Borne*
Boy .... Paul White
Girl .... Ivy Anderson
Rockets, Hi-Hatters, Ensemble

12. MADE TO ORDER
By Sid Kuller
First Tailor .... Pan
Second Tailor .... Skillet
Customer .... Pot

13. SHARP EASTER
Lyrics by Sid Kuller *Music by Duke Ellington*
The Loan Shark..................................... Herb Jeffries
The Streetwalker .... Marie Bryant
The Dandy .... Andrew Jackson
The Sweetman .... Henry Roberts
The Wolf .... Garbo
The Customer .... Pot
The Tailors .... Pan and Skillet

14. Finale Entire Company.

DUKE ELLINGTON'S ORCHESTRA
Johnnie Hodge .... Alto Saxophone
Barney Bigard .... Tenor Saxophone
Ben Webster .... Tenor Saxophone

Otto Hardwick .... Alto Saxophone
Harry Carney .... Baritone Saxophone
Rex Stewart .... Trumpet
Ray Nance .... Trumpet
Wallace Jones .... Trumpet
Joe Nanton .... Trombone
Lawrence Brown .... Trombone
Juan Tizol .... Valve Trombone
Jimmy Blanton .... Bass Viol
Sonny Greer .... Drums
Freddie Guy .... Guitar

GIRLS OF THE ENSEMBLE
Artie Brandon, Lucille Battle, Avanelle Harris, Ethelyn Stevenson, Myrtle Fortune, Alice Key, Doris Ake, Hyacinth Cotten, Millie Munroe, Frances Neely, Louise Franklin, Patsy Hunter.

CHOIR
Roy Glenn, Wesley Bly, Edward Short, Lawrence Harris, Louise Jones, Anna Dent, Evelyn Burrwell, Eloise Flenoury, Le Roy Antoine

THE ROCKETS
Henry Roberts   Andrew Jackson

THE HI-HATTERS
Clarence Landry   Vernod Bradley   Udell Johnson

VOCAL ARRANGEMENTS

Hal Borne   "Jump for Joy" Number
Assisted by Eddie Jones   By Eddie Jones

MUSICAL ARRANGEMENTS

DUKE ELLINGTON, WILLIAM STRAYHORN, HAL BORNE

ASSISTANTS TO MR. CASTLE
Patsy Hunter   Joe Stevenson

ASSISTANTS TO MR. HUBERT
Denny Winter   Herman Cherry

Costumes Executed by Hogan-Anderson and Vessie Cardinal
Sets and Draperies by California Scenic and Costume Company
Lighting Equipment by L. A. Stage Lighting Company
Shoes by Capezio
Men's Clothes by Arno

FOR THE "AMERICAN REVUE THEATRE"

General Manager . . . . Henry Blankfort
Company Manager . . . . Everett Wile
Press Representative . . . . Nate Krevitz
Stage Manager . . . . Jack Boyd
Assistant Stage Manager . . . . Joe Stevenson
Carpenter . . . . Ernest Parks
Electrician . . . . Norman Peterson
Assistant Electrician . . . . Sammy Thompson
Properties . . . . Dolly Case
Wardrobe . . . . Don Rhoda
Casting Director . . . . Ben Carter

GLOSSARY

all reet . . . all right
all root . . . all right
short . . . cheap car
rubber . . . good car
vine . . . suit
hame . . . job
fly . . . fine
groovy . . . in t e know
square . . . not in the know
sport my hen . . . show off my girl
kitten . . . girl
beat . . . tired
cut out . . . have to go
knock a scarf . . . eat a good meal
solid . . . fine

murder . . . fine
banta . . . girl
jump . . . joyful
killer . . . dandy
cat . . . fellow
lush . . . sot
juice . . . liquor
charge . . . marijuana
charge water . . . liquor
blow my top . . . enjoy
flip my lid . . . enjoy
snap my cap . . . enjoy
bust my conk . . . enjoy
don't drape that on me . . . don't kid me

dig this . . . get this
dig you later . . . see you later
pins . . . legs
gams . . . legs
dresses . . . girls
pants . . . boys
chick . . . girl
K.M. . . . kitchen mechanics
Jack . . . name for any fellow
Mike . . . other name for any fellow
skin . . . palm of hand
ice . . . jewelry
furburg . . . town far away
put you on the air . . . give me a cigarette
waitress . . . aviator

Ivy Anderson sings with the Duke Ellington Orchestra. Photographs and Prints Division, Schomburg Center for Research in Black Culture, The New York Public Library, Astor, Lenox and Tilden Foundations.

Duke Ellington at the piano in Central Park, May 18, 1947, performing in the "I Am an American" concert series. Harry Ransom Humanities Center, University of Texas at Austin.

to "dribble, fake and move past the man guarding you so that you had a clear path to the basket for a moment. Then you would try to drive in for a lay-up. If your path was blocked you would shoot a set shot if you had time; if not, you would pass." In traditional white basketball, players left their feet only for rebounds or blocks. Many coaches considered the jump shot a "hot dog" move that should be "confined to the playgrounds where it originated." Russell claims that strict disciplinarians threw players off their teams for such an offense. Jumping was "Negro basketball," and white coaches feared it would ruin the game. The jump was awkward, it threw players off balance, and the coaches believed it would be the downfall of anyone who used it.[70]

As the game evolved, the shot that had been standard for African Americans proved itself at the highest levels. Playing in the 1960s, Walt Frazier relied on the jump shot almost exclusively. "Except for shots off the drive," he said, "the jump-shot is the only shot I shoot, the only shot I've ever known. Basketball has become such a fast game, and the guys are so big and quick, that the jump-shot is the only realistic shot you can normally take."[71] Frazier could appreciate the two-handed shot, favored by formerly successful white players and coaches, but by the 1960s it could no longer keep up: "Red Holzman was a good guard in the days of two-hand shots. He's still a great shot. He can beat you just shooting from the center of the court, two-handed. But there's no speed in that shot."[72]

Ed Gottlieb was one white coach who didn't object to the jump shot. Gottlieb started coaching in 1918, and he recognized that the future of basketball lay in the entertaining, fast-paced, high-scoring game he'd witnessed in contests against the Renaissance and the Globetrotters in the early years of professional ball. Gottlieb, an immigrant from Kiev, founded the Sphas just after World War I. After World War II, the team members who remained became the nucleus of Gottlieb's Philadelphia Warriors, one of the original teams in the Basketball Association of America and the league's first title-holder (1946–47). When many other teams were folding, Gottlieb kept the Sphas going before the war and the Warriors afterward through a combination of careful money management and a gift for promotion. He hired local sportswriters Herb Good of the *Philadelphia Record* and Harvey Pollack of the *Bulletin* to handle public relations, he carried tickets in his pocket, and he personally roused the house during games. Gottlieb understood that fan excitement kept teams alive: in the 1930s he practically guaranteed a fight to patrons who came to the Sphas' home games at the Broadwood Hotel. But Gottlieb knew that even more than violence, it was the thrill of a high-scoring game that would draw fans. When many coaches in the American Basketball Association, and then the National Basketball Association, shunned the faster, flashier style, Gottlieb signed a series of high-scoring jump shooters, beginning with Jumpin' Joe Fulks in 1946, then Paul Arizin in 1950, and finally Wilt Chamberlain in 1958.

By 1954 more owners were beginning to agree that a faster, higher-scoring game would attract fans. One owner, Danny Biasone, took a mathematical approach to fan response and decided that the most exciting games were those in which each team took at least sixty shots. Dividing the forty-eight-minute game into 120 shots, he arrived at twenty-four seconds per shot and proposed that the league institute a new rule limiting to twenty-four seconds the amount of time a player holding the ball had to shoot. At first, someone from each team would stand on the sidelines with a stopwatch and yell "Time!" when the twenty-four seconds expired. By the end of the 1954–55 season, the rule was so successful that all teams had invested in shot clocks. Like the 1937 center court tip-off rules change, the 1954 twenty-four-second shot clock took the game another leap forward. Attendance at NBA games increased by 50 percent over the next two years, and the number of playoff games in which over a hundred points were scored more than quadrupled.

The Boston Celtics were a team trying to get into the new style. Coach Red Auerbach had a fast player in Bob Cousy, but he desperately wanted a big man who could jump. Coaching a summer resort team in the Catskills, Auerbach had the chance to work with sixteen-year-old Wilt Chamberlain and thought he had found his man. At the time, the NBA's territorial draft meant that each team had the right to take the top player graduating from college within its territory. So Auerbach tried to persuade Chamberlain to come to the New England area for college. Auerbach wanted to pay Chamberlain's family $25,000 to send him to Harvard. Gottlieb, coach of Chamberlain's hometown team, the Warriors, was also courting Chamberlain, trying to get him to stay near Philadelphia. But Chamberlain wanted to go elsewhere. So Gottlieb got the league rules changed to extend the territorial draft to high school players. The Warriors then claimed Chamberlain in the 1955 draft, four years before he was eligible to play.[73]

Auerbach moved on to the next big man, signing Bill Russell in mid-season after Russell returned from the 1956 Olympics in Australia with a gold medal. The six-foot-ten Russell had a seven-foot reach: he could jump from the floor and touch the top of the backboard. Russell reinvented defensive play through his left-handed strategic shot-blocking and leaping rebounds. Ironically, this primarily defensive player changed both the pace of professional basketball and its shooting style. Russell's impressive capacity for rebounding transformed the Celtics into the fast break team Auerbach had been trying to create. And Russell's blocking was so effective that other teams were forced to employ jump shots, like it or not. According to one estimate, by the spring of Russell's rookie year, 75 percent of all field goals in the NBA were jump shots.[74]

But the NBA was still a very small league—only eight teams—compared with the far larger number of college and high school teams, where the coaching philosophy changed much more slowly. Gottlieb recruited Wilt Chamberlain early, at a time when many coaches across the country were afraid that his style would destroy the game. Jimmy Breslin, after he observed Chamberlain playing for the University of Kansas, wrote an article for the *Saturday Evening Post* titled "Can Basketball Survive Chamberlain?" Chamberlain was a paragon of the black style: flashy, high jumping, high scoring, and so dominating that he could seem at times a one-man show. Russell was the leaping veteran, as some writers called him, but Chamberlain was a high-flying rookie, known early on for his jumping ability, and when he came into the league, it seemed as if the game had been transformed from one played below the net to one played in the air. In truth, the transformation had begun decades earlier, on the dance floors of Harlem, Philadelphia, and Boston, among players trying to outrun their opponents and keep from slipping.

Perhaps it is fitting that, although historians continue to pass over African American pioneers of the jump shot and fast break basketball, once black athletes carried this style into the NBA, their prowess could not be denied. Not that people didn't try to deny it. In a 1958 article for *Sports Illustrated*, fittingly titled "Basketball Is for the Birds," Shirley Povich wrote: "In a single generation, there has been a revved-up degeneration of basketball from a game to a mess. It now offers a mad confection of absurdities, with ladder-sized groundlings stretching their gristle in aerial dogfights amid the whistle screeches of apoplectic referees trying to enforce ridiculous rules that empty the game of interest."[75]

Even Bill Russell's defensive shot-blocking was called a "playground move," one that most coaches discouraged because they believed a good ball handler could fake out and then outmaneuver a shot blocker. But Russell was no ordinary shot blocker, and when coach Brick Swegle encouraged him to block as much as he wanted, Russell improvised and refined his blocking to a form so distinctive and effective it became known as "Russell moves."[76] Russell's NBA coach, Red Auerbach, once declared that Russell was one of the four players who had revolutionized basketball—the other three being Hank Luisetti with his one-handed running shot, big George Mikan with his pivot, and Bob Cousy, who, according to Auerbach, "made the game spontaneous, with split-second playmaking and the fast break."[77] Ironically, in the 1950 draft Auerbach rejected Cousy as too small. Instead, he asked Celtics owner Walter Brown to pick Duquesne's Chuck Cooper, the first African American drafted from college into the NBA. When Cousy's team folded, he became available again, and the Celtics literally drew his name from a hat of leftover players.[78] Even Auerbach would admit that it was Russell's rebounds and line-drive passes that made Cousy's fast breaks possible. And as an NBA coach, Auerbach can hardly be faulted for focusing on standout NBA players while ignoring so many others who preceded them. But historians ought to cast a broader net. Cumberland Posey, Dolly King, Doc Kelker, the New York Rens, the original Harlem Globetrotters, and generations of athletes playing for coaches such as Big House Gaines, John McLendon, Cal Irvin, and others in the CIAA Conference—such as Mark Cardwell at West Virginia State College, winner of the 1948 and 1949 CIAA championships—should get the recognition they deserve for the plays and moves they invented and developed, a style that dominates play at every level today.[79]

The novelist John Edgar Wideman recalls that when he played ball for the University of Pennsylvania in the 1960s, he missed the "spontaneity, the free-form improvisation and electricity of the playground game. Remember the early sixties before Texas Western's all-black five defeated Adolph Rupp's lily-white Kentuckians. . . . 'Playground move' was synonymous with bad move. Not *bad* move, but something undisciplined, selfish, possibly immoral. Twenty years later, coaches are attempting to systematize and teach the essence of the game invented on the playgrounds."[80] The jump shot, the fast break (from which it evolved), and the slam dunk are staples of contemporary basketball and should be credited with making the game the enormously popular spectator sport it is today. All were initially dismissed as "schoolyard," "playground," or "Negro" ball, even though most of these "playground" moves are part of a carefully designed offense that now dominates the highest levels of play. The experimentation and improvisation of black players have pushed all basketball players beyond what was once thought possible.[81] And black players have long since proved what they could do if allowed to move from outdoor playgrounds into the finer training and playing facilities originally reserved for whites only.

The term "Negro basketball" is no longer used, but phrases like "playground ball," "street ball," or "hotdogging" serve the same purpose, and surprisingly, these phrases are still used to describe a cultural style in a derogatory manner. What is surprising, however, is not the derogation but the refusal to admit the obvious: this is a strategy that wins games and thrills crowds. Clarence Gaines liked to remind people of Earl "the Pearl" Monroe, the New York Knicks star who played for Gaines at Winston-Salem in 1967, when Gaines became the first black coach to win an NCAA Division II title. The 1968 Olympic team rejected Monroe and refused to let him play because of the same ball-handling tactics that won the title for Winston-Salem. They said he was "showboating," a racially loaded term that harks back to the 1936 Jerome Kern musical Showboat—a musical, incidentally, in which actor and singer Paul Robeson, a great college athlete, starred and sang "Old Man River," in dialect. As late as 1996, "Big House" Gaines, one of the winningest coaches in the history of the game, remained disdainful of white coaches who criticized his players and the African American style in general in favor of a more "disciplined" or "fundamental" approach—as if the fast break didn't also have its fundamentals and discipline. "They talk about their 'discipline,'" he said. "I don't think it's that disciplined—they're just doing the best they can."[82]

The Slam Dunk

Even after coaches admitted the effectiveness of the fast break and the scoring potential of the jump shot, resistance to the third point in black basketball's triangle offense remained. The slam dunk—an in-your-face form of "intimidation through improvisation," to quote Nelson George—has no parallel in any other sport. A football player may spike the ball and dance in the end zone after making a touchdown, a baseball player may make a victory

run around the bases, but no other sport allows the athlete to celebrate his individuality at the moment of triumph, to "personaliz(e) the act of scoring." [83]
And even more obviously than the jump shot and the fast break, the slam dunk
returned the locus of power from the owners and coaches to the players.

The NCAA banned the slam dunk in 1967 and didn't bring it back until
1976, the year Julius Erving showed the nation how stunning the dunk could be
at the American Basketball Association's first-ever slam dunk contest. People
called it the "Lew Alcindor Rule"—after Kareem Abdul-Jabbar, a seven-foot-
tall freshman from UCLA who was annoying coaches with his in-your-face
stuffs. Of its banning, Jabbar wrote, "The dunk is one of basketball's great
crowd pleasers, and there was no good reason to give it up except that this and
other n[egroes] were running away with the sport." [84] Hunter College coach
Robert Bownes explained: "Look, if a guy is seven feet tall, he is going to score
from in close whether he stuffs or just lays the ball in. That rule wasn't put in
to stop seven-footers. It was put in to stop the six-foot-two brothers who could
dazzle the crowd and embarrass much bigger white kids by dunking. . . .
Everyone knows that dunking is a trademark of great playground black athletes. And so they took it away. It's as simple as that." [85]

Coach Don Haskins of Texas Western University, starting in 1961, hated the
dunk, too. Haskins recruited African American players from across the country to bring to his El Paso team, but he chafed at their style. One of the star
players for the Miners was David Lattin, a spectacular dunker from Houston.
Lattin remembers, "He called it showboating, and he'd be spinning around
out there on the practice court like an apple standing on two toothpicks."
Lattin said of his team: "We were a Porsche that he was making us drive 55
miles per hour. Was he really gonna put his best player on the bench because
he went behind his back? He figured that out and relaxed." [86] Even so, Haskins
insisted on rigorous defensive play and a disciplined passing offense. He took
his Miners to the NCAA Division I championship in 1966 and made history by
starting five black players against Adolph Rupp's all-white Kentucky team—
and winning 72 to 65. Texas Western often started with five black players, but
never had Haskins played an entire game with only his seven black athletes. In
this game, he did.

Ironically, playing against a team known for its fast break, Haskins started
with three guards to try to slow Kentucky down. Evidently, the tactic worked.
Coach Clarence Gaines was there watching, and couldn't believe how boring

the game was: "Haskins's all-black starting NCAA Division I team played nothing like the all-black CIAA teams had been playing for 15 years. The black players for Texas Western played more like a white team than they did a black team!"[87]

Haskins admitted that racial discrimination was never far from his mind. "I never said anything about this way back in the past," he recalled. "I didn't think it was anybody's business." But Haskins grew up in Enid, Oklahoma, playing basketball with his co-worker Herman Carr. "I think the thing that enlightened me the most," he said, "one day in August, '46 or '47, we went out to get a drink. We were both hot and sweating. Herman went to the 'colored-only' fountain and I started toward the other fountain, the 'white-only.' I was pretty thirsty and it kind of made me sick at my stomach because I'd become very close to Herman."[88]

Whatever Haskins's intentions, African Americans across the county were profoundly aware of what it meant to start five black players in a nationally televised championship game. "Believe me, black people realized it," said Texas Western's Harry Flournoy. "I remember a friend of mine telling me he was watching the game on television when our starting lineup was introduced. He saw the first black player and didn't think anything of it. Then the second was introduced and he didn't make too much of it. But then the third black player was announced and he leaned forward in his chair. And then the fourth and he was on the edge of his chair. And then a fifth and he almost fell out of that chair."[89] Black high school players all over the country suddenly believed that they might aspire to a Division I program. Charlie Scott, then a senior at Laurinburg Institute in North Carolina, recalled, "Being black, how could you not see the significance?" He became the first black basketball player at the University of North Carolina. Bob McAdoo, then fourteen, remembers walking around his high school—almost all white—with his head held higher. He, too, went on to play for North Carolina.[90]

If African Americans knew the consequences of such public flouting of unwritten rules, Haskins learned. "The worst time of my life was the next few weeks after we won the national championship," Haskins says. "It didn't really dawn on me what this was all about until that time."[91] Haskins estimated the number of hate letters he received at forty thousand. Everyone from Adolph Rupp to *Sports Illustrated* accused the players of being mercenary thugs with prison records, even though the graduation rate of Haskins's players at

El Paso exceeded that at many other universities, including the University of Kentucky.

To this day, Haskins disputes the notion that the win was an upset. Texas Western had run away with every game but one that season. Although his players drove him crazy because they didn't believe they could lose, Haskins never doubted his team. "Since when is it an upset for five black guys to beat five white guys?" he later asked.[92]

Undeniably, Haskins used race to inspire the team. Miner Nevil Shed remembers Haskins suggesting that his players go over to the Wildcat bench to shake hands with the opposing team, knowing that the Kentucky players would refuse.[93] David Lattin remembers Haskins telling the team that he had heard Rupp say five black players would never beat five white players. Early in the game Lattin made a resounding dunk, an announcement of what was to follow. Future NBA coach Pat Riley, who made 19 of Kentucky's 65 points, recalls it as such. "I was a little intimidated," he admits.[94] One year later, in 1967, the NCAA banned the slam dunk. "After that one dunk I had on Pat Riley in the first half," Lattin believes, "Rupp was so disgusted that he went to the NCAA rules committee and had the dunk banned from college basketball for ten years. That one dunk, can you believe that? He was such a powerful coach, a big figure, that he had the dunk taken out of college basketball for a decade." If anything, Lattin understates the case: he stuffed the ball three times in that game.[95]

Sometimes people make history unintentionally. That doesn't make it any less historical. In the wake of the 2006 movie about this game, *Glory Road*, critics fell all over themselves convincing the public that Haskins wasn't trying to make a racial statement—he was simply trying to win a game. Well, so was Adolph Rupp, but he didn't sign a black athlete until 1969—Tom Payne from Louisville, who spent only a year at Kentucky. In those days, winning a championship with seven black players *was* a racial statement. So was the slam dunk. It may have been a feel-good movie, but to the Texas Western players, it was a feel-bad season. Not one of three black seniors from the championship team was chosen in twelve rounds of the NBA draft. Tommy Kron of Kentucky went in the third round. The following year David Lattin, like Pat Riley, was a first-round draft pick. But by then the NCAA had banned the slam dunk. It should have been called the David Lattin Rule. History may have forgotten him, but Pat Riley hasn't. We shouldn't either.

The Soul Focal Moment

Long after the dunk was readmitted to basketball, this crowd-pleasing move continued to rub some people the wrong way. For former coach John Wooden, winner of ten national titles, the dunk is unnecessary showmanship—exactly what is wrong with contemporary basketball. "I'm very much against showmanship, perhaps more than I should be. If a UCLA player passed the ball between his legs or behind his back, I'd have something to say to him real quickly, and I'd say it to him on the bench," remarked Wooden in 2000, sounding like Nat Holman objecting to the one-handed jump shot nearly half a century earlier. But Wooden is particularly opposed to the solo artistry of the dunk shot: "I don't like it when they're all by themselves and they do a 360 [degree] dunk. That's not necessary. If I want to see showmanship, I'll go see the [Harlem] Globetrotters and I'll enjoy it." [96] What Wooden calls "showmanship" is a series of moves that were once thought gratuitous and antithetical to winning basketball—except by African American players: passing behind the back, dribbling between the legs, and spectacular slam dunks. Yet all of these moves have proved to be useful elements in any winning arsenal. Children's basketball drill teams across the country begin with dribbling between the legs and passing the ball behind the back—not because the intent is to make the children into miniature Globetrotters, but because better ball handlers make better players. Dribbling between the legs protects the ball from defenders, and behind-the-back passes are more difficult to defend.

The "showmanship" that has increased box office attendance since the 1980s by an order of magnitude is one element of an African American aesthetic that pervades many forms of expressive culture. Michael Eric Dyson lists three important characteristics of this aesthetic, all of which are present in basketball's jump shot, the fast break, and most obviously the slam dunk. The first trait reflects the "will to spontaneity," or improvisation—the spur-of-the-moment elaboration and refinement that depend on a lifetime of discipline and dedication to craft. The second trait—"stylization of the performed self"—highlights the individual strengths of a ballplayer or a musician and builds on them, so that Abdul-Jabbar's skyhook, Magic Johnson's baby-hook, or Alan Iverson's crossover dribble becomes a trademark move. Similarly, musicians in Duke Ellington's orchestra had tones and styles so unique, and Ellington was so intimately familiar with them, that his musical manuscripts bear the individual names of his musicians, not the instruments they played.

Finally, there is the use of "edifying deception"—subverting or defying perceived limitations.[97]

The slam dunk isn't very different from similar improvisational moves performed by jazz artists, who seldom are accused of showing off but rather are seen as being virtuoso performers. Part of the essence of such improvisational artistry is something composer Olly Wilson calls the "soul focal moment," a point of unity between audience and player that occurs when a player—whether musician or athlete—exceeds the demands of the situation with exceptional grace and flair but also with control.[98] The soul focal moment celebrates individual virtuosity but also reaffirms loyalty to community by performing a feat that underscores the assumed knowledge players and audience share. In a soul focal moment the player doesn't go for the sure shot, the easy shot. Instead, the player performs the unexpected with style. Charlie Parker transforms a routine break in "Night in Tunisia" into a historic moment of improvisation. Playing in the NCAA semifinals in 1955, Bill Russell comes down with a rebound while he has his back to the board. Without turning around, he jumps and swings the ball backward over his head and down into the basket.[99] In a memorable championship game in 1991, Michael Jordan (Game 3, Bulls vs. Lakers) goes up for an easy right-handed dunk and then suddenly, and unnecessarily, switches hands to bring the ball down from the left side of the basket.

Through artistic deception, the soul focal moment defies ordinary limitations of time, gravity, and human capacity—and it is risky. Sarah Vaughan might run out of breath and ruin the intonation; Parker might hit a note outside the changes; Jordan could be trading an easy dunk for a missed layup (or vice versa). Part of the appeal of the soul focal moment is that it stretches the limits of risk: the great artist knows his or her limits, and they exceed ours—something that we know and feel at the time, which is what allows us to appreciate such a moment. The virtuoso artist or athlete transports us beyond our own limits as we vicariously hitch a ride. The British critic Simon Frith is talking about the soul focal moment when he says: "Our joyous response to music is a response not to meanings but to the making of meanings. This response involves self abandonment, as the terms we usually use to construct and hold ourselves together suddenly seem to float free."[100]

Some objections to stylish moves in basketball ostensibly hinge on the assumption that individual virtuosity detracts from the team. But it is possible to consider moments of showmanship in a different context—not as taking away from but rather adding to team performance. The soul focal moment is transcendent, one in which the performer raises the audience above ordinary experience into an awareness of the extraordinary reach of human possibility. Like all displays of human virtuosity, the soul focal moment is a sanctifying experience, one that stirs up a crowd, joins people together, erases boundaries and divisions, and touches the soul. It fills the whole of one's auditory or visual consciousness with such elaboration and refinement that there is, at that moment, nothing more to be said. These soul focal moments—what Ralph Ellison calls "true jazz moments"—are flashes of transcendence.[101] Rules, limits, and barriers between people disappear as all—performer and audience alike—fuse in a moment outside time. The soul focal moment is showy, to be sure, but this is not a one-person show, for the soul focal moment elevates a community, and its master might be the ultimate team player.

Of course, it is hard to ignore the irritating taunt implicit in the slam dunk. The dunk is showmanship; the dunk is unnecessary. It is gratuitous, and it says much more than "two points." By emphasizing style, the dunk trivializes score. When styling is spectacular enough, it doesn't matter who wins the game. Suddenly, the game has changed: what matters now is not *whether* you score but *how* you score. When a child finds himself on the losing end of a footrace, he will often cry: "I didn't lose—I wasn't racing!" But the dunk is the opposite. It is the taunt of a winner whose action says, "I'm winning, and I couldn't care less." The dunk is a score that makes you forget the score. The dunk is what Kenneth Burke in *Language as Symbolic Action* calls a "dramatistic negative": it is a way of indicating the negative through an affirmative action. The dunk is a double positive, two "yeses" that make a "no." The dunk is a form of cultural defiance historically used by those who have no other way of saying "no"—one of many such gestures that both defy and define American culture.

But if we continue to frame the issue as a debate between style and winning, we miss the most important outcome of this cultural revolution. What were once "stylish" or risky moves are now winning moves. The fancy dribbling and passing, the fast break, the jump shot—all once considered to be unnecessary showmanship—have become staples of the game. Experimentation and improvisation might appear playful, gratuitous, or risky. But it is through playing with the possibilities of the present that innovators create new possibilities, new parameters, and new standards of performance. There was a time in basketball when the baskets had bottoms and there were no backboards, when players dribbled the ball in the air above their heads, when the only jump was the center jump, and blocking a shot was a boneheaded move. The man who invented basketball thought he had gotten it right, and he did not consider changes in the game to be improvements. Yet even James Naismith acknowledged levels of skill that he could not have foreseen, and plays that evolved simply because players developed the skill to enact them. There was a time when the slam dunk was considered a risk. Today, in our culture and perhaps around the world, the phrase "slam dunk" is above all a synonym for "a sure thing." [102]

CHAPTER 7 : THE BROWN BOMBER : JOE LOUIS

Compared to the high-flying Lindy Hoppers or the fast-breaking, jump-shooting, flashy-passing, slam-dunking basketball players of the previous chapters, Joe Louis was positively ground-bound. Solid, soft-spoken, and powerful, as a representative figure Joe Louis seems to defy the airborne aesthetic of the late 1930s. But while Louis kept his feet on the ground, thousands of spectators did not. And while much of America was jumping up and down, celebrating his successes, Louis himself became a springboard for the aspirations of black Americans.

As the most recognized black man of the 1930s, Louis was the first in the twentieth century to achieve widespread popularity among white Americans. And Louis played an important part in the revolution in American sports that began in the 1930s and continues to this day. Boxing, which had been in decline, surged in popularity, and other spectator sports seemed suddenly more important, too. In a time of increasing international tension, athletes such as the 1936 Olympians and Joe Louis achieved ambassadorial status. As they represented the United States to the world, they conferred citizenship on all African Americans. Louis's fame continued into the war years, until Louis became the iconic, if laconic, patriot of World War II. At a time when the armed forces were segregated and only a small fraction of servicemen were black, how did a black man become one of the best-known faces in the American military? What allowed Americans to accept a black man as their cultural representative?

Playing sports often took first- and second-generation ethnic Americans down the road to full citizenship, as if the sporting events of their new country were part of a long rite of initiation. Traditionally, boxing had featured white ethnic Americans, particularly the Irish. John L. Sullivan, son of Irish immigrants, became heavyweight champion in 1882 and held that title for ten years, afterward maintaining a vaudeville and melodrama career that lasted until 1915. Jews were also prominent in boxing—as fighters, as managers, as promoters, and, most important, as fans. So helpful was it to be Jewish in boxing that in the 1930s the fighter Max Baer wore the Magen David (Star of David) on his trunks, even though he was not a practicing Jew, had only a limited claim to Jewish heritage on his father's side, and had been raised a Catholic. Dan Parker of the *New York Daily Mirror*, who catered to a Jewish audience, said, "The closer Max Baer got to New York the more Jewish he became." [1]

But fighters of African descent could not travel this passage to legitimization. Although John Sullivan established his reputation through a national tour offering $1,000 to any man who could last four rounds against him, he steadfastly refused to fight Peter "Black Prince" Jackson, who won the Australian heavyweight championship in 1886. Several African Americans won championships in lighter weight classes, but no black athlete had the chance to fight for the heavyweight championship before Jack Johnson. Historians rank Joe Jeannette, Sam McVey, and Sam Langford as the equal of any white boxer of the day, but none could book a fight with a white boxer. And after Johnson won the championship in 1908, he steadfastly refused to fight African Americans, depriving them of the chance to compete for the championship. When Johnson finally succeeded in securing a fight with reigning champion Tommy Burns, John L. Sullivan denounced Burns, saying: "Shame on the money-mad champion! Shame on the man who upsets good American precedents because there are Dollars, Dollars, Dollars in it." [2] Their 1908 World Championship match in Sydney, Australia, drew little attention—although Jack London covered it. But the following year, as Johnson successfully defended his title five times against white challengers, public antipathy toward him grew. Johnson verbally taunted and physically humiliated his opponents, flashed his gold teeth at the crowds, and boasted to reporters. Fond of jewelry, dramatic attire, fast cars, and beautiful white women, Johnson flouted all the conventions of a segregated society. His 1910 fight against retired champion Jim Jeffries attracted more attention than any other sporting event ever held in the United States. But the racial disturbances that followed in such places as Uvalda, Georgia, and Pueblo, Colorado, as well as Houston, New York City, and Washington, D.C., resulted in the deaths of at least eight African Americans. [3] Twice indicted for violating the Mann Act of 1910—forbidding the transportation of women from one state to another for immoral purposes—Johnson was convicted and sentenced to a year in prison in 1913. He left the country and defended his title twice in France before finally losing to Jess Willard in

1915 in Havana. For the next nineteen years, no black boxer could negotiate a championship fight.

Willard restored the color line to boxing. Even though he defended his title only once between 1915 and 1919, he toured a country full of cheering crowds. When he lost to Jack Dempsey on July 4, 1919, Dempsey, too, swore that he would not fight black challengers, thus avoiding a bout with Harry Wills, the number-one contender for the title. Dempsey defended his title in 1920, once in 1921, and twice in 1923, becoming one of the most famous men in America and the country's richest athlete, earning over $500,000 from exhibition matches and movies in 1924 alone—an amount worth many millions of dollars today. Under pressure from black voters, the New York Boxing Commission banned Dempsey from boxing in New York State because of his refusal to fight Wills, so Dempsey's losing 1926 title fight against Gene Tunney was held in Philadelphia. When Dempsey met Tunney the next year for a rematch in Chicago's Soldier Field, over 100,000 spectators attended, creating gate receipts of more than $2.5 million. Letters to Dempsey numbered five thousand a day in the weeks before the fight. Like sports in general, boxing in particular had become mass entertainment, a spectator sport of enormous scale and profitability, second only to baseball. But just a few years later, during the economic depression, gate receipts dropped as people found themselves forced to choose between eating and entertainment, and boxing promoters began looking for ways to reinvigorate the sport.

"On the Rise"

Joe Louis was a young amateur of nineteen when John Roxborough offered to manage his career. Roxborough, a former basketball player, was a respected Detroit realtor and numbers operator with a reputation for helping young black men. After winning the light heavyweight crown for the Detroit Golden Gloves, Louis agreed to turn professional. "Okay, I'm ready," Louis told Roxborough. "But you have to tell my mom[m]a."[4]

Born to sharecroppers in 1914 in rural Alabama, Louis took part in the Great Migration, leaving the South for Detroit with his family in 1926 after a frightening encounter with the Ku Klux Klan. When Louis left trade school in 1931, he found that his cabinetmaking skills couldn't land him a job. His mother scraped together money for violin lessons in hopes that her son could make a living as a musician, but Louis found a different way to use his talented hands.[5]

Roxborough introduced Louis to Chicago numbers operator and nightclub owner Julian Black, who agreed to finance Louis for the first several months of his professional career.[6] Black managed several fighters in Chicago, and Roxborough convinced Louis that the only way to avoid becoming another burned-out, broke black boxer was to go with a black manager. The son of a New Orleans lawyer, Roxborough was brother to Charles Roxborough, Michigan's first African American state legislator.[7] "Mr. Roxborough was talking about Black Power before it became popular," Louis recalled in his autobiography.[8] Together, Roxborough and Black had, as Lewis Erenberg puts it, the "criminal backgrounds and business skill" to "navigate through the murky world of shark-like promoters and greedy gangsters who traditionally had treated black fighters as mere cannon fodder for promising young white boxers."[9]

Black placed Louis with Charles Henry "Jack" Blackburn, former lightweight champion and ex-convict, who would be Louis's trainer for the rest of his career. Louis and he called each other Chappie. Blackburn sold Louis on his training program with hard talk about the politics of boxing: "He kept telling me that the cards were stacked against me because I was a black fighter opposing white fighters. He told me that I could not win on points alone. I had to go for the knockout, so there'd be no doubt. His words were, 'Negro fighters do not go to town winning decisions.' "[10]

Louis was a shy and truly modest man, and he understood the paradox facing him: to rise above all others in his profession, he would need to stay in his place. Roxborough instructed him: "We never, never say anything bad about an opponent. Before a fight you say how great you think he is; after a fight you say how great you think he was. And for God's sake, after you beat a white opponent, don't smile."[11] As Louis put it: "My backers were not about to let their investment in me be messed up by any kind of scandal. They told me I had to live my life both professionally and personally a certain way. They remembered how Jack Johnson had ruined boxing for blacks, especially for black heavyweights."[12] Reporters, hoping for more of a story, often criticized Louis for his dead pan. But the truth was, he could not afford to show any emotion, because any emotion he showed would be twisted and misinterpreted.

Louis quickly learned the racial politics of boxing. After several victories in Chicago, he was set for his first big fight in Detroit when his manager, Roxborough, was called before the Michigan State Boxing Commission. The commissioner, two white fight managers, and the sports editor of the *Detroit Free Press* issued an ultimatum: either Roxborough would take on a white co-manager or Louis couldn't fight in Michigan. Roxborough refused, and—facing the likelihood of an overflow crowd—the commissioner backed down. Even mild-mannered Louis remembered the incident as sheer racial harassment: "Those white people couldn't stand to see a black on the rise, and if you were moving up, they wanted a piece of you for free." [13]

At the end of 1934, his first year as a professional, Louis had won all twelve of his fights, with ten knockouts and two decisions. He was becoming a hero to African Americans, but in a way that confused him: "A lot of black people would come to me and want to kiss me, pump my hand. I thought they were congratulating me on my fighting skills. Now they started saying things like 'Joe, you're our savior,' and 'Show them whites!' and sometimes they'd just shout, 'Brown Bomber, Brown Bomber!' I didn't understand, then." [14]

Louis was a fighter to watch, but the first thing about him that the white press saw was his color. The papers called him the Detroit Negro, the dusky challenger, the colored pugilist, Brown Bomber, Dark Destroyer, sepia slugger, mahogany maimer, dark dynamiter, dusky David from Detroit, sable cyclone, tawny tiger-cat, saffron sphinx, dusky downer, Mike Jacobs's pet pickaninny, shufflin' shadow, saffron sandman, heavy-fisted Harlemite, coffee-colored kayo king, murder man of those maroon mitts, tan-skinned terror, chocolate chopper, mocha mauler, tan Tarzan of thump. [15]

Segregation penetrated every aspect of the press. White newspapers covered whites only, which meant that as a rule, only white brides, politicians, clergy, athletes, and entertainers appeared in them. The prominent political activist and labor leader A. Philip Randolph was mentioned in the *New York Times* on three occasions between 1935 and 1940, and only once on the front page. [16] At the same time, black newspapers had trouble gaining access to major news events. Louis recalled: "Seems like the Negro press couldn't get ringside tickets for the fight like the rest of the press could get. The promoters did not right out say they didn't want no n[egroes] in the press section, they just said it real polite: 'Sorry, no ringside tickets for the weekly press.' Well, that automatically eliminated all the Negro press. Negroes can't afford to support a daily press." [17]

Louis's phenomenal drawing power broke these rules. By 1935 his reputation and popularity had attracted an ambitious promoter named Mike Jacobs, who thought he could break through the color line and get Louis a chance at the heavyweight title. A former ticker scalper, Jacobs controlled a syndicate of scalpers and was eager to tackle Madison Square Garden's control of boxing in New York City, particularly its monopoly over the heavyweight division. With three ambitious newspapermen—Damon Runyon, Edward J. Frayne, and Bill Farnsworth—Jacobs formed the 20th Century Sporting Club and then waited for the big fight. Roxborough had turned down an offer from Jimmy Johnston, Madison Square Garden's promoter, following a conversation in which Johnston told Roxborough that Louis wouldn't be allowed to win too many fights because he was "a n[egro]." Roxborough replied, "So am I," and hung up.[18] Unlike Johnston, Jacobs told Roxborough that he wanted Louis to win every fight with a knockout if he could, and that he'd do his best to get Louis a championship fight. Jacobs met with Louis early in 1935. Louis remembered: "He told me that there was a kind of silent agreement between promoters that there would never be another black heavyweight champion like Jack Johnson. He told me how Jack Dempsey had run all over the country to avoid fighting Harry Wills, a black fighter. And he wanted me to fight Primo Carnera. If I could fight, he'd get me a shot at the title, and he'd make a lot of money for me."[19]

Jacobs used his journalist partners to saturate the Hearst national newspaper chain with coverage of Louis, and he got the attention of other newspapers by using his private railroad car to take nearly thirty New York sportswriters to Detroit to watch Louis fight the six-foot-six Italian, a former carnival strongman who had arrived in the United States only five years earlier. The Louis-Carnera fight was scheduled for the summer of 1935, and the buildup to it turned the twenty-one-year-old Louis into the most famous African American in the country. White papers approvingly printed John Roxborough's seven commandments to Louis:

1. He was never to have his picture taken along with a white woman.
2. He was never to go into a nightclub alone.
3. There would be no soft fights.
4. There would be no fixed fights.
5. He was never to gloat over a fallen opponent.

6. He was to keep a "deadpan" in front of the cameras.

7. He was to live and fight clean.[20]

The June 25, 1935, bout marked Louis's first appearance in New York. Black fans traveled in caravans from most major cities east of Mississippi to see him fight; an estimated 3,000 came from Louis's hometown of Detroit. Among the 65,000 fans were such respected community leaders as Walter White of the NAACP, the Reverend Adam Clayton Powell Jr., Duke Ellington, and Howard University's Ralph Bunche. Some 400 members of the press made reservations for the Madison Square Garden arena, including Al Monroe of the black weekly *Chicago Defender*. Sitting as an equal alongside writer Damon Runyon, Paul Gallico of the *New York Daily News*, and radio host and *New York Daily Mirror* columnist Walter Winchell, Monroe saw Louis knock out Carnera in the sixth round of the fight.[21]

Louis's defeat of Carnera was front-page news across the country. No African American before Joe Louis had received so much front-page coverage; the headlines were followed by praise of Louis's skills. For different reasons, both black and white newspapers stressed Louis's African descent. Many white writers tried to sensationalize the event through dramatic primitivist imagery. David Walsh of International News Service wrote, "Something sly and sinister and perhaps not quite human came out of the African jungle last night to strike down and utterly demolish the huge hulk that had been Primo Carnera, the giant." In his syndicated column for the *New York Daily News*, "The Sportlight," Grantland Rice, one of the best-known and most bigoted sports writers of the day, called Louis the "jungle killer," "bushmaster," and "Brown Cobra." He alluded to the fighter's "speed of the jungle, instinctive speed of the wild," and declared that "Joe Louis was stalking Carnera, the mammoth, as the black panther of the jungle stalks its prey."[22]

Black newspapers celebrated Louis's victory and emphasized the political implications of the match. At a time when Benito Mussolini was threatening to invade Ethiopia, one of the few independent black countries in Africa, African Americans identified with the Ethiopians, and Louis's victory over the Italian Carnera was a symbolic defeat of white supremacist forces and fascism. African Americans had a new hero, a David who had defeated an Italian Goliath. Young black couples celebrated by Lindy Hopping in the streets while jukeboxes blared.[23]

For white Americans the victory was complicated, as was Louis's defeat of former heavyweight champion Max Baer three months later. Many white Americans were not yet able to leap beyond racism into a sense of national pride. Giving black men a chance to assert their equality could only lead to trouble. Conventional wisdom, and the press, held that the absence of African Americans in athletic competitions was the logical result of their complete racial inferiority. Now the press began to explain their successes by presuming a natural racial affinity for athletic achievement. An editorial in the New York Daily Mirror asserted, "In Africa there are tens of thousands of powerful, young savages that with a little teaching, could annihilate Mr. Joe Louis." The New York Sun declared that "the American Negro is a natural athlete. The generations of toil in the cotton fields have not obliterated the strength and grace of the African native." And Grantland Rice stated unequivocally: "The great Negro boxer is rarely a matter of manufacture, like many white boxers. He is born that way." [24] Before Louis's heavily publicized September 24, 1935, match with Baer, Paul Gallico delivered a column that dehumanized Louis absolutely. Only today is it clear, as it could not have been to white readers in 1935, how little the piece had to do with Louis and how much with the prejudices of the columnist and his readers:

Louis, the magnificent animal. He lives like an animal, untouched by externals. He eats. He sleeps. He fights. He is as tawny as an animal and he has an animal's concentration on his prey. Eyes, nostrils, mouth, all jut forward to the prey. One has the impression that even the ears strain forward to catch the sound of danger. He enters the arena with his keepers, and they soothe and fondle him and stroke him and whisper to him and then unleash him. When the leash slips, he fights. He prowls from his corner cruelly and stealthily, the way the lion prowled into the Roman arena when the bars were raised and stood blinking in the light for a moment and then headed for the kill.

He lives like an animal, fights like an animal, has all the cruelty and ferocity of a wild thing. What else dwells within that marvelous, tawny, destructive body? The cowardice of an animal? The whipped lion flees. The animal law is self-preservation. Is he all instinct, all animal? Or have a hundred million years left a fold upon his brain? I see in this colored man something so cold, so hard, so cruel that I wonder as to his bravery.

Courage in the animal is desperation. Courage in the human is something incalculable and divine. It acquits itself over pain and panic.[25]

Few American journalists offered such speculations on the "cruelty and ferocity" of the Nazi regime. It was easier to see the shadowy side of humanity in a soft-spoken dark-skinned American.

The black press, too, called Louis the "Brown Bomber," but whereas the white press focused on Louis's physical being, the black press emphasized his intelligence and machinelike precision. Prior to his 1935 fight with Paulino Uzcudun, the "Bounding Basque," the *Pittsburgh Courier* declared Louis a "brilliant young fistic blaster."[26] After his knockout victory against Uzcudun, the *Courier* headlined Louis as a "Perfect Fighter."[27] George Schuyler wrote that watching Louis was akin to observing a "master surgeon conducting a clinic in the operating theater of a famous hospital," surrounded by helpers clad in white like so many nurses and assistants. Louis's technique was flawless, Schuyler wrote, as he applied "the scalpel in the form of his slim, powerful arm to the patient." Louis moved "cooly, scientifically, jabbing, feinting, appraising. Once in a lifetime one sees a master like this perform."[28] After his 1937 defeat of Max Schmeling, *Courier* headlines called Louis a "fighting machine."

Characterizations of Louis as skilled, scientific, or machinelike grounded him in contemporary American culture. Rather than explaining his prowess as a function of his African or southern black heritage—primitive or backward in the mind of white America—the black press showed that Louis's skill was a thoroughly modern development, and furthermore that Louis was equal to the challenges of life in twentieth-century urban America.

White writers who managed to portray Louis as something other than a primitive African or backward southerner still used stereotypes. In an article for *Ring* headlined "Better Get Those White Hopes Ready!" Nat Fleischer called Louis "clever," a fighter who had beaten Carnera through "a masterly presentation of scientific boxing and clouting such as has not been seen in an American ring since Dempsey was in his prime." Yet, according to Fleischer, Louis achieved his final victory by waiting to unleash his "cave-man instinct until he saw his opening."[29]

No matter how clever his fighting might be, many writers seemed determined to chalk it up to instinct, and they piled on other examples of Louis's "instinctive" or "natural" inclinations. R. G. Lynch of the *Milwaukee Journal* wrote in a profile of Louis: "The hulking, lazy brown boy might have been lolling in a cabin doorway down in Alabama, listening to somebody inside making mouth music. Instead, he lounged in a huge easy chair . . . and played jazz records on a squeaky portable phonograph." In the *New York Journal*, Bill Corum reported: "There isn't an ounce of killer in him. Not the slightest zest for fighting. He's a big, superbly built Negro youth who was born to listen to jazz music, eat a lot of fried chicken, play ball with the gang on the corner, and never do a lick of heavy work he could escape. The chances are he came by all those inclinations quite naturally."[30]

In truth, like many Americans of his generation, Louis did love jazz and had at one time hoped to become a trumpet player like his idol, Louis Armstrong. He took his jazz records wherever he went, since they relieved the tedium of traveling and training. "If it hadn't been for the music, I don't know what I'd have done," said Louis. "I brought my Victrola [on the road]. Hot damn! Let me tell you, that railroad car was all set up with outlets. They even had standby electricity for when we were parked. I brought my Duke Ellington records and played my favorites, 'Caravan' and 'I've Got to Be a Rug Cutter,' [meaning a jitterbug or Lindy dancer] with my friend Ivy Anderson singing. Then my favorite, Jimmie Lunceford."[31] Although Louis was a frequent guest of Duke Ellington and rode to more than one fight in Ellington's car, to his ears, Lunceford was the best, a combination of Ellington, Calloway, and his other favorite dance bands. Louis admitted to the press that he could dance "when I can't duck it," and affirmed that he loved "hot dance music."[32] The black press had a name for Louis's walk back to his corner after each victory; they called it the "Joe Louis 'Truck' " after a popular dance.[33] Was Louis different from others—or even from other fighters—in liking the jazz bands and tunes of the day? Hardly. Hours before his championship fight with James J. Braddock, Louis received a package from Braddock's camp with a message in a form anyone would have understood: it was a recording, the popular Gershwin ballad "They Can't Take That Away from Me."

There was another connection between Louis and jazz music and dance that not many people were aware of, but one that made sense in the world of African American entertainment. Andrew H. "Jap" Sneed, Detroit's most successful dance promoter and manager of the Plantation nightclub, was also president of the Detroit Athletic Association. Early in Louis's career, after he won the 1933 Golden Gloves title, the DAA formed a committee to find a manager for him. Sneed spent months trying to persuade Roxborough to take charge of Louis's career and successfully wooed him away from another promoter who hoped to gain Roxborough's support for light-heavyweight champion John Henry Lewis. It was Sneed who got Roxborough to watch Louis fight, whereupon he agreed to take on the young boxer. Without Sneed's persistence and Roxborough's ultimate assent, Louis might have remained a minor success instead of the national phenomenon he became.[34]

By the time of Louis's June 19, 1936, fight against the German boxer Maximilian Schmeling, Louis had developed a huge reputation. Spending prior to the fight at Yankee Stadium was expected to reach a quarter of a million dollars. Seventy percent of Harlem's hotel rooms were booked in advance. Restaurants took on additional crews of waiters, and several nightspots were booked for private parties.[35] When Louis went down in the fourth round, radio listeners fell silent in disbelief. Louis finally went down for good, and the crowds of listeners clustered around loudspeakers and private radios began to disintegrate. In Harlem, what would have been a giant victory party became a somber scene. Children cried, and the police called to quell any rioting had little to do. Street vendors loaded down with Joe Louis emblems, pins, pictures, and lapel buttons "stood dolefully at street corners."[36]

Black newspapers ran story after story trying to explain the defeat. Trainer Chappie Blackburn was said to blame the loss on the "damn motion pictures," explaining that the newsreel distributors "were afraid that Schmeling might be knocked out in the first round, so they asked Joe to take it easy for the first three rounds."[37] Others suspected that Louis had been doped.

Louis spent several days recuperating from his loss to Schmeling and afterwards wrote: "In those three days I did a lot of reflecting and thinking. It was all my fault, entirely. I was too damn sure of myself. Didn't train properly, and between the golf and the women and not listening to what Chappie said, it's a wonder I wasn't killed in the ring. I let myself down, I let a whole race of people down because I thought I was some kind of hot shit." Louis knew better than anyone else that every fight was symbolic, and he bore the weight of this one especially heavily: "People took the loss bad, too. They say that folks in Chicago's 'Little Harlem' rioted that night—people actually stoned streetcars. And in New York a girl took my loss so bad that she attempted to drink poison in a drugstore. She had to be taken to a hospital."[38] He renewed a rigorous training and fighting schedule, hoping for a match with the reigning U.S. champion, James J. Braddock. Less than two months after his loss to Schmeling, he defeated Jack Sharkey in Yankee Stadium, and by November the fight with Braddock was "practically assured," front-page news for African Americans.[39] Louis continued to fight throughout 1936 and 1937, defeating Eddie Simms in eighteen seconds in Cleveland in December 1936.

The buildup in the white press to the 1937 Louis-Braddock championship fight in Chicago's Comiskey Park drew a sharp contrast between the two fighters. Although Braddock had no more education than Louis and nothing in his career to indicate any special intelligence, reporters claimed that the battle was between wit and instinct, intelligence and brute force. Jack Miley of the *New York Daily News* wrote: "Joe was a natural fighter. He will never be any better than he was the day he first pulled on a glove. He performs by instinct and nobody will ever be able to pound anything through his kinky skull."[40] Louis had no illusions about the political implications of his championship opportunity. "I was the first black man in twenty-nine years given a chance to get to the top," he wrote afterwards.[41]

The June 22 fight drew a crowd estimated between 45,000 and 70,000, with three of every ten tickets going to African Americans.[42] Louis recalled:

> Tickets were selling from $3.75 to $27.50 for ringside. A whole lot of black people helped to fill up those bleachers. They must have saved real hard to get that money together. Half of them must have been on welfare, but Lord knows what they sacrificed to see me. I had a responsibility to them. Later, I heard trains, cars and busloads of black people were coming from all over the country. All the black hotels were filled. Black people were sleeping in hotel lobbies, renting space to sleep over in night clubs and cafes. And there was a fair share of black people at ringside, those who could afford it—the gamblers, the doctors, the lawyers, the gangsters. Most of the black folks, though, were sitting around their radios, making little parties, chipping in on beer or booze, and waiting to cheer for me or cry for me.[43]

Under a full moon, Louis knocked out Braddock in eight rounds to become the youngest champion in history. He was twenty-three and only the second black titleholder ever. White reporters devoted more coverage to Braddock's courage than to Louis's skill, but the black press was ecstatic. The *Pittsburgh Courier* issued a special edition to cover the event, calling Louis the "perfect fighting and boxing machine" with "reflexes of almost unbelievable swiftness," a "piston-like left," and a right with "the devastating force of a cyclone." [44] Bill Nunn declared it "perhaps one of the greatest heavyweight battles in all history," and Chester Washington claimed, "It was one of those never to be forgotten masterpieces of the art of self-defense." [45]

Louis's win ignited celebrations in black communities across the country. "People all over were celebrating the win," said Louis. "In Chicago they stayed up all night shouting and running through the streets. They burned bonfires on corners, they drove taxis all over; they say that a thousand people were out all night. And in Harlem—thousands and thousands marched up Seventh and down Lenox all night long." [46] Some sixty thousand white and black fans took over the South Side of Chicago, "swirling, careening, madly dashing from house to house . . . yelling, crying, laughing, boasting, gloating, exulting . . . slapping backs, jumping out of the way of wildly-driven cars . . . whites and blacks hugging . . . the entire world, this cosmic center of the world tonight, turned topsy-turvy." [47] Louis's mother reported that hundreds of people gathered outside her home in Detroit. Louis and his wife, Marva, heard noises outside their home on South Michigan Avenue and went to investigate. "The cheers, the yells almost had me crying," he remembered. "Marva and I had to come out, I don't know how many times, and wave at the people. Black people were calling out saying, 'We got another chance,' 'Don't be another Jack Johnson,' 'We're depending on you.' " [48]

In 1938 Louis got to fight Schmeling again. Press coverage leading up to the match maintained the usual dichotomy: black newspapers stressed Louis's careful preparation and training, while the white press held that Louis was a natural. Bill Corum of the *New York Journal-American* captured that viewpoint in his story: "There are certain gifts that the Negro race, as a race, and Louis, as an individual, have as a heritage. The ability carefully to work out a methodical plan and adhere to it, is not among them. That's for Schmeling." [49] Increasingly, and especially in a fight with so many nationalist overtones, white Americans were willing to claim Louis as a symbol but had not yet made the leap to accepting him as a person.

German coverage, too, seemed to have a split personality. On the one hand, the Nazi press complained bitterly that the United States "sanctimoniously lectured the rest of the world about tolerance" but was itself deeply discriminatory. Other commentators wrote as if Americans and Nazi Germans were actually allies at heart; they had nothing but praise for America's painfully obvious racial prejudice.[50] Most Germans believed that the majority of America would, as in the 1936 fight, root for their "Maxie."

The reality of Louis as an economic force is impossible to dismiss. Yet to say that Joe Louis was accepted into the ring because he made money for promoters is not enough: he became a moneymaking proposition because Americans were on the verge of a drama that was not about race but rather about nation.[51] On the day of Louis's fight with Schmeling, picketers carried signs outside Yankee Stadium that read "Down with Hitler and Mussolini," while Louis told fans he was fighting "for America against the challenge of a foreign invader. . . . It is the good old U.S.A. versus Germany."[52] Americans had to make the choice between "supporting a white Nazi or a black American."[53] At a time when German politics promoted Schmeling as the champion of racial purity, many American fans were willing to admit Louis as a hero who stood for the whole diverse country. But acceptance was not the dominant emotion in Yankee Stadium that night in 1938.

Although the event was not sold out, it marked one of the first million-dollar gates for boxing in many years.[54] Among the seventy thousand fans in Yankee Stadium were Cab Calloway, Bill Robinson, the Mills Brothers, Ethel Waters, Jimmy Rushing, and Louis's special friend Duke Ellington, as well as Walter White, Roy Wilkins, J. Edgar Hoover, and Fiorello La Guardia.[55] But for Louis, many of whose fans sat far from the ring, there was only "tepid applause and a few boos."[56] Years later, Schmeling recalled walking through the infield as if running a gauntlet as a hostile crowd threw banana peels, cigarette butts, and paper cups, and this memory is often cited as evidence of America's loyalty to Louis. But it cannot be true. Even in the dugout, much less the infield of Yankee Stadium, Schmeling would have been far out of anyone's throwing range. Broadcasting to audiences in Germany, the German radio announcer Arno Hellmis declared, "Everyone is shouting and applauding" for Schmeling.[57] One African American reporter confirmed this account, noting indignantly that the crowd "saw fit to give Schmeling, a Nazi, a greater hand than it did an American-born world champion."[58] Another writer complained, "No challenger in memory of the oldest scribes was ever given such a welcome."[59] Wishful history aside, Louis did not begin the fight as America's favorite.

That night, everywhere, people had their radios tuned to the fight—in homes, cars, clubs, and on the streets—some 60 million listeners, or 57.2 percent of the American radio audience, the largest in radio history, at a time when the top-ranking shows boasted ratings of 30 to 35 percent. Not until President Roosevelt declared a state of national emergency in the spring of 1941 did a larger audience tune in to a radio program.[60] Worldwide, listeners topped 100 million, as the largest audience in world history hunched over radios in Kingston, Berlin, Warsaw, British Guiana, South Africa. So much of South America was listening that the fight was broadcast in Spanish and Portuguese. In Atlanta, W. E. B. Du Bois and friends gathered to listen, as did Woody Guthrie in Santa Fe, Studs Terkel in Chicago, and a young Jimmy Carter on a peanut farm in Plains, Georgia.[61] Across the country, wrote Frank Marshall Davis, 14 million "brown men, women and children cussed and prayed in 14 million ways for Joe to come through. Probably never before in American history were so many black voices silent."[62]

In the shortest heavyweight title fight on record—one that lasted only two minutes and four seconds—Louis leveled Schmeling, cracking his spine in at least two places.[63] Davis declared it a victory for all those millions of black Americans: "It was as if each had been in that ring himself, as if every man, woman and child of them had dealt destruction with his fists upon the Nordic race of Schmeling and the whole Nazi system he symbolized. It was the triumph of a repressed people against the evil forces of racial oppression and discrimination condensed—by chance—into the shape of Max Schmeling."[64] Louis's biographer sums up the significance of that fight to the twenty-four-year-old prizefighter this way: "If Louis had lost, he would have been criticized as a boxer and derided as another losing Negro. Few human beings face tests like that the Schmeling fight posed for Louis, a single event that will decide whether a life's work will be a success or a failure, with no second chances and the whole world watching."[65]

"Fight of the Century—Joe Louis vs Jim-Crow"

Louis's victory provided the cultural glue to bind Americans together in a way no other person or event of the day had done or would do again until Pearl Harbor. If Americans were to claim his victory as their own, they had to examine at least their rhetoric, if not their hearts. Overnight, questions about Louis's athletic abilities disappeared. Dave Walsh of the *Philadelphia Record* wrote, "It was the finest boxing and hitting that I and Schmeling ever saw."

Dan Parker of the *New York Daily Mirror* declared: "Louis has finally come into his full estate as a great world's champion. If any one doubts his greatness after his masterful job last night, he's plain plumb prejudiced."[66]

Even newspapers for southern readers grudgingly accepted Louis's athletic superiority. O. B. Keeler of the *Atlanta Journal* wrote: "Joe Louis now is heavyweight boxing champion of the world, and so far as this correspondent can see there is nothing to be done about it. Our fastest runners are colored boys, and our longest jumpers, and highest leapers. And now our champion fighting man with the fists is Joseph Louis Barrow."[67] Other papers noted the paradox of the American position. The *Boston Globe* commented that "brown Joe was accepted by multitudes as the representative of world democracy . . . [which] is strange when the undemocratic treatment of Negroes by many who boast of their own attitude toward freedom and equality is recalled." The *New York Post* suggested that the "fact that a Negro happens to be the heavyweight title-holder stirs no resentment, rouses no racial feeling" indicated a remarkable leap in tolerance.[68]

For African Americans, there was little equivocation: Louis's victory over one white man was a victory for all African Americans over all white people. One headline in the *Pittsburgh Courier* captured the sentiment: "Fight of the Century—Joe Louis vs Jim-Crow."[69] Impromptu celebrations in black communities across the country dwarfed previous high spirits. Thousands gathered on the streets of Indianapolis, Kansas City, and Cincinnati, and along Central Avenue in Los Angeles. Joining them were many Jews. Even in southern cities such as Memphis and Mobile, crowds paraded and danced in the streets until police dispersed them. Along Lenox Avenue in Harlem, bootblacks offered revelers a "Joe Louis shine": it took only two minutes and four seconds.[70] Estimates of the crowd in Harlem reached as high as 500,000.[71] Richard Wright called the public revelry after the second Schmeling fight "the largest and most spontaneous political demonstration ever seen in Harlem."[72]

German writers took up where the American press had left off, continuing to describe Louis as a savage jungle beast surviving in the ring on the basis of instinct and brute force. Some Germans determined that Louis could have won only through the use of typical American trickery.[73] Louis's victory was so disruptive to Nazi propaganda that propaganda minister Joseph Goebbels refused to allow footage of the fight to be shown in Germany.[74]

Louis's first match after Schmeling was against John Henry Lewis, another standout African American fighter, and promoter Mike Jacobs kept ticket prices low, believing that white customers wouldn't pay to see two black boxers. Madison Square Garden sold out. Until he joined the army in 1942, Louis successfully defended his title seventeen times, with fifteen of those victories won by knockouts. No champion had ever fought so often or with such complete domination. And the laconic Louis became one of the most widely quoted celebrities of the era. Before his fight with Billy Conn, on June 18, 1941, Louis was asked whether he thought he could catch up with his nimble opponent. Louis answered, memorably, "He can run, but he can't hide."[75] When asked to speak before a benefit fight for the Navy Relief Society in Madison Square Garden, Louis said simply: "I have only done what any red-blooded American would do. We gon do our part, and we will win, because we are on God's side," thus coining one of the most commonly used slogans of the war.[76]

Louis was not admired by all African Americans. Some, particularly the upper middle class and intellectuals, believed that Louis helped to maintain a one-dimensional view of African Americans. When, as the editor of the NAACP's Crisis, Roy Wilkins tried to attract a wider audience by publishing an article on black athletes, complete with a cover photo of Joe Louis and sprinter Jesse Owens, he titled the photo "Owens and Louis, Our Ambassadors."[77] And yet the success of such athletes worried Wilkins, who editorialized: "We do not advise our race to hitch its wagon to a boxer, or base its judgments of achievement on the size of a black man's biceps or the speed and power of his left hook. . . . Those who maintain that a Negro historian or editor or philosopher or scientist or composer or singer or poet or painter is more important than a great athlete are on sound ground."[78] The Amsterdam News, reflecting the ambivalence of its middle-class readers, urged that "Dr. Carter Woodson's achievements in history, Dr. Ernest Just's discoveries in zoology, Dr. W. E. B. Du Bois' new book, "Black Reconstruction," Dr. Charles Houston's victory in the University of Maryland [desegregation] case ought to give us greater pride in achievement than a victory in any sporting event."[79]

The same black bourgeoisie that repudiated Louis, "rejecting the idea of having the 'genius' of the Negro race represented by a mere prizefighter," also rejected jazz, swing, and the dances of the Savoy Ballroom.[80] Their criticism misses the point. No other athlete of the day, and no other African American, was more respected and revered than Joe Louis, who became, in the words of Gerald Early, "the greatest, the most expansive and mythical blues hero in twentieth-century America, nothing less."[81] Fighting to become a champion in a world that refused him social equality, Louis defeated a host of opponents more powerful than those he met in the ring. As Louis's biographer Chris Mead wrote, "historians recognize W. E. B. Du Bois and A. Philip Randolph as the most important black leaders of the 1930s; white Americans of that era would have been hard pressed to recognize their names, still less their faces."[82]

While some black intellectuals may have believed a mere boxer an unworthy model to emulate, Louis was getting an average of three hundred letters a day from fans, many of whom wrote to tell him that they were naming their sons after him.[83] The feelings of one eighteen-year-old college student likely represented the black majority: "For years whites have kicked Negroes about, and I'm happy somebody came along who could kick the stuffing out of the toughest 'hombres' the whites could put up against him."[84] Black intellectual George Schuyler recognized the importance of athletes like Louis and Owens. And not just for their symbolic significance. In his column in the *Pittsburgh Courier*, Schuyler wrote:

> The accomplishments of Dr. Joseph Barrow in the squared circle and the achievements of Prof. Owens on the cinder path have reflected much credit and glory upon the group and certainly deserve as much respect as the efforts of some of the higher mendicants who have received the Springarn Medal. It strikes me as being just as commendable to be the world's outstanding track man or acknowledged master of the pro-ring as it is to write some songs, act in a play, produce some medical books or corral a group of well-fed colored ladies and gentlemen in London, Paris or Lisbon ostensibly to name the entire Negro race while wolfing caviar and champagne.[85]

When Joe Louis returned to Detroit in 1935 after beating Carnera, one of the first things he did was to attend the Calvary Church with his mother "to give thanks to the Lord." That morning, he discovered, the sermon was dedicated to the topic of Joe Louis. "The Reverend J. H. Maston . . . talked about how God gave certain people gifts and that these gifts were given to help other men. My gift was fighting," said Louis, "and through my fighting I was to uplift the spirit of my race."[86] Preachers were the strongest purveyors of the middle-class uplift position—an argument that often advocated patient struggle and the need to earn the rights that others claimed simply by virtue of being born American. Louis, an undereducated youth who spoke through his fists, represented few middle-class values. When the Reverend Maston anointed Joe Louis, a *fighter*, the new prophet of racial uplift, this was a sure sign of shifting cultural authority.

Blues scholar Paul Oliver has written about Louis's special role in relation to the blues music of his time: "There are no blues devoted to the achievements of Paul Robeson, George Washington Carver (the Black scientist) or Ralph Bunche (Black politician and diplomat), though these figures would probably have been known to the more literate and especially the city-dwelling singers."[87] Yet Louis's 1935 victories over Carnera and Baer inspired countless blues songs. Memphis Minnie McCoy recorded "He's in the Ring (Doin' the Same Old Thing)" and "Joe Louis Strut." Ike Smith recorded "Fighting Joe Louis," George Dewey Washington the "Joe Louis Chant," and Lil Johnson "Winner Joe (the Knock-Out King)" within a year after Louis's knockout of Carnera. Billy Hicks and the Sizzling Six recorded "Joe the Bomber" after Louis's heavyweight championship in 1937, and Bill Gaither recorded a song about Louis's victory over Max Schmeling in the 1938 rematch. Richard Wright wrote the lyrics to a song Paul Robeson recorded with the Count Basie Orchestra in 1940, "King Joe." The record sold forty thousand copies within two months of its release.[88]

Louis's fame reinforced itself, eclipsing that of all other African Americans: between 1933 and 1938 Louis got more front-page exposure in the *Chicago Defender* than any other Negro. Perhaps the white press did consciously promote Louis, the humble, soft-spoken athlete, at the expense of better-educated, more eloquent, or more "representative" African Americans; but to say so does not diminish his importance to a generation. Economist Thomas Sowell recalls: "How he fared in the ring mattered more to black Americans than the fate of any other athlete in any other sport, before or since. He was all we had."[89] And if the promotion of Louis at the expense of more politically or intellectually astute African Americans was part of a conspiracy to maintain control, it certainly backfired.

Richard Wright was a young poet when Louis knocked out Max Baer on September 24, 1935, and he marveled at the reaction in Chicago: "The blacks began to remember all the little slights, and discriminations and insults they had suffered; and their hunger too and their misery. And the whites began to search their souls to see if they had been guilty of something, some time, somewhere, against which this wave of feeling was rising." Young black men took to stopping automobiles and streetcars, demanding to know, "Who yuh fer—Baer or Louis?" Wright said that Louis had uncovered dynamite in the midst of African Americans, dynamite that could explode if things didn't change, soon: "Four centuries of oppression, of frustrated hopes, of black bitterness, felt even in the bones of the bewildered young, were rising to the surface. Yes, unconsciously, they had imputed to the brawny image of Joe Louis all the balked dreams of revenge, all the secretly visualized moments of retaliation, AND HE HAD WON!" Wright stated it as clearly as one could: "Joe was the consciously-felt symbol. Joe was the concentrated essence of black triumph over white." [90]

Lena Horne was singing with Noble Sissle in Cincinnati on June 19, 1936, the night that Louis lost to Schmeling, and she could hardly continue her show. She later recalled: "Joe was the one invincible Negro, the one who stood up to the white man and beat him down with his fists. He in a sense carried so many of our hopes, maybe even dreams of vengeance. But this night he was just another Negro getting beaten by a white man." Her mother scolded her for getting so emotional about a prizefighter who was no relation to her, and Horne shouted back, "He belongs to all of us." [91] Millions of African Americans felt that loss personally. The *Pittsburgh Courier* headlined "Harlem in Mourning over Louis Setback" and denied that there had been racial "disturbances." Instead, "bystanders were stricken dumb." [92] As Maya Angelou puts it: "If Joe lost we were back in slavery and beyond help. It would be true, the accusations that we were lower types of human beings." But when Louis won, he was "Champion of the world. A Black boy. Some Black mother's son. He was the strongest man in the world." [93]

Louis's Legacy

Although he gained fame as a boxer, Joe Louis functioned effectively as both a symbolic and a real agent for social change. When the Daughters of the American Revolution refused to let the renowned black opera singer Marian Anderson perform at Constitution Hall in the nation's capital in 1939, Louis invited her to his training camp. Anderson sang the national anthem before a Louis fight. In 1941, when the National Urban League sponsored a radio program pressing for desegregation of the defense industry, skits about Louis dominated the show, which ended with Louis himself appealing for equal

participation by African Americans. Louis contributed thousands of dollars to naval relief through benefit fights and made notorious the state of segregation in the navy. As a soldier, Louis refused segregated seating on camp buses and complained so effectively about the American-imposed segregation of a theater in England that General John C. H. Lee ordered the theater desegregated. And it was Louis who went to the commanding general of Fort Riley to ask that Jackie Robinson—all-American football player from UCLA—also be allowed to play baseball on the camp team.

Louis's modesty and patriotism combined during World War II to make him the "most famous black man in history," a symbol of national unity "representative of American manhood and masculinity."[94] Louis's words "We'll win because we're on God's side" captioned a poster bearing a photo of a uniformed Louis thrusting a bayonet at viewers. That a majority of Americans could look at this image of a powerful, bayonet-wielding black man and feel proud to be on his side was nothing short of miraculous.

In addition to his prominent role in promoting nationalism and his participation in the National Urban League radio campaign for "fair play" in the defense industry, Louis fought for desegregation in education. After the war, during the 1950s, Louis helped to expose discrimination in the world of professional golf. "I stand for right and work for it hard 'cause I know what it means not to have the rights what God give us," Louis said.[95]

In succeeding generations, prominent African Americans acknowledged Louis's impact on their lives. Lena Horne, Maya Angelou, Malcolm X, and Jesse Louis Jackson found in Joe Louis a model for high achievement, an inspiration for high expectations.[96] Dizzy Gillespie wrote that he identified with Louis and often felt he was carrying a similar responsibility: "Black people appreciate my playing in the same way I looked up to Paul Robeson or to Joe Louis. When Joe would knock out someone, I'd say, 'Hey . . . !' and feel like I'd scored a knockout. Just because of his prowess in his field and because he's black like me."[97]

Even more important than the individual inspiration Louis gave thousands of African Americans was the insight of political awareness. Author and journalist Renata Adler has written about fan response as a form of political expression: "Every bravo is not so much a Yes to the frail occasion they have come to make a stand at, as a No, goddamn it to everything else, a bravo of rage. And with that, they become, for what it's worth, a constituency that is

political. When they find each other, and stand and roar like that, they want, they want to be reckoned with." [98] Victory celebrations across the country—except in the South–were not private: they were public. As black Americans streamed onto the streets, they formed, in Adler's words, "a constituency that is political." Louis might have been, as Mead calls him, "a revolutionary by coincidence," but the revolution he inspired continued for the next several decades. [99]

Joe Louis—and other outstanding athletes and entertainers of the day—were conspicuous black achievers in a racist society that discouraged black achievement. They symbolized—and demonstrated—the hope of fulfillment in a world that otherwise offered little . However much the elite deplored mere physical accomplishments, it was these very acts that gave the prospect of any improvement at all to the lives of hundreds of thousands of African Americans. To demean or ignore such achievements because they happened in the gymnasium or dancehall instead of the laboratory or halls of academe is to discount the value of symbolic action in the lives of ordinary people.

CHAPTER 8 : RACIAL UPLIFT AND CULTURAL PERMISSION

Triumphs in African America must be measured against contemporary attitudes toward achievement. Sadly, a series of community riots in the United States formed a national pattern of white retaliation against black success. Riots from 1898 to 1906 resulted in several hundred lynchings. The tensions that erupted in those communities were sparked by fears of African American autonomy and self-determination. They were a warning to black America: Do not overstep your bounds. The Scottsboro case of 1931, in which nine black youths were charged with raping two white women on a train, is perhaps the best-known event in which African Americans were punished for crossing an invisible line that was nevertheless as real in the consciousness of most Americans as that of Mason and Dixon.

One of the most carefully documented of these riots against black accomplishments took place in Tulsa, Oklahoma, in 1921, when a thirty-five-square-block area known as Greenwood burned to the ground. At the time, oil-rich Oklahoma contained more all-black towns than any other state, and boasted thirty African American newspapers.[1] Some eleven thousand African Americans lived in the part of Tulsa known as Greenwood, which was also home to a large entertainment district where the "Territory Bands" such as those of Count Basie and Jay McShann cut their chops. Of Greenwood, W. E. B. Du Bois wrote: "I have never seen a colored community so highly organized as that of Tulsa. . . . The colored people of Tulsa have accumulated property, have established stores and business organizations and have also made money in oil. They feel their independent position and have boasted that in their community there have been no cases of lynching. With such a state of affairs, it took only a spark to start a dangerous fire."[2]

The spark for this torching of a successful middle-class community was a casual encounter between a nineteen-year-old black shoeshine boy and a seventeen-year-old white female elevator operator, but the fuel was nothing more nor less than white indignation. Lawyers, doctors, dentists, teachers, carpenters, elevator operators, nurses, and bookkeepers ran for their lives as a lifetime of work and savings literally went up in smoke. As many as three hundred people were gunned down or clubbed to death as they fled from the holocaust, or died in the flames. Tulsa police called to defend the finer houses of Greenwood doused them with kerosene and deputized white Tulsans as they fired on their black neighbors. Survivors remember airplanes dropping nitroglycerin and kerosene bombs while machine guns took aim at those trying to escape the mob.[3]

The entire business district of black Tulsa—Negro Wall Street—perished, along with the 191 businesses that Greenwood supported. The Dreamland Theater, the *Tulsa Star*, and the Stradford Hotel were among the institutions gutted in that riot, along with the law office of B. C. Franklin, father of six-year-old John Hope Franklin, who planned to be the first Negro president of the United States and instead became a revered historian.

As the flames died down, looting began. One African American resident remembered, "Men were carrying out the furniture, cursing as they did so, saying 'These [damn] Negroes have better things than lots of white people.'"[4] Dr. R. T. Bridgewater, assistant county physician, recalled: "On reaching the house I saw my piano and all of my elegant furniture piled in the street. My safe had been broken open, all of the money stolen, also my silverware, cut glass, all of the family clothing, and every thing of value had been removed, even my family bible. My electric light fixtures were broken, all the window lights and glass in the doors were broken, the dishes that were not stolen were broken . . . even the phone was torn from the wall."[5] The city paid only the white citizens who lost property in the riot and discussed ways of reclaiming what had been black-owned land. City commissioners discouraged a nationwide fund-raising effort and promised to begin a rebuilding fund but didn't. Then the city brought charges against several prominent African Americans, including hotel owner J. B. Stradford, for inciting the riot. Insurance companies refused to compensate the victims for their losses, white-owned banks refused to lend them money, and lumber companies refused to sell them lumber for rebuilding. So devastating was the aftermath that for the first time in its history the American Red Cross came to the aid of a "man-made" disaster, spending some $100,000 on the Greenwood relief effort. Eighty years later, when the Tulsa Race Riot Report recommended paying minor reparations to the few remaining survivors, one such Tulsan, Kinney Booker, was asked what he would do with the money were it forthcoming.

"I'd use it to move as far away from here as quick as I could, that's what I'd do," said the eighty-six-year-old man, who, as a child of six, had watched his father led away at gunpoint.[6]

When white Oklahomans burned Greenwood, the hardest hit were the most successful African Americans, those closest to white Tulsa. A similar case was that of Rosewood, Florida, a black community in central Florida wiped out by white invaders in 1923. In Detroit in 1925 a black doctor named Ossian Sweet was besieged by a white mob when he bought a house in a white neighborhood, igniting a riot and bringing Clarence Darrow to Detroit to defend Sweet. The NAACP's Walter White recalled defending his home from white mobs in the Atlanta riots of 1906. While he and his father stood on their front porch, White heard a man calling to his companions to burn down the house because it was too nice for Negroes: "In the eerie light Father turned his drawn face toward me. In a voice as quiet as though he were asking me to pass him the sugar at the breakfast table, he said, 'Son, don't shoot until the first man puts his foot on the lawn and then—don't you miss!' "[7] In that riot, officially twenty-five black people and one white person were killed. The fair-skinned, nearly blond White and his father believed that only their skin color had saved them from death.

"Revolt against Weariness"

In the late 1930s, more and more people began crossing the color line, propelled by the successes of others more prominent than they. On a broad scale, African Americans were giving themselves *cultural permission*: authority to be part of the culture, and sometimes to excel. Simply put, because of the public victories of people like Joe Louis, Jesse Owens, Duke Ellington, and Count Basie, some African Americans believed that the time had come when they could cross a certain line without getting beaten up. In many cases, they were right. And the cases in which they were wrong only strengthened cultural resolve.

The journalist Russell Baker, who lived on the border between white and black Baltimore in the 1930s, described what happened when Joe Louis defeated James Braddock to become heavyweight champion. Black residents, "seized by an instinct to defy destiny," streamed out of their homes toward "white territory": "Men in shirt-sleeves, women, boys and girls, mothers carrying babies—they moved down Lombard Street almost silently except for a low murmur of conversation and an occasional laugh. . . . Joe Louis had given them the courage to assert their right to use a public thoroughfare, and there wasn't a white person down there to dispute it. It was the first civil rights demonstration I ever saw, and it was completely spontaneous, ignited by the finality with which Joe Louis had destroyed the theory of white superiority."[8] That day nobody shot at them or beat them or chased them, in part because Joe Louis had just beaten a white man publicly and gotten away with it, but also because a series of cultural victories had shifted the weight of moral authority.

Deeply felt cultural permission laid the foundation of the civil rights movement of the next thirty years. The political activities of that time are called a movement rather than a rebellion precisely because they were so broad-based and because they proceeded with an assumption of moral authority, an assumption of the right to inhabit, on equal terms, the very streets of this nation. Athletes, musicians, and dancers found that their music and steps and jumps were accepted long before they themselves were welcome on the streets of most white communities. But the cultural expressions that led them there are the physical manifestation, the embodiment of an internal, felt entitlement not just to walk the street but to create, innovate, excel—in a street sense, to own that street.

In 1937, the year that "One O'Clock Jump" was recorded, when air steps became common, and when basketball changed forever, Richard Wright published an autobiographical sketch called "The Ethics of Living Jim Crow" in the Federal Writers' Project collection *American Stuff*. Wright described several lessons in his "Jim Crow education," all of which were, he said, dedicated to the single purpose of learning to "*stay in your place*."[9] African American men, women, and children who jumped—athletes, dancers, and otherwise—were refusing to stay in their place, and the many instances of the jump throughout African American culture should be read as a record of that refusal. While many ordinary African Americans were challenging Jim Crow segregation, others publicly defied the enfeebled Jim Crow stereotype on stage and in dancehalls, clubs, gymnasiums, and YMCAs, and on the streets of their neighborhoods.[10]

Jazz music, dance, and basketball were three cultural practices through which African Americans challenged those in power, and the jump was a key ingredient of that challenge.[11] Through the powerful, assertive, and identifiably black jump, men, women, and adolescents reclaimed a central gesture of African American culture, defying the Jim Crow stereotype by reclaiming Jim Crow's jump. Jump tunes, the athletic jitterbug, and the jump shot helped to form a new black image: not self-deprecating or shuffling but self-assertive and literally uplifted.

Many African American leaders did not see such forms of culture as uplifting. To them, vernacular dance and jazz music were degrading, the very thing to avoid for the sake of political and social advances. In 1914 Adam Clayton Powell Sr. complained of the effect of "the tango, the Chicago, the turkey trot, the Texas Tommy, and ragtime music" on black people, "in the movement of their bodies about the home and on the street. Grace and modesty are becoming rare virtues." [12] Twenty years later Ralph Matthews, theatrical editor of the *Afro-American*, wrote that the ability to "dance with feverish abandon" the "dances reminiscent of the levee and the plantation" simply confirmed the stereotypes that white audiences held about African Americans. [13]

The "feverish abandon" Matthews noted in the dances he abhorred was indeed reminiscent of the levee and the plantation, which thousands of African Americans had abandoned for the city. And while the dances they brought with them may have confirmed certain stereotypes for white (and black intellectual) Americans, at the same time they resisted stereotypes through the public display of powerful, graceful, and sensual black bodies.

For African American intellectuals and political leaders such as Walter White and Roy Wilkins of the NAACP, jazz and blues and the dancing that went with them did not seem to register as important cultural contributions. Wilkins was a journalist for the *Kansas City Call* from 1923 to 1931, peak years for Kansas City jazz. Yet in his autobiography he does not once mention music in the town where he lived for all those years. In 1931 he moved to Harlem, but with the exception of one interview with Fats Waller, he recalls no music during his life in the capital of Black America, either.

Frank Davis notes that blues and jazz were "noisily rejected by Negro 'strivers' as a group." In the 1920s and 1930s it was "fashionable for souls trying to be 'cultured' to condemn such music as 'low class' and 'a disgrace to our people.'" [14] In the middle of the Harlem Renaissance, Langston Hughes's jazz and blues poems elicited harsh words from the African American intelligentsia. Reviewing Hughes's poetry collection *The Weary Blues* in 1926, Countee Cullen wrote: "I regard these jazz poems as interlopers in the company of the truly beautiful poems in other sections of the book. . . . I wonder if jazz poems really belong to that dignified company, that select and austere circle of high literary expression which we call poetry." [15] A year later, when Hughes published *Fine Clothes to the Jew*, the Negro press denounced him, his work, and the world he wrote about. The *Pittsburgh Courier* proclaimed "Langston Hughes Book of Poems Trash," and the *Amsterdam News* sank even lower: "Langston Hughes—the Sewer Dweller." [16] But Hughes could not imagine his poetry, "derived from the life I know," without the "meanings and rhythms of jazz." For Hughes, jazz was "one of the inherent expressions of Negro life in America; the eternal tom-tom beating in the Negro soul—the tom-tom of revolt against weariness in a white world, a world of subway trains, and work, work, work; the tom-tom of joy and laughter, and pain swallowed in a smile." [17]

When members of the black intelligentsia did not outright reject jazz in music, poetry, and dance, they simply ignored it. Writing for the *Journal of Negro History* in 1947, the white critic Morroe Berger noted that the journal "from its inception in 1916 through the issues of 1946 did not publish a single article on jazz or a single review of a book on jazz." [18] Berger continued: "Leaders of Negro communities have spoken out against the influence of jazz. This is to be expected of those 'race leaders' who believe that Negroes can improve their status mainly by acceptance of the standards of the white community, which clearly disapproved of jazz as barbaric and sensual—characterizations which Negroes have tried to dissociate from themselves." [19]

The tension between elite leaders and popular culture reflected an ongoing struggle to define racial progress. While the notion of racial uplift included claims for the social advancement of all blacks, historically the message of race advancement through self-improvement carried a strong middle-class bias—and, by the 1930s, a bias toward the middle class of an older generation. [20] Younger innovators ignored moralizing political leaders and went about the task of spontaneous cultural transformation through creative expression. "Let the blare of Negro jazz bands and the bellowing voice of Bessie Smith singing the blues penetrate the closed ears of the colored near-intellectuals until they listen and perhaps understand," Hughes wrote. "Let . . . [them] cause the smug Negro middle class to turn from their white, respectable, ordinary books and papers to catch a glimmer of their own beauty. We younger Negro artists . . . intend to express our individual dark-skinned selves without fear or shame." [21]

In Defiance of Gravity

Although jazz, swing music and dance, and sport were especially important forms of cultural assertion and rebellion because they involved so many
ordinary African Americans, the jump carried over even into forms of art that
were highly individual. The two best-known African American modern dancers, Katherine Dunham and Pearl Primus, also overtly or obliquely challenged
white cultural dominance through their dancing, and both relied on African
traditions to do so. Infusing their contemporary artistic choreography with
indigenous traditions, they, like jazz musicians and dancers, ran the risk of
being called to task for confirming stereotypes or primitivist notions. But each
was more concerned with art than with the opinions of the African American
intellectual elite.

Dancer and aspiring anthropologist Katherine Dunham made her New
York debut in the Negro Dance Evening on March 7, 1937, an event that offered New Yorkers a history of African-influenced dance. The program opened
with dances of Africa and, in a storyline that was both chronological and
geographic, continued across the Atlantic with slave dancing and spirituals.
After an intermission, the second half of the program included contemporary
American social dances such as the Lindy Hop and truckin' and concluded
with modern stage dance. By claiming African dance as the root of contemporary African American social and art dance, the organizers of the Negro Dance
Evening also established an African basis for contemporary American culture.
At a time when virtually no one was prepared to acknowledge the African
American roots of American popular culture, to claim that the most popular
dance forms in America had African roots was downright seditious.

Such a bold claim for African heritage was considered outrageous. Even
black intellectuals wanted to distance themselves from Africa, believing that
acknowledging this connection was a form of primitivism; that is, it reinforced
a stereotype of African Americans as natural, primitive people. The error of
this thinking, of course, was in presuming that African culture was primitive,
in ignoring the sophistication of African culture and cultural aesthetics. The
Negro Dance Evening offered a chance to elevate both African and African
American dance by claiming historical authenticity for both.

Dunham had grown up in Illinois, where she excelled in theater and athletics in high school. At the University of Chicago she studied dance and anthropology, hoping that by looking at the intersection of art and anthropology,

she could find out why people dance as they do. In the early 1930s Dunham embarked on an ambitious project, a comparative study of primitive dancing. She planned to study Native American dance as well as dancing in the African diaspora, including Afro-Caribbean and African American cultures. In 1935, under a grant from the Rosenwald Foundation, she traveled to the Caribbean to begin her fieldwork. Dunham observed and then danced with communities in Haiti and Jamaica, and she drew heavily on these experiences throughout her career as a dancer and choreographer. Dunham's own great-grandparents were Haitian, and in Haiti she found that her dancing skills gave her prestige in the communities she visited. It was assumed that, because of her prowess, she had spiritual powers. Before she left Haiti, Dunham was initiated as a spiritual guide, or *obi*.

Upon her return to Chicago in 1937, Dunham choreographed and performed her *Haitian Suite* before traveling to New York to present it at the Negro Dance Evening. Her most ambitious project of those years was *L'Ag'Ya* (1938), performed in Chicago through the Federal Theater Project, a federally funded work program for artists. In *L'Ag'Ya* Dunham did not replicate but rather interpreted dances from many different places in the Caribbean, using steps that she had not only observed but also danced. It included the Creole mazurka, the beguine, the Cuban habanera, and the Brazilian majumba. The first scene of the piece recreated daily life in a small Caribbean fishing village. Then the second moved to the jungle, where animal cries and steady drumming accompanied slow dancing. The culture depicted here was that of the Jamaican Maroons, descendants of escaped slaves living in remote areas of the island. Dunham emphasized a step that she had observed among the Maroons she visited in Jamaica—one in which a male dancer in second position, legs spread wide apart and knees bent, hops back and forth, from left to right. In other words, the focus of this scene was a jump.

In the 1940s, at the peak of the jitterbug's popularity, another dancer, Pearl Primus, commanded attention with her spectacularly high jumps. Although Primus was only five-foot-two and stocky rather than lithe, one critic said that she could "outjump any man."[22] Born in Trinidad in 1919, Primus came to the United States with her family at the age of two. An excellent student, she received a degree in biology from Hunter College, studied at the New School for Social Research, and hoped to work as a laboratory technician. Like the jazz arranger Fletcher Henderson, who had a degree in chemistry, Primus was unable to find work in her field. So, like Henderson and many other educated African Americans, she turned to entertainment.

Although she had no formal dance instruction, Primus had been a track and field athlete in high school, and from that training she crafted a career, first by replacing a no-show dancer in the production *America Dances*, and then, when that show finally closed, by gaining a scholarship to the New Dance Group. There Primus studied with Martha Graham and German immigrant Hanya Holm, widely considered two of the four founders of modern dance (the other two being Doris Humphrey and Charles Weidman). With Trinidadian Beryl McBurnie—also a Martha Graham student—Primus studied the dances of the Caribbean. As a graduate student in anthropology Primus toured the southern United States. Then in 1949, like Dunham, Primus received a grant from the Julius Rosenwald Foundation to study dance in Central and West Africa. In the Belgian Congo she learned the dances of the Watusi, who named her *omowale*, "child returned home."

Even though reviewers connected Primus's leaps to Africa, she began using them in her dances long before her trips there. Primus's choreographed solo works from the early 1940s include *African Ceremonial*, *Strange Fruit*, based on the poem by Lewis Allan about a lynching, and *Rock Daniel*, an interpretation of Langston Hughes's poem "The Negro Speaks of Rivers." Her 1943 dance *Hard Time Blues*, based on a song about sharecroppers by the folksinger Josh White, depicted the life of southern slaves and sharecroppers, using leaps and jumps as signs of defiance—not just defiance of gravity but also of a life of permanent deprivation.[23] Referring to a scene in *Strange Fruit*, Primus said, "The hurt and anger that hurled me to the ground in that solo were translated into an anger that took me into the air in *Hard Time Blues*."[24] A 1944 concert at the Ninety-second Street YMHA presented a chronological exploration of African and African American dance, beginning with Africa, then moving to Harlem dancehalls, and ending with modern dance. Reviewing this concert in the *Amsterdam News*, Nora Holt described Primus "leaping from the heart of a dark continent and spreading its symphonic beauty through an unbounded universe in a story of freedom . . . unstemmed and thunderous."[25] The choreography may have leaped out of Africa, but American segregation built the emotional foundation of Primus's work.

Modern dancer and choreographer Martha Graham believed that the way people move reveals much about the character of their society. Dance is a stylized version of everyday physical life. "The psyche of the land is to be found in its movement," she wrote in 1935. "It is to be felt as a dramatic force of energy and vitality. We move; we do not stand still. . . . In the dancer is to be mirrored the tempo and essential rhythm of his country." [26] In the late 1930s and early 1940s the tempo was up, and the essential rhythm of the country was jumping—whether in vernacular dance, social dance, or high art.

The cultural historian Lawrence Levine wrote: "There has been far too great a concentration on organized movements and on the articulate middle-class and upper-class Negroes upon whom the title of 'Negro leaders' has been bestowed. The larger masses of lower-class and lower-middle-class Negroes, who are anything but inarticulate in their own lives, have thus been rendered silent, and this silence in turn has been interpreted as acquiescence or apathy. Failure to understand the reaction of the Negro masses has stemmed directly from failure to look seriously at their lives and their culture." [27] I would suggest that this failure has diminished our understanding of the whole of American culture, and in particular of American popular culture.

As the energy of African American dancers, musicians, and athletes coalesced into political legislation, the jump—in music, dance, and basketball—transformed American popular culture in ways so complete we scarcely remember a time without it. Indeed, as the next chapter shows, one can fairly say that there has scarcely been a time without it. But its remarkable resurgence in the 1930s transformed the jump, a historical gesture of celebration and defiance, into a cultural exclamation point.

CHAPTER 9 : JUMP JIM CROW

African American secular music is full of words that mean different things on different levels in different arenas that are somehow all connected. "Ragtime" may refer to a genre of music, to the "ragged time" (syncopation) characteristic of the music, to African American clog dancing, to the head rags dancers often wore, to the rags that were hoisted outside a barn or meeting hall to signal a dance, or to rags stuffed in the cracks of cabin walls to block out Sunday's morning light, in hopes of prolonging the night.[1]

John S. Wright talks about the tangled legacy of meanings for the term "boogie-woogie": "The boogie-woogie was simultaneously a fast-stepping, Kansas City Jazz–influenced piano blues in which the bass figure comes in double time; it was the knee-flexing jitterbug one danced in accompaniment; it was a racial epithet; it was a wartime moniker for enemy aircraft; it was an intransitive vernacular verb connoting the uninhibited pursuit of pleasure; it was a reference to the devil and all the troubles associated with him; and it was, less openly but no less significantly, a southern euphemism for a case of secondary syphilis."[2] The word "roll," from "rock and roll," connotes "work, struggle, sexual congress, dancing, having a good time, and shooting dice."[3] In 1930s and 1940s America, "swing"—as verb, adjective, and noun—was so pervasive and yet so variable, so context dependent, that it became one of those words that if you had to ask its meaning, you wouldn't understand the answer.[4] So, too, do "blues," "jazz," "scat," and "rap" convey different levels of meaning while bridging them.

The jump seemed to occur in every part of African American life. It was a lively dance, a bouncy kind of tune, a way of partying, a basketball move, a children's game, a synonym for "joyful." To "jump in" meant to become involved; to "jump salty" meant to become suddenly angry. The word also had sexual connotations.[5] "Jumping" could be a state of mind and a way of behaving: nervous, excited, playful, energetic, joyful, angry, or simply having fun.

Nat D. Williams, a longtime patron of the working-class clubs on Beale Street in Memphis, recalled that in the liveliest hours at the clubs, "you did what the spirit told you. If it said, 'Jump up and kick,' you jumped up and kicked." In addition to its vague connection with spiritual possession, jumping seemed to have African roots: "Sometimes if you took a notion to go native, . . . you'd be there jumping yourself and look over in the corner, and there's another friend over there doing the same thing."[6]

In African American communities in the rural South, "jump" was a term for certain kinds of children's play, sometimes but not always involving actual jumping. The dance step "Jump for Joy"—a "strongly restrained Charleston step, with the high side kick eliminated"—was used in several children's jumping games, including "Juba," "Elephant Fair," "Little Sally Walker," "Josephine," and "Sir Mister Brown."[7] "Jump That Jody" was another children's jump, and mothers would often jump their babies up and down on their laps to strengthen their legs, chanting the words "jump that Jody," which sounds very much like "jump for joy" when repeated quickly; Georgia Sea Islander Bessie Jones recalled, "The old folks would tell us to jump them so their legs wouldn't be bowlegged."[8] The words to "Miss Lucy" tell listeners to jump.[9] "Shoo Turkey" was, in Jones's words, a "pretty little jump," while "Elephant Fair" was "a hard jump; it's good for you, makes you strong."[10] For African Americans, the jump was associated with youth, vitality, muscular strength, and athletic conditioning.[11]

In 1887 Charles W. Chesnutt published the first of many stories drawing from his childhood in downeastern North Carolina. Based on a hoodoo tale he had heard from his father-in-law's gardener in Fayetteville, "The Goophered Grapevine" told of conjure practices during the time of slavery. In this story, the ex-slave Uncle Julius McAdoo recalls what happened when an elderly man used the sap from a conjured grapevine to regain his youth: "En nex' spring, w'en he rub de sap on ag'in, he *got young ag'in*, en so soopl en libely dat none er de young niggers on de plantation *could n' jump, ner dance*, ner hoe ez much cotton ez Henry."[12] For Henry, the sap from the goophered grapevine was a fountain of youth. And the signs of this youth were his ability to work, dance, and jump. Whether the jump in this story is a form of play, a kind of dance, or a jump for joy, Henry does it in celebration—because he is young and strong again.

"Jump" in the African Diaspora

Africans carried a rich culture of sports all over the diaspora, gaining a reputation for extraordinary athletic prowess, particularly in foot racing, jumping, and dancing. Even in ancient times the speed of African or "Aethiopan" runners was legendary; Herodotus wrote that they were "exceedingly fleet of foot—more so than any people of whom we have information." [13] Along with wrestling, foot racing, stick fighting, hunting, and fishing, jumping was and remains an important part of athletic competitions throughout Africa. Jomo Kenyatta, prime minister and then president of Kenya from its declaration of independence in 1963 until his death in 1978, studied anthropology with Bronislaw Malinowski, a pioneer in a method of research based on firsthand contact and observation. In 1938 Kenyatta published *Facing Mount Kenya: The Tribal Life of the Gikuyu*, in which he wrote about the importance of traditional dances in physical education in Kikuyu culture: "Special care is devoted to physical development, and many of these dances are the means of providing healthy and bodily exercise. . . . [A]part from these dances, the boys have their games of wrestling, running and *jumping*, sparring with sticks and shields, lifting weights and stones and clubthrowing." [14] These athletic games represent more than child's play. Deeply rooted in cultural beliefs and needs, they help to create social and physical health, building physical skills and preparing children for the complicated social interactions necessary for group survival.

The legendary King Charles of Albany had been enslaved in Angola and brought to New York as a very young boy in the early years of the eighteenth century. One acquaintance later wrote of the time shortly after the Revolution when King Charles, in full ceremonial dress, had placed him on his shoulders and "leaped a bar more than five feet in height." [15] Free barber William Johnson, who kept a diary from 1835 to 1852, recorded, "I made a jump or 2 with the boys this Evening and beat Bill Nix about six inches in a one-half hamon Jump." (A "hamon" is a jump with no running start.) [16] Slaveholders encouraged such activities. Fugitive slave Henry Walton Bibb's 1849 *Narrative* tells of slaveholders who, when they wished to have "a little sport of that kind, they go among the slaves and give them whiskey, to see them dance, 'pat juber,' sing and play on the banjo. They get them to wrestling, fighting, jumping, running foot races, and butting each other like sheep." [17]

Slaveholders used athletic prowess as a way of gauging health. Freeman

Solomon Northup was kidnapped and sold into slavery in 1841, at the age of thirty. The narrative of his years of slavery, published in 1853, describes his auctioning in New Orleans. Northrup and a group of other slaves "were . . . paraded and made to dance," and one small boy "was made to jump, and run across the floor, and perform many other feats, exhibiting his activity and condition." In his 1857 novel *The Garies and Their Friends*, freeman Frank J. Webb wrote about a slave who "had been fifteen years before sold on the auction-block in the neighbouring town of Savanah—had been made to jump, show his teeth, shout to test his lungs, and had been handled and examined by professed negro traders and amateur buyers, with less gentleness and commiseration than every humane man would feel for a horse or an ox."

At the other end of the spectrum, countless Africans crossing the Atlantic jumped to their death rather than endure slavery. Jumping overboard was common enough to compel slave traders to keep their cargo in chains. It was commonly believed that Africans preferred death by drowning to the horrors that awaited them. Born in 1756 and taken captive when he was eleven from what is now Nigeria, Olaudah Equiano related shipboard punishments so severe that he "would have jumped over the side; but I could not; and, besides, the crew used to watch us very closely who were not chained down to the decks, lest we should leap into the water; and I have seen some of these poor African prisoners most severely cut for attempting to do so." But there is also reason to believe that many Africans jumped with the hope of swimming back to shore and to freedom. Born free in Massachusetts in 1799, Nancy Prince remembered vividly her African stepfather's tale of just such an event somewhere off the eastern coast of the United States: "I have heard my father describe the beautiful moonlight night when they two [her stepfather and another captive] launched their bodies into the deep, for liberty." As her stepfather told it, he escaped discovery because "it was supposed we were drowned, as many had jumped over-board on the voyage, thinking they could get home to Africa again." On March 16, 1737, off the coast of Basseterre, Saint Kitts, more than a hundred slaves from Africa's Guinea Coast jumped overboard together in what became a mass suicide but might well have been intended as a slave rebellion. The 1853 novel *Clotel*, by fugitive slave William Wells Brown, recounts the case of "one woman who had been taken from her husband and children, and having no desire to live without them, in the agony of her soul jumped overboard and drowned herself." Even this jump of suicide was yet one toward freedom, as Brown explains: "She . . . sighed for freedom, but not the freedom which even British soil confers and inspires, but freedom from torturing pangs, and overwhelming grief."

Jumping had its place in many different slave festivals and celebrations in the United States. Jonkonnu (Christmas masquerade), Election Day, Mardi Gras (preceding Lent), and Pinkster (spring festival, around the time of Pentecost) processions across the country featured energetic revelers, such as those observed in Saint Mary's, Georgia, on December 27, 1843, "some dancing, some walking & some hopping, others singing, all as lively as lively can be." [18] According to the ethnographer Mura Dehn, the winner of nineteenth-century cakewalk contests was "whoever jumped the highest." [19] The jump could also signify the beginning of wedded life as African American couples in the South jumped over a broomstick. [20] Annie Louise Burton, born a slave in Alabama in 1860, recalled: "If a slave man and woman wished to marry, a party would be arranged some Saturday night among the slaves. The marriage ceremony consisted of the pair jumping over a stick. If no children were born within a year or so, the wife was sold." [21]

A famous description of jumping in the performance of African American dancer William Henry Lane, otherwise known as "Juba," comes from Charles Dickens on a visit to New York in 1842: "Single shuffle, double shuffle, cut and cross-cut; snapping his fingers, rolling his eyes, turning in his knees, presenting the backs of his legs in front, spinning about on his toes and heels like nothing but the man's fingers on the tambourine; dancing with two left legs, two right legs, two wooden legs, two wire legs, two spring legs—all sorts of legs and no legs—what is this to him?" [22] This turning, spinning, springing performer was only the most noted of the African American dancers who inspired their colleagues and their audiences throughout the nineteenth century.

"Remaking a cruel world"

Globally, the single most prevalent American art of the nineteenth century was minstrelsy, drawing on the actions, humor, song, and dance of African Americans. Minstrelsy traveled as far south as Santiago de Chile and as far west as the California mining camps during the gold rush. [23] Minstrels were heard in South Africa as early as June 1858, and by the 1880s, residents of Durban, South Africa, could choose from a plethora of local troupes such as the Blackbirds, the Snowdrops, the Apache Minstrels, the Umgenis, the Diamond Minstrels, and the Iroquoi Minstrels.[24] Although there were some black artists who performed in blackface during minstrelsy's early years, it was not until after the Civil War that troupes of African American performers began to "black up." Minstrelsy provided training and employment and was instrumental in the development of ragtime, vaudeville, and black musical theater.[25]

"Jump Jim Crow" was perhaps the first popular portrayal of African Americans as "jumpers," the first great international American hit song and one of the most popular pieces of the nineteenth century. Tradition has it that a minor actor named Thomas Dartmouth Rice saw a disabled African American man working in a stable near the Louisville theater where Rice was performing in 1830.[26] According to the old story, as the man worked, he sang to himself, and on the chorus of his song, he'd turn and give a little jump. Yet the historian W. T. Lhamon insists that far from being the creation of a single performer, whether Rice or the stable hand, "Jump Jim Crow" was part of a black folk pattern, a "widespread African-American folk dance impersonating—delineating—crows."[27] Over the course of his career, Rice took the Jim Crow persona from the original "Jim Crow" song and dance through several original plays in which he was the featured character.[28]

Although Rice and later performers invented hundreds of verses for "Jump Jim Crow," the words of the chorus nearly always remained the same: "Weel about and turn about and do jis so, / Eb'ry time I weel about I jump Jim Crow."[29] Surprisingly, these lines echo the following description of the sacred Haitian possession dance invoking the African god Legba, guardian of the crossroads: "When a person is mounted by this loa, one of the things he may do is to go about limping, since Legba is thought of as an old man with one lamed leg. . . . Sometimes a person mounted by this deity may dance or spin around with a kind of cane-crutch called a Legba-stick, around which he twines his leg. Under conditions of possession, the spinning and twirling often become a true acrobatic feat."[30]

The deformity, the spinning around, the acrobaticism of the dances are undeniably similar. So is the limp. At the time Thomas Dartmouth Rice was said to have observed the Jim Crow dance among southern African Americans, little more than thirty years had passed since the revolution in Santo Domingo, when thousands of Haitians migrated to the United States, so it is possible to consider Haitian origins for Jump Jim Crows. But even if we discount the likelihood of direct transmission of the dance from Haiti to the American South, one could fairly state that here is an American dance with identifiable African-derived traits that are found in other areas of the diaspora. One of those traits was the jump. In Santo Domingo (and in parts of the southeastern and Gulf Coast United States) to this day, social dances are called "jump-ups." In the Bahamas, hand-clapping jumpers provide entertainment at festivals. The festival dance at Carnival in Trinidad is called "jump and wine." In several countries the name Munah means "jump," and is given to babies "so charismatic that your heart would jump . . . when you saw them." [31]

White minstrel performers had plenty of contact with African American singers and dancers and often drew ideas from black entertainers such as Juba or the legendary Jim Crow. Rice's assemblage "Jump Jim Crow" was the best-known dance in all minstrelsy, and in Rice's extensive and ever-evolving repertoire, and for the duration of his career Rice was called either "Jim Crow" Rice or "Daddy" Rice. [32] Rice played "Jump Jim Crow" to packed houses in London in 1836; Hindu minstrels performed it in Delhi. [33]

As a song, "Jim Crow" functioned as political satire, entertaining its male fans with endless raucous verses, up to forty-four in one version. [34] But it was the dance, not the tune, that made "Jump Jim Crow" an international craze. [35] The *New York Tribune* carried an article in 1855 that noted: "Never was there such an excitement in the musical or dramatic world; nothing was talked of, nothing written of, and nothing dreamed of, but 'Jim Crow.' The most sober citizens began to 'wheel about, and turn about, and jump Jim Crow.' It seemed as though the entire population had been bitten by the tarantula; in the parlor, in the kitchen, in the shop and in the street, Jim Crow monopolized public attention." [36]

The dance "Jim Crow" was so popular that on one occasion it was offered as an explanation for the public nuisance created by several African American children dancing in front of a paint shop. An attorney argued: "What colored child can be expected to withstand the temptation of listening to 'Jim Crow'? Yes, your Honor, if they will play 'Jim Crow,' the little boys and girls will 'do jist so,' as they have done." [37] Musicologist Dale Cockrell, who unearthed this account, queries: "Could it be that during this period 'Jim Crow' and kindred songs functioned for black people much as they did for common white people, as songs of subversion, songs about movement, the body, and laughter, about how the performance of joy and pleasure could remake a cruel world?"[38]

If "dancing" or "jumping" Jim Crow was bi-racial subversion, the term "Jim Crow" came to mean something very different. Tom Rice himself was never a member of a minstrel show, but his character Jim Crow became a stock minstrel figure, a quaint plantation rustic who often played in opposition to the other popular minstrel stereotype, the ridiculous citified dandy Zip Coon. Long after the tune faded from memory, the genial, shuffling Jim Crow remained a standard minstrel character. Whether from the minstrel stereotype or the political versions of the "Jim Crow" song, the term "Jim Crow" became the unofficial name for the civil segregation statutes that reached their peak during the first two decades of the twentieth century, although the phrase was used to describe segregation as early as 1838.[39]

The phrase "jump Jim Crow" might have been a reflexive statement, a command for the dancer to jump in the middle of what was otherwise a flat-footed performance.[40] No one "performed" Jim Crow: everyone "jumped" Jim Crow. Accounts pun relentlessly on this "jumping," underscoring its evocative nature. One of Rice's early biographers, Molly Niederlander Ramshaw, couldn't resist noting that " 'Jim Crow' had, indeed, jumped high and far from a Louisville stable-yard." Yet, she adds, the legion of " 'Jim Crow' imitators who wheeled about on their heels throughout the nation . . . still jumped many leagues behind the master."[41]

The Jim Crow dance persisted into the early twentieth century and is performed to this day across the South, from Florida to Indiana.[42] Clarence Dotson, a top dancer of the 1920s, did a number called "Jumpin' Crow" that began with a little jump and a headshake and continued with what he called throwing a "fit."[43] Marshall Stearns suggests that the 1930s dance truckin', or "Trucking," was a later transformation of the Jim Crow dance: "In Trucking, the shoulders are often hunched up, one above the other, the hips sway in Congo fashion, and the feet execute a variety of shuffles while the index finger of one hand wiggles shoulder-high at the sky."[44] The only difference between "Trucking" and "Jump Jim Crow" seems to be that "Trucking" moves straight ahead, while "Jump Jim Crow" was performed in a circle. One scholar suggests that Jim Crow was the source of Little Richard's limp and Chuck Berry's duckwalk.[45]

Other African American dances incorporate jump steps or steps with a little hop, which is sometimes followed by a side kick—a move that survived in the familiar Charleston. "Jump Dem Bars" is a flat-footed jump typical of nineteenth-century African American folk dance.[46] The "Buzzard Lope" was a narrative dance whose first two lines instructed one to jump: "March aroun'! Jump across!"[47] It called for "arms high and wide like the wings of a bird, along with a cute shuffle and hop," and when it died out, another dance with similar winglike arm movements, body rocking from side to side, and a hop took its place.[48] In West Africa, turkey buzzards are called "Jack Crows," and in the West Indies, they are called "John Crows."[49] The connection to Jim Crow in name and gesture is obvious.

A more urban version of the "Buzzard Lope" is the "Eagle Rock," named after the Eagle Rock Baptist Church in Kansas City. Like the shout, the Eagle Rock included the "high arm gestures associated with evangelical dances and religious trance." The dance spread north and south, gradually "discard[ing] the hop for a shuffle that could be performed at a crowded house-rent party."[50] More than sixty years ago, folklorist Harold Courlander stated unequivocally that such moves as the "shimmy, crawl, shuffle, strut, and jump" are drawn from "Negro and not European tradition. In them, one can see concepts of posture and motion which are related, even if distantly, to those of the African dancer." Furthermore, the indefatigable Courlander (who later wrote the novel The African, on which Alex Haley based much of Roots) asserted that he had witnessed "secular dances in South Africa, Ghana, and Nigeria in which certain passages occurred which were virtually indistinguishable from what in this country go by the name of Cake Walk, Shuffle, and Strut."[51]

An obvious remnant of jumping Jim Crow is the jump "Knock Jim Crow," which Bessie Jones always thought was a song and dance about a bird. Bess Lomax Hawes compares the Rice lyrics to those Jones recited for her:

Rice: I kneel to the buzzard,
          I bow to the crow,
          And eb'ry time I w'eel about
          I jump jis' so.
          W'eel about an' turn about an' do jis' so,
          An' eb'ry time I w'eel about I jump Jim Crow.

Hawes: Where you going, buzzard?

Where you going, crow?

I'm going down to new ground

To knock Jim Crow.

Up to my kneecap,

Down to my toe,

And every time I jump up,

I knock Jim Crow.

The action to accompany this dance is described thus: "Step on right foot, raise left leg with knee straight (like a high goose step) and clap hands together around it; repeat, raising alternate legs." [52]

According to Marshall and Jean Stearns, "Jump Jim Crow" was more a "syncopated hop in the flat-footed Shuffle manner" than a jump. [53] Contemporary descriptions of the dance Rice incorporated into his stage act call it a "jig and shuffle." [54] Joseph Ireland, writing in 1867, noted Rice's "shambling negro gait." [55] The Stearnses believe that even the jig of "Jump Jim Crow" was a "syncopated hop in the flat-footed Shuffle manner rather than a jump 'high up,'" and the chief feature of the dance was the "rhythmic circling *before* the jump." [56] This qualifier is important, because the rhythmic circling and flat-footed shuffle were defining characteristics of African American dance, part of the important religious ritual known as the ring shout. [57]

The Ring Shout

African American slaves who were forbidden to dance drew a distinction between dance, in which the legs crossed, and a shuffle, in which the feet slid over the ground without crossing. In the ring shout, the most formal of the many sacred slave dances, worshippers shuffled across the ground in a counterclockwise circle. James Weldon Johnson, born in 1871, remembered "seeing this dance many times when [he] was a boy. A space is cleared by moving the benches, and the men and women arrange themselves, generally alternately, in a ring, their bodies quite close. The music starts and the ring begins to move. Around it goes, at first slowly, then with quickening pace. Around and around it moves on shuffling feet that do not leave the floor. . . . The music is supplemented by the clapping of hands. As the ring goes around it begins

to take on signs of frenzy. The music, starting, perhaps, with a Spiritual, becomes a wild, monotonous chant." [58]

When worship services moved indoors, the ring shout did too, and it
changed as it became enclosed and surrounded by pews or benches. What
had once been a horizontal, circular movement now often became vertical.
At many points during the service, if the congregation could not dance in a
circle, worshippers stamped their feet or threw their arms in the air, as did
those listening to the preacher at one 1864 service, "the women sitting around
him, rocking & swaying & throwing up their arms." [59] The cultural historian
and folklorist Roger Abrahams notes, "We tend to think of shouting . . . in
the standard English sense of referring to noisemaking, but it means the holy
way of moving the whole congregation whether through vocal or movement
vocabulary," a way of "moving together while playing apart." [60]

Worshippers also jumped. When English clergyman Ebenezer Davies heard
a black minister in Baltimore preach to a group of five or six hundred African
Americans, their enthusiastically physical response so shocked him that he
had to leave the meeting: "The laughing, the shouting, the groaning, and the
jumping were positively terrific." [61] African Methodist Episcopal bishop Daniel
Alexander Payne complained in his 1886 memoir of preachers who encouraged emotionalism in their congregations: "Such preachers never rest till they
create an excitement that consists in shouting, jumping and dancing." [62] Landscape architect Frederick Law Olmsted reported on a black church he visited
in New Orleans: "Sometimes the outcries and responses were not confined to
ejaculations . . . , but shouts, and groans, terrific shrieks, and indescribable
expressions of ecstasy—of pleasure or agony—and even stamping, jumping,
and clapping of hands were added. . . . I was once surprised to find my own
muscles all stretched, as if ready for a struggle—my face glowing, and my feet
stamping—having been infected unconsciously." [63] Olmstead's use of the pas-
sive voice here is instructive; he takes no responsibility for what he considered
the powerful "infectious" potential of African American expression.

Jumping could get a person into trouble. Courlander reports an elderly
man's description of an "unfortunate experience" after jumping in church:
"Well, don't you know, them folks all shouting, rockin', and reelin', and me
in the middle; and I ask you if it wasn't the Holy Ghost that come into me,
who was it? Those feet of mine wouldn't stay on the ground in no manner,

they jumped around and crossed over, back and forth, and the next thing I know they turned me out of the church."[64]

Not many mainstream Protestant churches encourage jumping as part of the worship service, but jumping remained in African American holiness or sanctified churches (Pentecostal, Church of God in Christ, Church of God Apostolic, Church of Holiness Science, Fire Baptized Holiness Church). The theology of these churches follows the same general pattern: First, one is saved, meaning one makes a commitment. Second, one is sanctified, meaning a change in lifestyle. Finally, one is filled with the Holy Ghost, or possessed by the Holy Spirit. Divine possession can take many forms: speaking in tongues is one manifestation of the spirit, but holiness people were known as "Holy Rollers" because they jumped, shouted, danced and "fell out" for Jesus. In other words, the holiness churches continued an African orientation toward religious rituals, one of total bodily engagement. It is not out of place to move with the spirit in the holiness churches, and in some situations, movement is absolutely required. In the holiness church, you gotta jump when the spirit says jump.

Dancer Frankie Manning remembered going to church with his grandmother: "In most Baptist churches, when the preacher's getting deep down and he's talking to the sisters and brothers, they start carrying on, and sometimes you'll see somebody jump up. But in revival meetings, the Holy Rollers do that constantly."[65] Dancer Bill Bailey recalled: "Father was a preacher in a Holy Roller church, I guess that's where I got my start dancing. The congregation stamped its feet and clapped its hands, and I'd sit there and use my heels in an off-beat rhythm to what they were doing—we worked up a lot of swing."[66] Jazz trumpeter Dizzy Gillespie attributed much of his early rhythmic and harmonic inspiration to the sanctified church in South Carolina, saying, "I first learned the meaning of rhythm there and all about how music could transport people spiritually." Gillespie's family worshipped at a Methodist church, but on Sunday evenings he would sneak over to the sanctified church to hear the Burch brothers on snare drum, bass drum, cymbal, and tambourine: "They used to keep at least four different rhythms going, and as the congregation joined in, the number of rhythms would increase with foot stomping, hand clapping, and people catching the spirit and jumping up and down on the wooden floor, which also resounded like a drum." The rhythm-centered worship of the sanctified church permeated American culture. Gillespie said: "Even white people would come and sit outside in their cars just to listen to the people getting the spirit inside. Everybody would be shouting and fainting and stomping. . . . People like James Brown and Aretha Franklin owe everything to that Sanctified beat. I received my first experience with rhythm and spiritual transport going down there to the well every Sunday, and I've just followed it ever since." [67]

In the early 1990s, ethnographer Timothy Nelson spent a year in a nondenominational church in Charleston, where he observed the many responses encompassed under the term "shouting." Some were quite athletic, as he described in his field notes for one Sunday morning worship service during the hymn of praise, when energy was high, and several people were beating tambourines in time to the organ and drums.

> Abruptly, a middle-aged woman right in front of us started dancing vigorously with her legs, all the time holding her arms straight down at her sides. She held her eyes squeezed shut and shook her head from side to side, suddenly appearing oblivious to those around her and to the service in general. An usher came into the row and took her by the hands to draw her out into the center aisle. Once into that more open space, she began to jump and spin around at the same time—faster and faster until she was just a blur. Another usher joined the first and they linked arms, forming a protective enclosure around the spinning woman. She jumped and spun this way for over a minute, then collapsed and lay prostrate on the floor and seemed to be unconscious. [68]

Not all shouting was as athletic as this instance; sometimes, says Nelson, it was more of a "hopping and skipping style of dance, moving back and forth across the floor." [69] But jumping of some sort was usually involved. The worshippers Nelson observed believed that shouting was a genuine response to the Holy Ghost and the impulse to dance "in the Spirit," an expression of joy and praise to God and evidence of God's presence in the worship space. Nelson described "shouting" as "clapping, only with the whole body rather than just the hands." [70] He did point out, however, that from the perspective of the person doing the shouting, the transition from hand-clapping to shouting is not gradual but a radical break between ordinary and ecstatic consciousness: in a genuine shout, the person shouting has entered a different state of consciousness and has been overcome by the presence of God. Although another term for shouting is "getting happy," shouting is an involuntary withdrawal from consciousness, a trance state or a sign of what other cultures might call spirit possession.

The shout is what remained in worship after the ring shout moved indoors. But the ring shout's circular motion was retained in many worldly forms. Lydia Parrish, who observed geographically isolated descendants of slaves in the Georgia Sea Islands just after the turn of the twentieth century, recorded a rice dance that used a "shout song" in two parts, one slow and the second much faster. To thresh the rice, the dancers stripped the grain from the straw by hand and laid it out on a clean floor, walking around on it with a "pre-liminary scuffle." Then, with a "quick and effective dance step," the shouters scuffed off the outer husk while singing: "Make a jump, jump for joy! / Make a jump, jump for joy!" This faster section of the shout was sung "as two hops were made on one foot while the other did the scuffing."[71]

The closing number of nearly all minstrel shows was the "Walk Around," or cakewalk, a secular shout.[72] The cakewalk also had slave origins: on some plantations, on Sundays or special occasions, slaves dressed in their best finery and paraded in a circle—some say mocking their masters—and the grandest was awarded a cake. In minstrelsy, the cakewalk is a high-stepping grand march, done in circle, that often incorporates a circular kick to the side. The cakewalk made the transition to musical theater, where it inspired dancers during the first decade of the twentieth century. The Charleston, Texas Tommy, turkey trot, and many other vernacular dances of the time contain trace elements of the cakewalk—namely the side kick—as does the longest-lived of its progeny, the Lindy Hop. And other elements of the shout remained as well. According to one knowledgeable observer of the day, "Of all the dances yet originated by the American Negro, [the Lindy Hop] most nearly approaches the sensation of religious ecstasy."[73]

In the early years of minstrelsy, the Jim Crow dance may have been quite athletic, drawing on a long and widespread heritage of jumping as a way of expressing vigor and vitality.[74] But as minstrelsy evolved throughout the nineteenth century, "Jump Jim Crow" lost the powerful connections it originally had with African American culture. As "Jim Crow" came to mean less a dance and more a minstrel stereotype, its chief physical feature was not an athletic or powerful jump, a true expression of jubilation, but rather the shuffle, with all its connotations of slavery and subjugation. "Jim Crow" became synonymous with civil and political segregation and oppression, and acquired a life of its own as a vivid symbol for the same. In 1935, several black rights groups joined to form an umbrella organization they called the National Negro Congress. Among its officers were representatives from the International Ladies' Garment Workers' Union, the Brotherhood of Sleeping Car Porters, the Workers' Councils of the National Urban League, several churches, the League of Struggle for Negro Rights, the Federal Workers Education Project, the International Workers' Order, the Harlem Labor Committee, the National Y.W.C.A., Howard University, the Social Action Committee of the Phi Beta Sigma Fraternity, and both the Communist Party and the Communist Party Opposition. This extraordinarily diverse group, headed by A. Philip Randolph and John P. Davis, gathered in Chicago on February 14, 1936, to advance the cause of economic and civil rights for African Americans in the United States. A poster for the National Negro Congress portrayed a powerful black fist enclosing and crushing a struggling blackbird.[75]

In a stunning cultural turnabout, African Americans now had to kill Jim Crow before they could be free to express the power and exuberance that jumping, and Jim Crow, had once represented.

CHAPTER 10 : UPWARD MOBILITY : PULLMAN PORTERS, A. PHILIP RANDOLPH, AND POLITICAL CHANGE

The same year Joe Louis leveled James Braddock to win a world championship, an unspectacular group of men, known more for their deference than for their power or political prowess, won a victory of no less historic proportions. The 1937 contract between the Brotherhood of Sleeping Car Porters and the Pullman Company was the first ever signed by a black union in the United States. With that contract, railroad porters became the most politically powerful group of African Americans in the country, at a time when they still made their living by serving white people.

When George Mortimer Pullman began hiring former slaves as railway workers, he insisted that his porters be literate. Their first task was to read the 217-rule employee manual, including instructions on how to cut hair and how to pour an Old Fashioned Kentucky Colonel Mint Julep. But their fundamental obligation was to maintain the wall of racial separation between themselves and their customers. Although porters wore uniforms that clearly identified them, the uniforms were unnecessary. Never would a passenger be mistaken for a porter so long as passengers were white and the porters black, and the Pullman Company hired the darkest men they could find. A company directive insisted, "Do not hire a light complexioned man." [1]

George Pullman hired the first porter for his sleeping cars in 1867. By 1870 porters had become essential to the Pullman experience, and by the turn of the twentieth century, the Pullman Company was largest employer of African Americans in the United States. Pullman's criteria were clear: porters were to be between twenty-five and forty years of age, and no shorter than five-foot-seven but not taller than six-foot-one so they could easily walk through the cars. Although Pullman at first required only literacy, soon the company was demanding a grammar school education, and by the 1920s the Pullman Company hired only high school graduates. Some applicants received home visits, in which interviewers questioned family and neighbors about the character and moral stability of potential porters. Many were turned down because they were too light-skinned. Porters could not have sideburns or mustaches and had to wear one of two uniforms at all times: a black cap and blue jacket for receiving or discharging passengers and a white coat for making beds. Black trousers, white shirts, and black shoes completed the uniform, although when not on duty, porters were permitted to change into slippers. To be hired, a porter needed at least $15 to buy a uniform and a cap.

Mobility and Exploitation

The Pullman Company leased its cars to railway carriers, for which they served as hotel rooms on wheels. The Pullman sleeper became an American institution, not just a novel experience but for many travelers a luxurious one as well—as E. B. White described it, a "perfect thing, perfect in conception and execution, this small green hole in the dark moving night, this soft warren in a hard world." Part of the mystique of taking a Pullman sleeper was the chance to live as the wealthy do, for just one night—the chance to be served. At their most successful, the Pullman cars accommodated over 100,000 people a night, more than all the nation's top-flight hotels combined. And, as White observed, the Pullman had an advantage over a hotel room: "A hotel room can sometimes be depressing it stands so still." [2]

From the turn of the century onward, the country had become more and more segregated, and a job as a Pullman porter was one of very few that offered a black man the prospect of advancing into the middle class. Even government jobs, which had been available to African Americans, were segregated. Postal jobs had once been highly prized, but when President Woodrow Wilson's postmaster general, Albert Burleson, resegregated the post office in 1913, Negroes who had held front office jobs found themselves sorting and delivering mail, and many Southern postal workers lost their jobs altogether. African American doctors, lawyers, and judges combined numbered only half as many as the Pullman porters.

Although porters worked as menial servants for white railway customers, within their home communities they were respected members of society. They wore starched uniforms and worked indoors. Furthermore, they traveled the country, which made them, in the eyes of the community, nearly as worldly as black musicians and athletes. Porters accepted their place in black society as leaders, and when not in uniform they emulated the white passengers they served. They took suits or sport coats with them on the road, carried their belongings in briefcases, and looked for other ways to represent the middle class they were pleased to inhabit. Larry Tye, who wrote about the porters in *Rising from the Rails*, interviewed many former porters. One retired Pullman employee, Harold Reddick, noted that his travels as a porter had helped his son in school: "His teacher used to ask my son, 'How did you know so much?' My son could identify things because as a Pullman porter, I came into the passenger's refuse," by which he meant newspapers from around the country.[3]

New Orleans porters and doctors joined to form the city's first black Mardi Gras organization, the Original Illinois Club, an elite social club of fewer than fifty members. Its founder, Wally Knight, was a Chicago Pullman porter who hoped to instruct young people in social etiquette. The dance school he formed in 1894 continued to present annual debutante balls for young African Americans at Mardi Gras into the twenty-first century. The Original Illinois Club Ball was traditionally an elaborate affair hosting over seven hundred guests. The year 2006, following Hurricane Katrina, was the first in over a century when the Illinois Club could not muster enough middle-class New Orleanians to support the annual Mardi Gras event (the group reunited in 2007, along with several other black, middle-class clubs).

Being a Pullman porter could be a stepping-stone to later employment, too. Former Pullman porters had their pick of jobs at the finest hotels and restaurants in the country. And thousands of ambitious college students held summer jobs with the company. Thurgood Marshall, the United States' first African American Supreme Court justice, worked for Pullman in the summer of 1930. Roy Wilkins also worked as a Pullman porter, as did Benjamin Elijah Mays, president of Morehouse College and the first black president of the Atlanta school board.[4] Wilkins found his work as a waiter grueling, but it provided him with his "first sense of the sweep and expanse of the country. For the first time I began to look beyond the comfort and safety of St. Paul to the larger, harder world beyond."[5] Sadly, some African Americans discovered that their college degree was not a guarantee of employment, and many returned to the Pullman Company after college.

If the Pullman Company provided upward mobility for thousands of African Americans, it offered actual mobility to just as many who had never before left the limits of their hometown. To his black friends and neighbors, the well-traveled porter personified sophistication, and many communities depended on the porters to bring them news from other parts of the country. The stories Pullman porters carried back home helped fuel the Great Black Migration.

Many porters lived in the South, and what they told of life in Chicago, New York, or Detroit was nearly unimaginable to the mill workers and sharecroppers they left behind. In the words of one writer, if the migration was "the Flight from Egypt, then the Pullman porter was Moses."[6]

Porters ferried black newspapers such as the Chicago Defender and the Pittsburgh Courier from publishers to their contacts along the trains' routes. By 1920 the Defender had a paid circulation of over 100,000, and its greatest readership was in the South. Porters were able to read these and other newspapers that passengers left on trains. Then they bundled them up and dropped them at stops along the route or tossed them off the train to people waiting along the tracks. A former porter from Florida said, "I used to bring those papers home off the train out of New York, and it'd be a couple days before that news would be in our Tampa papers."[7]

Porters also imported and exported music up, down, and across the country. They bought records in Chicago and New York and sold them in the South, where listeners got their first exposure to jazz. Traveling with musicians like Duke Ellington, Count Basie, Louis Armstrong, and Fats Waller, porters were the first to hear the latest show business gossip and to see the newest fashions. This cultural railroad that the porters constituted worked in both directions, also bringing the blues and bluegrass to northern cities. Porter Joseph Strowder remembers: "When we would go South we'd go into black neighborhoods and talk to the people we were dancing with. The music there was different, they had a whole lot of blues, whereas we were used to swing and jazz and all that."[8]

Yet the porter's life was one of undeniable privation. The porter was responsible for making beds, or in porter parlance, "making down" beds. He would pop the upper berth down from the ceiling and create the lower by folding down opposing seats, adding cushions, headboard, and linen. Once the beds were made, the porter served the travelers, fetching water, helping passengers to the toilet, adjusting heat or opening windows, and waking sleepers in time for their stop. He would greet the passengers, keep cars clean of embers and soot, polish spittoons, set up card tables, and keep coolers stocked with ice. The porters' sleeping quarters were behind a curtain in the train's smoking room, which also doubled as the men's bathroom.

In 1926 porters worked an average of 343 hours a month. They often went without sleep altogether and seldom got more than three hours' rest on any one night. Even those few hours were likely to be interrupted by a passenger ringing for an extra pillow or blanket. When a porter joined the company, he signed a contract waiving any damages in case of injury. He was not provided with meals but rather had to pay half-price for them. He had to provide his own shoe polish and pencils, had to buy one blue uniform from Marshall Field every year, and had to pay for dry cleaning. If any towels, blankets, or combs went missing—stolen by passengers—the porter paid to replace them. If the porter required lodging on the road, he paid for that out of his wages, too. Such expenses averaged $33 a month, and often constituted half of the porter's salary.[9] Even though porters represented 44 percent of the Pullman workforce, they accounted for only 27 percent of the payroll. Porters relied heavily on tips, and customers sometimes took advantage of their position in a relationship of financial dependence. For many customers, part of the appeal of the Pullman porter was the temporary thrill of having a personal servant. Porters reported ridiculous requests from customers. Plumping up pillows was the least of it. Could the porter please tell a joke? What about a little dance? Could he please let the passenger rub his head for good luck?

Such humiliations stayed on the train. In his own community, by comparison to his neighbors, the porter was often relatively well off. Through their travels on trains, the porters witnessed a better way of life, and even though it might be beyond their grasp at the moment, they vowed they would have it for their children. Perhaps it was the constant exposure to and reminders of the American dream that account for their political activism, for no group other than the NAACP worked harder, longer, and more constantly for civil rights than the International Brotherhood of Sleeping Car Porters.

A. Philip Randolph and the Civil Rights Movement

Political activist Asa Philip Randolph spent his lifetime working for civil rights, and one of his first successes was with the Brotherhood of Sleeping Car Porters, which he organized in 1925 and over which he presided from 1929 to 1968. Randolph's path to the Brotherhood began in 1917, when he and his colleague Chandler Owen were hired to edit the monthly magazine for the Headwaiters and Sidewaiters Society of Greater New York, the *Hotel Messenger*. Soon the editors dropped "Hotel" from the title and relaunched the magazine as the *Messenger*, with a masthead proclaiming it "The Only Radical Negro Magazine in America." The *Messenger* achieved a circulation of 26,000 and became the most widely read left-wing black journal in the country. Fully one-third of its readers were white. The *Messenger* condemned the United States for waging war abroad while American blacks had no democratic rights. At home it attacked Democrats, Republicans, and old-style African American leaders, among whom it included W. E. B. Du Bois. The journal declared war on Marcus Garvey and initiated a "Garvey Must Go" movement, calling him a corrupt demagogue and capitalist. When Garvey was finally indicted for mail fraud and it was revealed that he had held a secret meeting with Edward Young Clarke, the Imperial Wizard of the Ku Klux Klan, Randolph and Owen were vindicated in their views that Garvey's Back to Africa campaign served only himself and the interests of white racists.

In 1925, five porters who were trying to organize a union contacted Randolph. Financially strapped at that point in his life, Randolph later recalled, "I am not sure that I had ever seen a Pullman car then, much less ridden in one." [10] In this group of black workers, representing the only job market that blacks dominated, Randolph saw the potential for political change. Porters had been trying to organize since the turn of the century, battling company threats and spies. Randolph agreed to take on the presidency and decided to call the new union the International Brotherhood of Sleeping Car Porters—a name chosen for its international sweep and solidarity, and one that did not identify porters specifically with the Pullman Company. In so doing, Randolph became the most important black leader in the country. [11] His paper, the *Messenger*, became the official organ of the union.

In the absence of public support and enthusiasm from any other powerful black leader, Randolph single-handedly lobbied Capitol Hill. By 1934 he had helped persuade Congress to pass a law requiring companies to negotiate with unions chosen by a majority of their workers. In the summer of 1935, Pullman porters voted on representation, choosing Randolph's Brotherhood by a margin of 5,931 to 1,422. When the American Federation of Labor tried to take away the union's right to organize, the Brotherhood gained the international charter that made it a full-fledged member of the House of Labor. On July 29, 1935, representatives of the Pullman Company sat down with Randolph and representatives of the porters to begin bargaining.

Meanwhile, as the nation's economic depression continued and ridership and revenues on sleeping cars plummeted, railway workers announced a nationwide strike of 250,000 union members on August 25, 1937. When

Pullman porters threatened to walk out with them, the Pullman Company agreed to sign that same day. Twelve years to the day after Randolph and five Pullman porters had launched the Brotherhood in an Elks hall in Harlem, the union had gained its first contract—and the first contract ever to be signed with an all-black union.

The contract raised minimum pay for porters from $77.50 to $89.50 per month. Even more important to the porters was establishing a maximum number of hours of work per month—240 hours, the same as for conductors—with overtime for more. And the porters were guaranteed three hours' sleep for any trip under twelve hours, four after that (unpaid). Porters would be paid for preparing the cars before journeys, and they would be paid for seniority. They were given assurances that grievances would be handled quickly and fairly. The contract took effect October 1, 1937. Randolph estimated that the agreement represented more than $2 million to porters and their families.[12] One porter who went to work that year summarized the impact of that contract on the porters: "The union took them off their knees."[13]

Like the victories of black athletes at the 1936 Olympics, and like the victories of Joe Louis, the porters' contract resounded with African Americans across the country. The NAACP editorialized in the Crisis in November 1937: "As important as is this lucrative contract as a labor victory to the Pullman porters, it is even more important to the Negro race as a whole, from the point of view of the Negro's up-hill climb for respect, recognition and influence, and economic advancement."[14] The IBSCP was the first workers' organization to displace a company union and the first all-black union admitted as a full-fledged member of the American Federation of Labor (AFL), which granted the Brotherhood a charter in 1935.[15] The IBSCP Ladies' Auxiliary, the first international labor organization of black women, became a powerful force in the civil rights movement over the next several decades.[16] And as the head of the country's only black labor union, Randolph came symbolically to represent all black workers, the only African American leader who focused chiefly on the economics of being black.

Randolph succeeded where organizations such as the NAACP failed, for many reasons. First, throughout his career, like Joe Louis, Randolph insisted on working solely with and for African Americans. Hamstrung by ties to white business donors, the NAACP found it politically expedient to deemphasize economic realities at a time when one-third of the black population was on relief or receiving public assistance.[17] While the NAACP focused on civil rights, which were slow in coming, Randolph attacked economic injustice, with more immediate results. The NAACP focused on the legislative and judicial branches of the government, in Roy Wilkins's words, "carefully selecting lawsuits and political issues and working from on high in Congress and the Supreme Court."[18] But Randolph went straight to the president, twice gaining sweeping and immediate changes by executive order. And Randolph could count on the cooperation of other civil rights organizations and leaders, or at least on the absence of interference from them, because his work never threatened or competed with theirs. He worked one march at a time. Neither a politician, an educator, nor a preacher, Randolph was a labor leader, his constituency simply hundreds of thousands of black workers across the country. Yet in this group Randolph found the support he believed necessary to create real change. In a statement he issued to newspapers around the country, he wrote: "Only power can effect the enforcement and adoption of a given policy, however meritorious it may be. . . . Power and pressure do not reside in the few, and intelligentsia, they lie in and flow from the masses."[19]

In September 1940, Eleanor Roosevelt was in the audience when Randolph addressed the annual meeting of the Brotherhood. He spoke about the twin issues of a segregated defense industry and segregated armed forces. Although nearly a quarter of a million new jobs had been created in answer to Europe's need for arms, none was available for African Americans.[20] The general manager of the defense contractor North American Aviation declared: "Negroes will be considered only as janitors. . . . It is the company policy not to employ them as mechanics and aircraft workers." And in Kansas City, Standard Steel informed the Urban League, "We have not had a Negro working in 25 years and do not plan to start now."[21] Mrs. Roosevelt found Randolph's presention so convincing that she wrote to her husband, asking him, at the very least, to respond to Randolph's many requests for a meeting. On September 27, 1940, President Roosevelt finally met with A. Philip Randolph, along with Walter White, the executive secretary of the NAACP, and T. Arnold Hill, an administrator for the Urban League.[22] Roosevelt acknowledged that although there were few jobs for black workers in the defense industry, positions would be forthcoming in the military—even though at the time only 4,700 blacks had been permitted to join an army that was now half a million strong, and they filled only support positions in segregated units.[23] Other branches of the ser-

vice were closed to African Americans, and when Secretary of the Navy Frank
Knox insisted that he could not have black recruits sleeping on board his
ships, Roosevelt suggested that perhaps the navy could include Negro bands,
reflecting a vast misunderstanding of the seriousness of the issue.[24] For his
part, Roosevelt commiserated with Randolph and White, but even so, he could
not "confuse the issue of prompt preparedness with a new social experiment,
however important and desirable it may be."[25] The only outcome of the meeting was a press briefing that suggested that Randolph and White had agreed
to maintain the status quo, a summary that in no way reflected reality and did
real harm to Randolph's and White's standing with their constituencies.

Randolph was so incensed by this misrepresentation from the White
House that on a tour of Pullman conferences across the country, he began to
speak about the rights of all citizens to fair employment in the defense industry. Having decided that the conference method no longer worked, at every
stop he made, he proposed a Negro march, and his audience answered him.[26]
Randolph recalled: "In meeting after meeting, the 'forgotten black man'
could rise and tell an eager and earnest crowd about jobs he had sought but
never got, about the business agent of the union giving him the brush-off,
how he had gone to the gates of the defense plants only to be kept out while
white workers walked in, how he cooled his heels in an office and finally was
told with a cold stare 'no more workers wanted.'"[27] By late 1940, Randolph's
March on Washington Committee had branches in eighteen cities. Originally
aspiring to 10,000 marchers, in May 1941 Randolph claimed that he had persuaded 100,000 people to convene in Washington, and he started reserving
train tickets and making arrangements for food and lodging. The NAACP and
the Urban League joined black newspapers to publicize the march, but it was
the idea of porters actually organizing communities across the country that
most frightened the Roosevelts.

After refusing Randolph's many requests for a meeting, on June 18, 1941,
President Roosevelt called Randolph to Washington, along with Walter White,
on whom Roosevelt thought he might be able to rely for support, and the sec-
retaries of war and the navy.[28] Roosevelt told Randolph and White he could
not agree to a precedent that might create an endless series of marches and
violence. Randolph answered: "Well, Mr. President, we are not here because
we just simply want to march. We're here because the great masses of Negro

workers are going to the various munitions plant and they're being turned away. They can't get jobs. Others are getting jobs, and unless something isn't done, you're not going to be able to avoid trouble anyway." Randolph specifically asked Roosevelt for "an executive order requiring that all workers have a right to jobs in the munition plants and in other [defense] industries." [29] Although Randolph insisted that the federal government was the "worst offender" of all, Roosevelt refused to believe that the federal government discriminated against black workers, and he continued to insist that Randolph call off the march. "You can't manage a hundred thousand people," Roosevelt said. "No one can." [30]

"Well, Mr. President," Randolph responded, "we had in mind to invite you to address them," a suggestion that ended the interview. Roosevelt declared that not only was he not going to address any marchers, he simply would not allow the march to take place. [31]

The next step was a meeting among Randolph, Eleanor Roosevelt, Mayor Fiorello La Guardia of New York City, and Walter White. Randolph refused to back down, even to requests from Eleanor Roosevelt and La Guardia, who had appointed Randolph to the New York City Commission on Race in 1935. [32] La Guardia begged him to call off the march, saying: "Phil, this is dynamite. You can't do anything to control these people. I know something about masses of people and you can't control them." [33] But Randolph remained firm: "I cannot call this off, the people are ready to come to this march from all over the country: California and Chicago; Jacksonville, Florida; Atlanta, Georgia; all around the country. . . . [T]he people are without jobs; they're without bread. Somebody has got to do something." [34]

A second committee formed to try to persuade Randolph to back down. After five days of discussion, La Guardia agreed to side with Randolph in asking the president for an executive order to change employment practices, telling the group: "I'll break off from my former position and say to you that something has got to be done as Phil Randolph says. Now, I happen to know him and you're not going to change him. We'e not going to change him. You're not going to be able to change him, and he's not going to change for me or Mrs. Roosevelt or the President." [35] The committee that assembled to handle the matter drafted an executive order with which Roosevelt could agree—one that excluded the federal government. Randolph held firm and insisted that he would accept nothing less than an executive order banning discrimination in all defense jobs. On June 25, 1941, Roosevelt finally conceded and issued his Executive Order 8802. Randolph called off the march, set for July 1.

Executive Order 8802 forbade discrimination by defense contractors and established the Fair Employment Practices Committee to investigate cases of racial discrimination. It opened employment and economic opportunity to thousands of African American men, setting off a huge migration to the West Coast. Many had doubted Randolph's ability to mobilize a march of ten thousand Negroes. But Executive Order 8802 came into existence because the country and the president were convinced that ten times that many ordinary people were willing and waiting to march for equal rights. The *Chicago Defender* concluded, "Never before in the history of the nation" had Negroes "been so united in an objective and so insistent upon an action being taken." [36]

Marching On

Defense work opened the doors of factory employment to black Americans, and not just men. Women who had had no option other than domestic work suddenly found themselves out in the world, earning more money and enjoying the companionship of fellow workers. But if working for the defense industry sparked political awareness for thousands of African Americans, military service during World War II fanned the flames of civil rights.

Roosevelt's executive order was a compromise: while it desegregated the civil defense industry, it left the military segregated, and as the war continued, Jim Crow dominated most branches of the service. Race riots in major cities—Mobile, Alabama, and Detroit, Michigan—belied the image of a united America. Although advisers pleaded with the president to address the issue, and Eleanor Roosevelt wrote in her newspaper column, "My Day," that the situation put the nation "on a par with Nazism which we fight," Roosevelt refused to take up the cause. [37] Randolph continued to agitate for desegregation of the military, but he had to wait for a new administration for this next step to be taken in the fight for civil rights.

In the meantime, Randolph organized a Public Prayer Protest to rally support for the failing anti-lynching bill that was pending before Congress. Stung by accusations of atheism, in 1943 Randolph wrote a letter to the *Chicago Defender*, crediting his father (a Methodist minister), Jesus Christ, and Gandhi as the sources of his philosophy and methods of public protest. In later years he was to call his work in the 1941 March on Washington "applied Christianity."[38] Historian Cynthia Taylor writes that Randolph's work instituted specific strategies—public prayer protests, liberation theology, and civil disobedience—on which the civil rights movement of the 1950s and 1960s was built.[39] J. Holmes Smith, a former Methodist missionary in India and consultant to the Congress on Racial Equality, called Randolph a "distinctly American Gandhi."[40]

In November 1947, Randolph and Grant Reynolds, a prominent black Republican from New York, organized the Committee against Jim Crow in Military Service and Training. Although President Harry Truman had appointed a Committee on Civil Rights in December of 1946, which had issued a report in 1947 condemning segregation, particularly in the military, no steps were taken. Truman then sent a message to Congress in February 1948 suggesting federal action on several fronts: passage of an anti-lynching law, federal statutory protection for the right to vote, the elimination of poll taxes, and the desegregation of interstate travel by bus, train, or air. But at the request of the army, his message included no recommendation or draft legislation for desegregating the military. Truman simply instructed the secretary of defense to look into the matter of "alleged discrimination."[41] Randolph and Reynolds sent a series of letters to the president requesting a meeting, which were ignored until Truman's administrative assistant wrote a note to the president: "Phil Randolph, the signer of this letter, is an important Negro. He is the head of the Negro Pullman Porters Union, and is not a left-winger."[42]

In March 1948 President Truman finally received Randolph, Reynolds, and eighteen other African American leaders representing the Committee against Jim Crow. Randolph spoke for the group, asking Truman to take specific action "in the form of an executive order barring and banning Jim Crow in the Armed Forces, eliminating discrimination and segregation."[43] Truman replied: "Well that's right, our boys who fight for our country are entitled to just treatment. I will do something about it."[44] But he refused to specify exactly what he would do, or when. Then, according to Randolph, when he told the president that "the Negroes [are] not in the mood to bear arms for the country unless Jim Crow in the Armed Forces is abolished," Truman dismissed the group even before a photo could be taken.[45] Five days later the group of black leaders reconvened in New York City to announce that African Americans would refuse to serve in the military unless the armed forces banned segregation. Three days after that, Randolph boldly (and at some personal risk) testified to the same before the Senate Armed Services Committee, elaborating, when asked whether he understood the consequences of such mass civil disobedience: "We would be willing to absorb the violence, absorb the terrorism, to face the music and to take whatever comes, and we, as a matter of fact, consider that we are more loyal to our country than the people who perpetrate segregation and discrimination upon Negroes because of color or race."[46] A month later, on May 7, Randolph and eight supporters marched in front of the White House carrying signs saying, "Don't Join a Jim Crow Army." Randolph's own sign read, "If we must die for our country let us die as free men—not as Jim Crow slaves."[47] In June 1948, when Congress passed and Truman signed a selective service act with no provisions for civil rights and, in Randolph's words, "no safeguards for Negro youth," Randolph promptly organized the League for Non-Violent Civil Disobedience and planned protest marches in Chicago, New York, and other cities.[48] He wrote again to President Truman on June 29 and on July 15, renewing his requests for a personal meeting and an executive order. Truman did not meet again with Randolph, but finally, on July 26, 1948, he signed Executive Order 9981, which states: "It is hereby declared to be the policy of the President that there shall be equality of treatment and opportunity for all persons in the armed services without regard to race, color, religion, or national origin."[49] The order also established the President's Committee on Equality of Treatment and Opportunity in the Armed Services, which turned out to be vital, since army staff officers publicly insisted that the executive order did not apply to the army.[50]

Randolph's union didn't let up at that point, either.

In 1955 the Brotherhood of Sleeping Car Porters seized a moment in Alabama to begin a bus boycott, bringing into their leadership a young, unknown minister named Martin Luther King Jr., whose success was so brilliant that today it is his name that most people associate with the movement that began long before he was invited to join its ranks. Porter Edgar Nixon was past president of the Montgomery and Alabama branches of the NAACP and the first and only president of the Montgomery Division of the Brotherhood of Sleeping Car Porters. That year Nixon and the Women's Political Council targeted public buses as the means of taking a civil rights struggle from the courthouse to the streets. His experience working with the Brotherhood had armed him to assault a transportation monopoly. He recruited Rosa Parks, secretary of the Montgomery NAACP, as a test case for desegregation and posted her bond when she was arrested. Then he quickly organized a meeting at the largest and wealthiest black church in Montgomery, the Dexter Avenue Baptist Church, whose new pastor was the twenty-six-year-old King. As a porter, Nixon traveled much of the time and knew he might be unavailable at crucial moments. King was as green as Nixon was experienced in political activism, but Nixon appreciated King's eloquence and believed his naïveté to be a virtue: he was too new in the game to have made any enemies. Nixon insisted that King, not he, be made president of the newly formed Montgomery Improvement Association. King advocated a wait and see attitude, and only after Nixon publicly called King a coward did King agree to a full-scale boycott and to accepting the presidency of the MIA. Porters continued to fuel the movement.

If few people today remember that it was the political activism and machinery of the Brotherhood that launched the Montgomery Bus Boycott and King's career, fewer still know that A. Philip Randolph and the Brotherhood of Sleeping Car Porters organized the 1963 March on Washington for Jobs and Freedom that provided momentum toward the Civil Rights Act of that same year. Bayard Rustin, who had directed Randolph's Committee against Discrimination in the Armed Forces, served as Randolph's deputy. Although Randolph was its first speaker, he has been forgotten in the wake of King, Joan Baez, and the 250,000 protesters who showed up.[51] Randolph invited King to speak, and it was here that King gave perhaps the most famous oration of his career, the "I Have a Dream" speech.

Randolph's speech, while little remembered today, summed up not just the day's mission but that of the previous forty years: "Let the nation know the meaning of our numbers," he said. "We are not a pressure group, not an organization or a group of organizations. We are not a mob. We are the advance guard of a massive moral revolution for jobs and freedom."[52]

At its peak, the Brotherhood numbered twelve thousand. It gave its unflagging support to civil rights efforts from 1930 through 1965. "We spent a small fortune," said one of the union's officers. "It's the porters' gift."[53] From the members' monthly dues of a dollar and a half, the Brotherhood paid Randolph's modest salary, when he finally drew one, helped underwrite the Montgomery Bus Boycott, gave $50,000 to the March on Washington, and helped dispatch "freedom riders" across the South in 1961. The Brotherhood also helped black railroad firemen, brakemen, and switchmen, and supported political candidates who fought for civil rights. The union didn't simply dole out financial aid. When the 1963 March on Washington was over, a five hundred–man Brotherhood cleanup squad made sure that the streets were cleaned to Randolph's satisfaction.

Behind the scenes of all these activities was the Ladies' Auxiliary, putting up posters, passing out leaflets, and collecting change to support and promote whatever cause the Brotherhood had embraced. The union made plans to feed, house, and care for those on the front lines of many nonviolent protests. Without such skills and efforts, the threat of 100,000 people marching on Washington in 1941 would not have been credible, and the reality of 250,000 arriving in Washington in 1963 would have been a nightmare. The members supported the Committee against Jim Crow in Military Service and Training, and the National Council for a Permanent Fair Employment Practices Committee, an interracial effort Randolph had started in 1943. During the bus boycott in Montgomery, they collected money, got the word out, and kept up the organizing, planning, and promoting that made the second March on Washington possible.

Political scientist James Scott has written that in "rare moments of historical crisis . . . it is often assumed that there has come into being a new consciousness, a new anger, or a new ideology that has transformed class relations. It is far more likely, however, that this new 'consciousness' was already there in the unedited transcript and it is the situation that has changed in a way that allows or requires one or both parties to act on that basis." [54] A. Philip Randolph and the Brotherhood of Sleeping Car Porters truly are part of the unedited transcript of civil rights in this nation. Not one person in a thousand, or even a hundred thousand, if asked, could correctly identify Randolph as the architect of the 1963 March on Washington. Who today remembers the 1941 march that resulted in the first federal desegregation order of the twentieth century? What popular image of the Pullman porter paints him as a political activist? Who remembers the wives of these porters, the chambermaids and waitresses, passing out leaflets and making box lunches for the marchers?

And if no one remembers the accomplishments of the politically active, who thinks to attribute political motivation and momentum to the merely socially active, the shock troops of singers, dancers, athletes, and audiences who declared their intentions to be counted in this world through their uplifted voices, bodies, and spirits? Do we recognize them for what they were—the advance guard of a massive moral revolution for freedom?

CHAPTER 11 : JUMP FOR JOY!

Randolph scheduled his 1941 march on Washington for July 1. The next day, on the other side of the country, tickets went on sale at the Mayan Theatre in Los Angeles for a musical revue, one that tried to do on stage what Randolph had partially accomplished with his threatened march—to bury Jim Crow. In the title song of this show, "Jump for Joy," creator-composer Duke Ellington used one of his favorite musical devices to call to mind one of the most ubiquitous symbols of black life in America, one that harked back to Randolph's Brotherhood of Pullman Porters: Ellington closed the song with a long, blaring train whistle.

Since the mid-1800s the train had been an important symbol of industrial progress and of shifting fortunes, and even as other forms of transportation became more efficient, more exciting, or more popular, the train remained the symbol that seemed to conjure up the qualities of a changing national culture. Countless blues songs recalled the moan of a train whistle and the lonely but thrilling experience of traveling the country by rail. Some train songs spoke proudly of a new urban life, while others reflected nostalgically on country and family left behind.

Train songs were not limited to black culture. Country singer and former blackface actor Jimmie Rodgers, known as the "Singing Brakeman," once recorded a blackface sketch called "The Pullman Porters" (1930) and recorded many train songs as well, such as "The Brakeman's Blues" (1928), "Waiting for a Train" (1929), "Train Whistle Blues" (1929), "Hobo Bill's Last Ride" (1929), and "Southern Canon-Ball" (1930).[1] The wistfulness of such pieces assumed a more urban form when the Glenn Miller Orchestra made a hit with its 1941 swing recording "Chattanooga Choo Choo" (1941). The lyrics describe a nostalgic voyage from New York's Pennsylvania Station through the South (Carolina), complete with ham and eggs. The singer first addresses a Pullman porter—"Pardon me, boy"—asking for directions, and as the song continues, he asks the same porter for a shoeshine. Clearly the reminiscence is that of a white passenger who longs to ride the train back to the comfortable Old South, attended by solicitous black porters.

By contrast, Duke Ellington's signature piece, "Take the 'A' Train," recorded the same year refers specifically to an inner-city train—the subway to Harlem—and its lyrics describe the route that many African Americans took as they moved from their former lives into up-tempo, urban New York City. The Ellington orchestra's arranger and composer, Billy Strayhorn, wrote "Take the 'A' Train" in 1939 as a tribute to Ellington, using for his lyrics the subway directions Ellington had jotted down so that Strayhorn could find his apartment on Edgecombe Avenue in Harlem's elite Sugar Hill.[2] "Take the 'A' Train" was more than a hit swing tune; it turned the Harlem train route into a national symbol. If nineteenth-century slaves had followed the drinking gourd to freedom in the North, twentieth-century African Americans now knew how to take the 'A' Train to the capital of Black America.

The Ellington orchestra's "Happy-Go-Lucky Local," "Daybreak Express" and "The Old Circus Train Turn Around Blues" are standards, as are Count Basie's "9:20 Special" and "Super Chief," and Jimmie Lunceford's "Lunceford Special." But composers and songwriters went beyond paying tribute to trains in the titles and lyrics of their pieces. Just as blues musicians had done, jazz orchestras, particularly Ellington's, mimicked train sounds and incorporated a train-like chugging rhythm in many pieces. Albert Murray suggests that train whistles, rumbling boxcars, pumping pistons, and the "percussive explosions of locomotive steam" may have influenced blues musicians as strongly as the music of the church.[3] Joel Dinerstein calls trains the "sonic embodiment of modernity," a sort of "sonic social cement," as it called to mind industrialization in the form of vernacular music for dance audiences.[4]

Nowhere is the train onomatopoeia more appropriate than in "Jump for Joy," the title piece of Duke Ellington's 1941 musical revue. Ellington and his many collaborators designed the revue to document and inspire a new social conscience among African Americans, one that refused the Jim Crow restrictions of the South. It is no accident that the piece ends with the Ellington orchestra's signature train cry. Audiences who saw the musical or heard the piece knew the meaning of that train whistle. It signified a people on the move to a better life.

Duke Ellington, writer Sid Kuller, and lyricist Paul Francis Webster created

Jump for Joy in a series of meetings and long-distance collaborations through-out the winter and spring of 1941, finally opening the show in July. In January the Ellington orchestra had begun a seven-week engagement at the Casa Mañana in Culver City, near Los Angeles. Also in Culver City was the MGM film studio, where Sid Kuller was writing the screenplay for the Marx Brothers' movie The Big Store. Kuller started dropping in at the Casa Mañana after work to listen to Ellington. One night after the last set, he invited Ellington and his band to stop by his house on North Knoll Drive in Hollywood Hills. The jam session that began that Sunday morning lasted all the way till Monday, picked up again the next Saturday night, and resumed every weekend that Ellington was in town. Actor Jackie Cooper brought his drums to play. Mickey Rooney was there, hoping for a chance on the drum set. Soon people from all over Hollywood were showing up, "even really square people," according to Kuller. "That was one of the greatest qualities of Ellington. His music communicated with everyone on every level. They all adored him. Duke was so warm he would just charm everybody out of their boots."[5]

One Sunday in February, Kuller came home to find Ellington on piano and Sonny Greer on drums, playing with Mannie Klein, Lawrence Brown, Barney Bigard, Harry Carney, Ben Webster, and others. "Hey, this joint sure is jumping!" Kuller exclaimed, and Ellington responded, "Jumping for joy!" Kuller was struck with the phrase and quickly shot back, "A Negro musical—Jump for Joy, starring Duke Ellington."[6] Songwriter Paul Francis Webster was there, too. Webster had been trying to pull together an all-Negro musical called Rhapsody in Black, a title no one seemed excited about. But Jump for Joy—that sounded promising.

The talent in the room was extraordinary: screenwriters William R. Burnett and Hal Fimberg; actors John Garfield, Harry Ritz, and Harpo and Groucho Marx; actresses Bonita Granville and Lana Turner; actor and singer Tony Martin; Austrian-born composer-lyricist Walter Jurmann; songwriter Hal Borne; Italian-born composer and pianist Mario Castelnuovo-Tedesco; pianist-arranger Skitch Henderson; composer-arranger Billy Strayhorn; and the Ellington musicians Klein, Brown, Greer, Webster, Bigard, Carney, Johnny Hodges, Rex Stewart, Ray Nance, and Tricky Sam Nanton. By the time the sun came up, this group of talented music lovers had formed the American Revue Theatre with a handshake and a pledge of $20,000 from those present—nearly half the necessary financing. Further contributions—including $15,000 from producer Joseph Pasternak and $10,000 from actor John Garfield—finally brought the total budget to $42,000.[7]

Their goal, Ellington said, was to "correct the race situation in the U.S.A. through a form of theatrical propaganda."[8] Ellington wrote most of the score, with help from Mercer Ellington, Billy Strayhorn, and Hal Borne, while Sid Kuller and Hal Fimberg shared credit for the book. Kuller also directed the show. Other writers included poet Langston Hughes, Mickey Rooney, screenwriter Charles Leonard, and songwriter Otis Rene. Choreographer Nick Castle staged the production.

In Ellington's words, the show was supposed to "take Uncle Tom out of the theater, eliminate the stereotyped image that had been exploited by Hollywood and Broadway, and say things that would make the audience think."[9] The group intended to achieve that goal in an unprecedented way. "Traditionally, black humor had been performed by blacks for white audiences from a white point of view. Our material was from the point of view of black people looking at whites," said Kuller.[10]

Despite their serious political and artistic intentions, or perhaps because of them, the ever-widening circle of artists working on the show had a ball. They advertised it as "A Sun-Tanned Revu-sical." Although the cast was all black, the group behind the show could not have been more integrated. Together they wrote close to fifty sketches and musical numbers. The show generally included about thirty of these, but not always the same thirty. Hardly a night went by without changes because of ongoing discussions about the issues the creators and cast wanted to highlight. Ellington said they discussed "the Negro, the race, what constituted Uncle Tom, what constituted chauvinism, what constituted everything. . . . It was done on a very high level, pinpoint fine, and you get to see these things from all the different angles."[11]

Ellington worked on the show throughout the spring of 1941, collaborating with Kuller via mail and telephone. Meanwhile, Ellington's fifteen-member orchestra continued touring the West Coast and the Pacific Northwest in a series of one-night stands until they reached an extended five-day engagement at Salt Lake City's New Lake Theater. There Ellington composed one of the revue's most enduring numbers, "I've Got It Bad and That Ain't Good," and sent it to Paul Francis Webster with instructions that this piece was to be completed with singer Ivy Anderson in mind.[12] By the time the Ellington orchestra returned to Los Angeles at the end of March—for a one-week, five-show-a-day engagement at the Paramount—Webster had finished the song.

Ellington accumulated performers for the show as he toured, drawing on past relationships and fulfilling promises made years earlier. He had met dancer Al (Alfredo) Guster in Chicago in 1939 and told him to keep in touch. That spring he sent Guster a train ticket to Los Angeles. The comedy-dance team Pot, Pan, and Skillet—James A. Jackson, Eugene Ware, and Ernest Mayhand—were appearing at the Cedar Gardens in Cleveland in the late 1930s when Ellington first saw them. In April 1941 they happened to be working in Houston when the Ellington orchestra came through town. They went to hear Ellington, and he told them he needed them in Los Angeles. Pot, Pan, and Skillet turned down a national theater tour with Cab Calloway just to remain available to Ellington.

Comic actor Wonderful Smith was working as a parking attendant at the Grace Hayes Lodge when he read that Ellington's "all colored revue" was in preparation at the Mayan Theatre. Smith went to the theater to audition for production manager Henry Blankfort, who called him back for Kuller and Ellington. "Sid and Duke were a great audience," Smith remembered. "Sid really broke up. 'Where are you appearing now?' he demanded. 'Grace Hayes Lodge's parking lot,' I replied, '—parking cars.' They signed me up on the spot." So talented was Smith that when Charlie Chaplin dropped by to observe rehearsals, he advised Blankfort to take Smith out of general rehearsals, "because if he rehearses out in the open like he's doing now, Bob Hope's and Jack Benny's legmen will be down here to steal his material to use on the air."[13]

Ellington continued to compose until opening night, while staying at the Dunbar, a black hotel in Los Angeles. Blankfort had tried to book the band into a nearby Hollywood hotel but couldn't—the Hollywood Roosevelt would accept Ellington but not the band, and no other hotel would take any of the personnel. The musicians about to appear in a show condemning racial segregation could not find a hotel room in all of Hollywood. Two and a half weeks before the opening, with only half the proposed music written, Blankfort panicked and went to talk with Ellington at the Dunbar:

Duke was in the bathtub. Beside him was a stack of manuscript paper, a huge container of chocolate ice cream, a glass of scotch and milk, and

Jonesy [Richard Bowden Jones]. Jonesy was his valet, and his job was to keep adding warm water and let out cooling water to maintain a constant temperature in the tub for the Maestro. And Duke was serenely scribbling notes on the paper and then calling to Billy Strayhorn. Billy would take the notes and play them on the beat-up old upright piano in Duke's room. Duke would listen and then write more notes, which he would give to Strayhorn. The band seemed to be all on the same floor of the hotel—like a very long railroad flat—and the sound of Strays at the keyboard was like some kind of signal. Pretty soon you'd hear Ben Webster playing a line, then Ray Nance would start tooting from somewhere down that hall, Sonny Greer would come in with his sticks, and the music would start to form . . . Duke writing more and more notes for Sweetpea [Strayhorn] . . . Jonesy keeping the water just right . . . and about four or five hours later, two more songs for the show were finished.[14]

While Ellington was writing music, the rest of the cast was rehearsing round the clock at the Mayan Theatre. The well-known actress Dorothy Dandridge and Ellington singers Ivy Anderson and Herb Jeffries led a cast of sixty that included Pot, Pan, and Skillet; the Rockets (Henry Roberts, Andrew Jackson, and John Thomas); the Hi-Hatters (Clarence Landry, Udell Johnson, and Vernod Bradley); Marie Bryant, Al Guster, Roy Glenn, Paul White, and Wonderful Smith. The revue had no single director; Kuller, Webster, and Fimberg each directed the pieces he had written, while Nick Castle coordinated the dances. Poet Countee Cullen often showed up at rehearsals, and John Garfield was there every day. When Castle made the tactical error of directing his dancers to speak in dialect, they, with Blankfort's tacit encouragement, threatened to walk out on the show, and dialect was not mentioned again.[15]

Although Duke Ellington's name was the largest on the marquee, he and the orchestra performed from the pit, since union rules called for $30 per man if band members appeared on stage. Only trumpeter Rex Stewart played on stage—and loved it, calling Jump for Joy a "sprightly dream of a show, a joy-studded avant-garde revue."[16] The orchestra was one of Ellington's best lineups, with Ben Webster, Stewart, and Joe "Tricky Sam" Nanton at the peak of their talent, in addition to Johnny Hodges, Barney Bigard, Lawrence Brown, Juan Tizol, Otto Hardwick, Freddie Guy, Wallace Jones, Harry Carney, Sonny Greer, and Ray Nance. Billy Strayhorn was a newcomer on the scene, while Jimmy Blanton and Ivy Anderson were in their last appearances with the band.

Tickets went on sale on July 2 and the show opened July 10. Marlene Dietrich and Martha Raye were among the celebrities who attended the premiere. In the original opening scene, the cast buried Uncle Tom. While children ran around the stage singing, "He enjoyed himself, let him go!" Broadway and Hollywood producers tried to revive him with a hypodermic needle. This sketch was cut before opening night. Instead, the curtain rose on Ellington, in tails, at the grand piano, backed by a cast of sixty: this was, according to the program, the "Sun-Tanned Tenth of the Nation." Actor Paul White, who for years had played the part of a dancing shadow behind white bandleader Ted Lewis, took center stage, pursued by a ghost, whom he scared away with one "Boo!" Ellington, now in the pit, delivered this monologue:

Now, every Broadway colored show,
According to tradition,
Must be a carbon copy
Of the previous edition,
With the truth discreetly muted,
And the accent on the brasses.
The punch that should be present
In a colored show, alas, is
Disinfected with magnolia
And dripping with molasses.
In other words,
We're shown to you
Through Stephen Foster's glasses.[17]

Next, Al Guster, brilliant in pale chartreuse tails, tapped out "Stomp Caprice" atop the roofs of a Manhattan skyline, while Ellington and drummer Greer emphasized his tapping and reedman Carney underscored his slides and turns. Herb Jeffries and Dorothy Dandridge performed "Brown-Skin Gal in the Calico Gown," and Marie Bryant sang the peppy scat number "Bli-blip." Ivy Anderson brought the house down with the torch song "I've Got It Bad and That Ain't Good."

White, waving good-bye to friends from the deck of a steamship, began "I've Got a Passport from Georgia," with the words "Farewell, Charlie, so

long Joe, / Good-bye, Jim, and I do mean *crow*" and ended with these: "I've
got a passport from Georgia, / And I'm sailin' for the USA." [18] When Ku Klux
Klan members showed up demanding that Kuller cut the song from the show,
the writers defiantly added even more verses. But after a charred drawing of a
coffin appeared one night under the stage door, producers dropped the skit
from the lineup. The first act usually ended with "Uncle Tom's Cabin Is a
Drive-In Now," which talks about moving Uncle Tom's cabin from Caroline
to Hollywood and Vine, paying off the mortgage with income from selling
barbecue. Insiders who had eaten at Ivy Anderson's Los Angeles restaurant,
Ivy's Chicken Shack, howled when the huge ensemble number concluded:

> She gives you an autograph and takes a bow
> since UNCLE TOM'S CABIN IS A DRIVE-IN NOW
> UNCLE TOM'S CABIN IS A THRIVIN', JIVIN'
> FHA DRIVE-IN NOW! [19]

The title and opening song of the second act, "Jump for Joy,"—which in
production notes Ellington called a modern spiritual—depicted another de-
parture from Jim Crow Land, with an allusion to *Uncle Tom's Cabin* [20]:

> Fare thee well, land of cotton
> Cotton lisle is out of style
> Honey chile, Jump for joy
> Little Eve don't you grieve
> All the hounds, I do believe
> Have been killed
> Ain't you thrilled
> Jump for Joy.

> Have you seen pastures groovy?
> "Green Pastures" was just a technicolor movie.
> When you stomp up to heaven
> And you meet old St. Pete
> Tell that boy, "Jump for joy!"
> Step right in,
> Give Pete some skin,
> And jump for joy. [21]

"Jump for Joy" was full of the tongue-in-cheek social commentary that distinguished the entire revue. The only Technicolor in *Green Pastures* was its racism, for the movie was in black and white. And what could be more "uppity" than telling Saint Peter, "that boy," called here by the nickname "Pete," to jump for joy? The song is a celebration of the African American vernacular at a truly elevated—and heavenly—level.

The music communicates as powerfully as the lyrics. From a bottom-heavy first chorus, with baritone sax supporting a muted trumpet solo, the music proceeds to Ivy Anderson's thirty-two-bar vocal, and back to orchestra, with alto sax calling to a trumpet section response. But then the full orchestra kicks in with a heavy four-beat chugging near-jump rhythm while Ellington's trademark "train whistle" blares on top. The music moves the listener northward, away from the Mississippi River bottom, with train whistles in full cry to signal the jubilant escape:

Intro: saxes, riff / **A, A1:** muted trumpet solo / **B:** sax section / **A:** muted trumpet / **Tag**

   8   /   8 + 8   /   8   /   8   /   4

Transition/ A, A1, B, A: Ivy Anderson solo / **Tag**

   4   /   32 / + 4

A, A1: Alto solo-brass section / **B:** Brass section–alto solo / **A:** Alto-brass section / **Tag**

   16   /   4 + 4   / 8/ 4

C, C: Full orchestra in heavy 4-beat "chugging" with "train whistle" horns / **Tag**

   8 + 8   /4

Jump for Joy introduced the term "zoot suit" to America in a sketch performed by Pot, Pan, and Skillet: "You've got a zoot suit with a reet pleat and a stuff cuff and a drape shape." [22] Teenagers began showing up in the balcony with "unbelievably loud zoot suits, trying to compete with Pot," Kuller recalled. [23] The zoot suits were a "form of visual protest," said Frank Davis, a silent complement to the show's blatant anti-racist position.[24] The zoot suit sketch, "Made to Order," preceded the show's finale, "Sharp Easter," an Easter parade ending spectacularly with Pot wearing his brand new, made-to-order checkered zoot suit. His entrance generally brought fans to their feet.

The press raved about the show. Ed Schallert, drama editor for the *Los Angeles Times*, wrote, "Duke Ellington and his orchestra, heading a group of star singers and dancers, brought zest and class to the musical revue *Jump for Joy*." Schallert praised nearly every soloist by name, predicting a bright future for the show, "particularly with Ellington leading the way, because he has style and distinction. Furthermore, he works in an effortless manner."[25] One reviewer contrasted it with the road show production of *Cabin in the Sky*, then appearing six blocks away with an all-star cast, saying that *Cabin in the Sky* was Booker T. Washington, while *Jump for Joy* was Frederick Douglass.[26] Crowds were so enthusiastic that they simply refused to leave the theater: Ellington had the piano brought on stage, and the band followed, as did dancers from the audience. The producers feared they would lose their profits to the stage-hands, who had to be paid bonus wages for the hour or more after-show jam session and dance.

The show continued to evolve. Gene Ware recalls: "So many people were coming back three and four times a week that we would improvise and drop in new things every night just for them. . . . They would brag to us that this performance was the thirty-fifth or forty-first time they'd been there."[27] The creative staff met every night throughout the entire twelve-week run. By the end of July, Ellington had convinced them that *Jump for Joy* was neglecting the blues and jump music. He insisted on bringing in Big Joe Turner to remedy the oversight. Turner, who had met Ellington at least twelve years earlier, left a gig at Barney Josephson's Cafe Society in New York to join the show. Josephon's nightclub was the first truly integrated nightspot in white New York, and Turner had been there since it opened in 1938. Leaving could not have been an easy decision. "Duke didn't have no songs for me to sing when I got there," said Turner, "so I just sang some of my songs for awhile until he could write me some. We all lived in the Dunbar, so we would get together and play the piano in Duke's room, and we put together 'Rocks in My Bed.' He wrote that for me, and I helped him on that. . . . We did a bunch of songs for me to sing in my spot, and they went over so good that they put me all through the show, had me running back and forth on the stage all the time. Sometimes I sang 'Jump for Joy.' "[28] By August the *Herald-Express* reported: "No question about the Mayan these nights. The joint really jumps." [29]

Among the songs written for *Jump for Joy* were several that became either standards or minor hits. "I've Got It Bad and That Ain't Good" was a hit for Ivy Anderson, as was "Chocolate Shake"—a quick review of African and African American dance starting with Eve and Venus de Milo, stopping briefly in Africa with Stanley and Livingston, and ending up in Manhattan. Anderson's version of the title song, "Jump for Joy" became a hit as well. Although Herb Jeffries also recorded "Jump for Joy," he had more success with his recording of "The Brown-Skin Gal in the Calico Gown." Marie Bryant did well with "Bli-Blip," and the dance number "Subtle Slough" was given lyrics and reworked into the song "Just Squeeze Me." Mercer Ellington wrote even more music for a version of the show that ran in Miami for three weeks in 1959. Perhaps because the racist conditions that originally inspired the show had not disappeared, it was harder than ever to laugh at them, and the show's revival was short-lived.

Wonderful Smith's most memorable contribution was a one-sided conversation with President Roosevelt satirizing the New Deal and preparations for war, government efforts from which blacks had been excluded. The sketch was so effective that many feared the Republicans would use it as ammunition against Roosevelt in the upcoming campaign. Roosevelt had just signed his Executive Order 8802, forestalling Randolph's march on Washington, but the armed forced remained segregated, and African Americans remained disfranchised and disgruntled. As a companion event to Randolph's march, *Jump for Joy* was a formal celebration and public embrace of a widespread cultural movement, an artistic counterpart to and reinforcement of political intentions playing themselves out across the nation.

Jump for Joy played for 101 performances at the Mayan before it finally folded owing to diminishing profits; operating costs ran $7,000 per week.[30] Notes for the production indicate that Kuller and the company clearly intended to take the show on the road: "Let us all bear in mind that the show as is runs much too long and though it might be all right for Los Angeles, the moment we hit towns with a large suburban population, we will find that trains and busses have a way of departing on time and that a great many of our patrons must leave to catch them." [31] But the tour never came to be. A recording ban kept all music from the show off the air, which hampered efforts to create nationwide audience interest. And the recording ban also meant that the musicians and songwriters, whose livelihood depended on royalty payments, were already living under diminished circumstances and couldn't personally finance further shows. Nevertheless, it launched careers for many of its performers and gained increased respect for black artists across the country. Ellington called it "the hippest thing we ever did," and said that out of *Jump for Joy* came a "feeling of responsibility" that culminated in his long masterwork *Black, Brown, and Beige* (1943).[32] He considered *Jump for Joy* the "first social significance show," and of all his achievements, the one thing outside his music that he was most proud of was his part in producing it.[33] In the 1960s, when San Francisco demonstrators challenged Ellington to make a statement on civil rights, he answered, "I made my statement in 1941 in *Jump for Joy* and I stand by it."[34]

In *Stomping the Blues*, Albert Murray wrote, "Each masterwork of art . . . is always first of all a comprehensive synthesis of all the aspects of its idiom."[35] *Jump for Joy* used music, dance, comedy, dress, and speech to make a political statement. It remains an important marker of a cultural watershed, a moment when artists, determined to turn their backs on theatrical stereotypes, united with audiences in celebrating black culture. As remarkable an achievement as it was, *Jump for Joy* should not be considered exceptional. Rather, it was part of a broad cultural movement, one of many examples in which African American musicians, dancers, artists, and athletes, men, women, and children refused to maintain the Jim Crow shuffle, choosing instead to jump.

✻ AFTERWORD : JUMPING AS PLAY : AN AESTHETIC AND THEORETICAL PERSPECTIVE

In his introduction to the monumentally significant volume of essays, stories, and poetry titled *The New Negro* (1925), Alain Locke, the public voice of the Harlem Renaissance, wrote about a "new spirit awake in the masses," and said that a generation of African Americans was on the verge of a "spiritual emancipation." Locke spoke of a community entering "a new dynamic phase, the buoyancy from within compensating for whatever pressure there may be of conditions from without." Yet Locke believed his book would reach only the "thinking few," and not the "migrant massees, shifting from countryside to city," not the "multitude" of African Americans who felt only a "vague new urge" for dignity but had no idea how to achieve it.[1] The dynamism and buoyancy Locke spoke of as dormant, hidden, or, at best, nascent, were actually in full bloom, all around him. The multitude he dismissed were acting out solutions to social issues, theorizing through behavior. The double irony of the position of African American intellectuals of the Harlem Renaissance was that first, popular culture, or the culture of the masses, offered a solution to the intellectual dilemma of the decade: how to maintain individual style and creativity in an increasingly hostile world. Second, music, dance, and sports had become an everyday solution not just for one race but for many.[2] The expressive culture that bloomed in the midst of and following the Harlem Renaissance actually addressed the concerns of the larger national culture. Its influence spread rapidly, reached countless people of all races, and it has lasted to this day.

George Schuyler framed the problem facing modern society: "We live in a highly organized world in which the individual counts for very little."[3] But jazz, social dance, and basketball provided a counter-statement; they allowed individuals to assert their excellence as soloists even as they remained part of a "highly organized" ensemble. Built into the structure of these expressive forms were complex rhythms, improvisation and stylization, call-and-response patterns, and competitive interaction that required individuals to coordinate and synchronize their efforts. Thus, they offered a working model of balanced group and individual expression. As soloists stood to perform alone and then relinquished the spotlight to blend in with the group, big bands showed the rest of the country that it was possible to work in precision with others without losing a sense of individuality. The dancers who followed and inspired them did the same, offering 1930s Americans, in Warren Susman's words, a "pattern of large-scale participation and close cooperation."[4]

These aesthetic concepts have strong and demonstrably African roots. In the introduction to *Signifyin(g), Sanctifyin', and Slam Dunking* I outlined an aesthetic sensibility that is fundamental to African and African American expressive culture, using the following principles: (1) rhythmic and metric complexity; (2) individual improvisation and stylization; (3) call and response, or active engagement of the whole person with the community; (4) competitive artistic dialogue; and (5) the use of all of these strategies to create a group consciousness (elsewhere in this book called the "soul focal moment").[5] Together, these principles form a cultural aesthetic that is remarkably consistent in African-based cultures on both sides of the Atlantic. And it can be found in many forms of artistic expression, including music and dance, as well as in sports, ordinary speech, and humor.

Rhythmic and metric complexity in song, dance, and speech force the individual to become highly attuned to what the group is doing. Each person has a place in the whole, but the whole is complex, and you must pay attention if you are to find your own particular place. Once you have learned the group exercise, then you are encouraged to add individual flair, to improvise and stylize, as do jazz musicians, as did the Lindy Hoppers, as do basketball players. It is by mastering the tradition or the medium that you acquire the ability to improvise. Lindy Hoppers could not create their own steps without first learning the basics. Jazz musicians must completely master chord changes before they reach the point of improvising within the structure of those changes. Without mastery of theme, there can be no variations.

Call and response occurs in the music of many cultures: in Western music the same principle is termed "antiphonal" singing or playing. But call and response is a fundamental principle of African music, and given the cultural segregation of slavery, it is far more likely that the antecedent of call and response in slave music was African than Anglo-European. The back-and-forth nature of call and response spills over into many other forms of African and African American cultural expression. African American preachers employ call and response as a way of engaging the congregation in the sermon. In his essay "The Chanted Sermon," Albert Raboteau describes the chanted call and response of sermons in black churches as an "African-influenced performance style" in which preacher and listener "did not merely talk about God, they experienced his power, and found that in the experience, their own spirits were renewed."[6] Sometimes the call and response becomes competitive. The principle of call and response is at work in the dialogue between group and individual that defines jazz, or in the verbal exchange known as signifying—a kind of verbal poker in which each player raises the level of insult one notch. An action is taken, a dance step is made, a musical phrase is sung or played, and each is a call for someone in the community to respond. African American preachers and performers trained and gifted in this tradition expect to be interrupted by their audience. Their message calls for a response, and if they are good, they get one.

The expressive arts of Africa evolved as they did because they helped African communities to function: they were socially adaptive. The very structure of African music and dance and play connects singers and dancers to one another, but at the same time it allows them to discover and express their individuality. And as Africans migrated or were taken to other parts of the world, the aesthetic principles that bound their communities together in Africa allowed them to survive in strange new lands. In turn, these aesthetic principles proved to be the foundation of a new African and then all-American culture, beginning with the arrival of the first African immigrants.

To understand music, dance, and sports as key elements of a total cultural shift, one that crystallized in the 1930s, we have to understand how they connect with one another. More often than not, we study these subjects separately—if at all. There is musicology and sports history and history of dance, but not many scholars have begun their work with the premise that these forms of cultural expression are co-dependent.[7] As long ago as 1945, jazz critic, dancer, and choreographer Roger Pryor Dodge wrote an article for the *Record Changer* titled "The Dance-Basis of Jazz." In it he remarked dryly, "It seems quite strange that I should have to say that jazz is dance music—that it has a close bond with the dance, and that it is not mere coincidence that we find it enjoyable to dance to."[8] Dodge reminded his readers of the interdependence of dance and music in eighteenth-century Europe. Others have done the same with African music and dance. Robert Farris Thompson's essay "An

Aesthetic of the Cool" and John Miller Chernoff's *African Rhythm and African Sensibility* discuss music and dance as inseparable, interconnected expressions with overlapping formal aesthetic patterns.[9] In *Jazz Dance*, for many years the single authoritative text on the subject, Marshall and Jean Stearns traced the African roots of American social dances and reiterated the inseparability of music from movement. More recently, Jacqui Malone explored these connections in *Steppin' on the Blues*, an updated history of African American vernacular dance. For Malone, dance is "visible rhythm," and dancers are drummers who use their feet instead of sticks.[10]

In his comprehensive history *America's Musical Life*, the musicologist Richard Crawford credits his predecessor Gilbert Chase with insisting that the strength of American music lies in the performance of music rather than simply in composition.[11] In his book about the big bands of the 1930s, *Swing Changes*, the historian David Stowe echoes ethnomusicologists who believe that understanding music means thinking of it first as *music making*, which includes "audience, performance context, ideology, and mass media." But Stowe goes further, saying that we should think about music as *social practice*.[12] Albert Murray goes further still, insisting that one has to understand the *idiomatic roots* of African American artistic expression or one is in danger of missing "the essential nature of its statement."[13] This is not to say that Murray is an essentialist—far from it. But he believes that unless we understand where the music came from, we won't know what it is for. That is, to understand the music, we need to understand the culture that nurtures the musicians, audiences, and music making itself. Murray's *Stomping the Blues* locates the idiomatic roots of jazz in the dancehalls of the 1930s, where the music and dance were inseparable because they were integral components of vital cultural rituals.

I add to this mixture basketball, and a new degree of political awareness fueled at the time by a number of national and international successes for individual African Americans. Murray describes the dances that took place in the dancehall-gymnasiums as rituals of purification, affirmation, and celebration. To understand these rituals, he says, we have to look not at *playing the blues* but at *the blues as playing*. And by that he means not *playing music* but *playing* plain and simple. And if we are looking at playing, we might as well include playing basketball.

Murray's aesthetic framework came from anthropology, a subject he began reading while still in high school.[14] Studying anthropology led him to think of music and dance not as separate entities but as interconnected elements of rituals that support all human cultures. The theories that Murray found most helpful were those of pioneer scholars in the history and theory of play as ritual: Dutch historian Johan Huizinga and French intellectual Roger Caillois. As theorists who consider social rituals as play, they fall into a large group of romantic and post-romantic thinkers who glorified originality, freedom from rules and convention, and above all the imagination, beginning with the poet and historian Friedrich Schiller, who said famously, "Man plays only when he is in the full sense of the word a man, and he is only wholly a Man when he is playing."[15] To observe play is to watch the imagination at work. And if, as romantic thinkers believed, it is through the exercise of the imagination that we discover what is most true and authentic in ourselves, then we must pay attention to the play of the imagination to find the meaning of our existence. Even so, most such thinkers had in mind a highly idealized kind of play, such as poetic or musical play; otherwise they focused on the developmental value of play for children. Huizinga and Caillois are in the minority of play theorists in categorizing a wide variety of adult behaviors as play. For them and later theorists such as Clifford Geertz, adult play becomes a text to be interpreted, a way of thinking about culture. According to play theorist Brian Sutton-Smith, "Play is the way we used to speak of ritual."[16]

In *Homo Ludens: A Study of the Play Element in Culture*, first published in 1938, Huizinga defined play as a "culture-creating activity."[17] He maintained that "civilization arises and unfolds in and as play," and "real civilization cannot exist in the absence of a certain play-element."[18] Through repetition and re-enactment, play assumes fixed form and becomes cultural tradition.[19] In his study of contests or competitive play, Huizinga suggested that the desire to win or to succeed elevates the aspirations of humanity. Some have criticized Huizinga's vision of play as blindly rooted in the combative arena, but the comprehensive scope of his history of adult social activities provided the foundation for later scholars of play.[20]

Roger Caillois introduced his theory in his 1958 book *Man, Play, and Games* (*Les jeux et les hommes*), in which he divided play into four categories: competition (*agon*), chance (*alea*), vertigo (*ilinx*), and mimicry. Caillois suggested that these categories run in a continuum from *paidia*, or spontaneous play, to *ludus*, or rule-driven reenactment. Whereas *paidia* is "frolicsome and impulsive exuberance" both "anarchic and capricious," *ludus* is the opposite, an urge to control *paidia* with "arbitrary, imperative, and purposely tedious conventions."[21] *Paidia* is the "primary power of improvisation and joy," while *ludus* is the "taste for gratuitous difficulty."[22] *Paidia* creates disturbance and tumult; *ludus* embodies the urge to regulate that tumult. In Jacques Attali's terms, *paidia* is noise, *ludus* music.

It is easier to dismiss frivolity than cultural ritual. By adopting the serious categories of play, Murray gave weight to jazz as a fundamental ritual in American culture, one that not only offers a way of surpassing the restrictions of everyday life but also gives meaning to existence. Murray organized his book *Stomping the Blues* around play theory, starting with mimicry. Playing the blues, he wrote, is a kind of mimicry, a ritual representation of the blues emotion. At its most complex level, ritual reenactment becomes theater. To begin the blues ritual, one must acknowledge the blues "face to face," expose them for what they are. The face-to-face ritual Murray talks about as so necessary to performing the blues is also a reference to theater: to dispel and defeat the blues, the blues musician must look the blues in the face, put on the mask of the blues, and become the blues.

The concepts of competition and vertigo pertain as well. Vertigo runs the gamut from children's impulsive spinning round and round until they become dizzy, to complex ecstatic rituals such as those of religious dance (for example, in Sufism). In the swing dance, hundreds of embracing couples swirl for hours in a counter-clockwise direction—just as do dancers in most pre-industrial cultures, including those of Africa. The urge toward vertigo inspires a faster and faster swing tempo, as dancers and musicians reinforce each other in a vertiginous, grooving social ritual.

The desire for vertigo (*ilinx*)—that is, for transcendence, for being a part of something bigger than oneself, and for the ecstasy that comes with it—is the spark that ignites the social ritual. Years after he published *Stomping the Blues*, Murray remained interested in the ecstasy and sheer dizziness of this social ritual. "It's very important to concentrate on that vertigo," said Murray. "It's all about getting high," whether through listening, playing, or dancing to blues music.[23] And in fact, after 1936 the Lindy Hop became a strikingly literal form of getting high, as dancers began to swing, throw, or flip their partners into the air, a vertical expression of vertigo.

Competition (*agon*) was also an important element of the 1930s swing ritual.

Individual musicians often competed with one another in "cutting contests," and dancers also competed in contests, both spontaneous and organized, that led to ever more intricate and challenging steps. Albert Murray witnessed such contests firsthand, and on special occasions when whole bands battled one another, he says, "the excitement, anticipation, and partisanship would be all but indistinguishable from that generated by a championship boxing match or baseball game." [24]

The purpose of blues music as a form of play is to make people feel good, "to generate a disposition that is both elegantly playful and heroic in its nonchalance." Blues musicians "play" music, but they also play in the sense of *paidia*, playfulness, or in Murray's word, "gamboling," which is to say "fooling around or kidding around with, toying with, or otherwise having fun with." Blues music and dance are playful, spontaneous; they respond to the "excitement of the moment." [25]

It is in the nature of humans to repeat and reenact spontaneous play and at the same time to up the ante—to increase the difficulty. Out of the tension between the spontaneously playful and gratuitously difficult arises the artistic creation. And the blues idiom—which includes jazz—is one of these artistic creations, in Murray's words a "perfectly natural historical development," an "extension, elaboration, and refinement that was no mere embellishment but an evolution altogether consistent with the relative sophistication of the musicians involved." [26] It is the tendency toward gratuitous difficulty that transforms everyday bluesiness into art.

Competition and *ludus*, the urge for unnecessary difficulty, channel playfulness into improvisation and cultural ritual. Murray is emphatic on this point: "Blues-idiom merriment" is not like the "sensual abandon of the voodoo orgy or . . . the ecstatic trance of a religious possession." The blues ritual combines "spontaneity, improvisation, and control." [27] Jazz music and dance depend on striking a balance between playfulness and control that often escapes the notice of observers. Clearly, the entire evolution of jazz music and dance depends on a driving urge toward gratuitous difficulty. But in any one performance, music and dance must respond to the forces and energies of the moment. The performer must be willing to play not only with the possibilities of the music itself but also with the possibilities that the situation generates: extension, elaboration, and refinement; subversion, inversion, and infinite variation. [28] Gratuitous difficulty is achieved through elaborate play.

A case study in the tension between *paidia* and *ludus*—as well as in their complementarity—is the innovation of air steps in the Lindy Hop. Frankie Manning takes credit for bringing aerials to the Savoy Ballroom in a most spectacular way. He claims that he and his partner, Frieda Washington, worked on the step privately for months, which is to say, it was not simply a free-spirited, spontaneous move but rather a ludic, rule-driven reenactment that the two worked to perfection. Manning and Washington were competing with other dancers—an agonic form of vertigo—and drummer Chick Webb was watching the dancers. When Washington landed on her feet, he responded in sync with a resounding smack of the snare with both sticks. Manning and Washington's well-rehearsed, ludic play inspired Webb's spontaneous, paidic reaction, all of which was originally inspired by the desire for vertigo in the competitive context of the Savoy Ballroom.

Another example of the ludic and the paidic in expressive culture is the development of the fast break, jump shot, and slam dunk. Basketball began as an expression of *ludus*: not spontaneous play but rather the opposite, a game invented deliberately to control the playful impulses of a class of eighteen young men at a school for YMCA instructors—to train them in muscular and disciplined Christian principles. But the rules themselves created opportunity and enticement for improvisation—for play. Former player-coach Bill Russell has written: "If the players are turned loose within the rules, the game will work automatically; they will keep inventing newer and more glorious moves to counter the inventions of the other players. All that is required to choreograph the action is the ball; just throw it out there and the moves will gather around the ball wherever it goes. This is true of many major sports: the ball provokes the art all by itself." [29] And Walt Frazier said that when he was playing for the Knicks, the team had about five basic plays, and from there, they improvised: "It's like making up something—making a poem or something. . . . That's one of the joys of basketball—improvising. It's almost impossible to practice moves because most moves professional guys make are moves that are instinct. They are made up on the spur of the moment." [30] Even though Frazier used the word "instinct," what he was talking about was improvisation and play.

The cultural willingness to improvise is why today's basketball looks so different from the game invented in 1891. It is not simply that more than 80 percent of the NBA players and 90 percent of the stars are African American.

It is that the African American players have changed the game. And improvisation is the key. Remember what coach Clarence Gaines of Winston-Salem State said? "You have to learn to adjust and adapt to the defense. Most of the kids didn't have the movement, the rhythm, to innovate." [31] We are considering cultural innovation as a form of play, and play as a form of cultural innovation: the most free-form brand of basketball occurs on outdoor courts, or playgrounds, and is called "playground" ball. When John Edgar Wideman took his game from the playgrounds of his native Pittsburgh to the University of Pennsylvania, he found that he missed "the playground game," its spontaneity, its "free-form improvisation and electricity." Wideman missed *playing* basketball.

The jump—whether in music, dance, or sports—*is* the play principle in action. In jump blues, the music speeds up and becomes leaner, the Lindy Hop takes to the air, and dancers swirl and twirl away from each other in a secular simulation of a sacred ritual of ecstatic union. According to abolitionist Frederick Douglass, enslaved people sang "more to *make* themselves happy, than to express their happiness." Clarinetist Sidney Bechet wrote of African Americans: "My race, their music . . . it's their way of giving you something, of showing you how to be happy. It's what they've got to make them happy." [32] People sing and dance, writes Albert Murray, not to express the blues but to chase the blues away. Or to paraphrase Bill Russell, it is possible for musicians and dancers and athletes to jump because they're happy, but it's more likely that they're happy because they're jumping.

I once telephoned Albert Murray to ask his permission to reprint a chapter from *Stomping the Blues* in a volume I was editing. When I read him the title, *Signifyin(g), Sanctifyin', and Slam Dunking,* and then the subtitle, *A Reader in African American Expressive Culture,* he immediately objected: "African American? African? What's African about it? Do you know anybody more American than me?" Murray is an Americanist, not an Africanist. And yet he does admit that there are African components to the blues aesthetic. In *Stomping the Blues* he compares the tonal coloration of blues music to African talking drums. He devotes an entire chapter to dance, stating: "The underlying dance-beat disposition involved is obviously West African in origin, and so are the definitive stylistic elements that give the incantation and percussion—which is to say, blues music—its special idiomatic character." [33] The people for whom blues music was created are "dance-beat-oriented people. They refine all movement in the direction of dance-beat elegance. Their work movements become dance movements and so do their play movements; and so, indeed, do all the movements they use every day, including the way they walk, stand, turn, wave, shake hands, reach, or make any gesture at all."[34] In *The Omni-Americans* Murray writes: "There is, of course, no question at all that the ultimate source of the dance-orientation so central to the life style of most contemporary U.S. Negroes lies somewhere in the uncharted reaches of some region of prehistoric Africa." But, he continues, "the blues tradition, a tradition of confrontation and improvisation[,] . . . is indigenous to the United States."[35] Murray prefers to emphasize the Americanness of the blues aesthetic, whereas I would like to see more acknowledgment of African influences in American culture. Still, we are talking about the same thing: an urge toward improvisation, an orientation toward what Murray calls "elastic individuality," maintaining a balance between the individual and the community through improvisation and stylization.[36]

Increasingly, living in the United States requires almost continuous adaptation to new technologies. The problem that technology creates is this: How do human beings maintain their humanity in an increasingly industrial, or now postindustrial, environment? How do we maintain individuality and group identity without sacrificing one to the other? How can we be more than a microchip in a machine? And the answer is provided in expressive culture. Swing music and dance—and their sports counterpart, basketball—offered Americans a vision of how industrial society could function efficiently and smoothly without losing the unique contributions of individuals, a vision of the individual as both a standout and a team player. In 1970 Murray wrote:

> Someday students of machine-age culture in the United States may find that Negro slaves in the cotton field had already begun confronting and evolving esthetic solutions for the problems of assembly line regimentation, depersonalization, and collectivization. After all, the so-called Industrial Revolution had as much to do with the way personnel was used as with machinery as such. In any event Harlem and Detroit Negroes, for example, are neither terrified by the intricacies of contemporary technology nor overwhelmed by the magnitude of megalopolis. On the contrary, they seize every opportunity to get into the swing of things, almost always contributing vitality and new dimensions of elegance when they succeed.[37]

One way to understand the simultaneous appearance of many forms of one physical gesture—the jump—in late 1930s African America is to tether it to the general cultural obsession with flight and height. African Americans showed the rest of the country how to become like the *Spirit of St. Louis* or like Superman—how to leap tall buildings. As American technology took to the air, Americans took their music and their dance and their games to the air as well.

Music, dance, and sport of the 1930s had to adapt to a new technological culture because that was what Americans had to do to survive. But I am talking about something more than survival instinct. As Murray says: "Art is by definition a process of stylization, and what it stylizes is experience. What it objectifies, embodies, abstracts, expresses, and symbolizes is a sense of life. . . . What is represented in the music, dance, painting, sculpture, literature, and architecture of a given group of people in a particular time, place, and circumstance is a conception of the essential nature and purpose of human existence itself."[38] When we look at how people played—music, sports, and dance—in the 1930s, we get a pretty good understanding of what American culture was becoming and has since become: the best of American culture, the playful, experimental, bold, and innovative parts of American culture. And we see what we must do if we hope to do more than merely survive. As Ralph Ellison wrote: "Without the presence of Negro American style, our jokes, our tall tales, even our sports would be lacking in the sudden turns, the shocks, the swift changes of pace (all jazz-shaped) that serve to remind us that the world is ever unexplored, and that while a complete mastery of life is mere illusion, the real secret of the game is to make life swing."[39]

In the past few years, more than one management expert has suggested that the new model for corporate structure in information-based industries is that of the jazz combo or the basketball team.[40] On a basketball team, anyone can score. In jazz, anyone can solo. The new management approach encourages creativity, spontaneity, and improvisation from all—crucial elements in Murray's blues idiom, the African American aesthetic of both jazz and basketball. The jazz-basketball-blues aesthetic is one of invention, improvisation, a take-what-you-got-and-go-with-it approach to life. The game plan may change at a moment's notice. While a basketball coach may stand on the sidelines yelling, "Don't shoot! Don't shoot!" his next comment is just as likely to be a murmured, "Nice shot." In a postindustrial culture, industrial models no

longer serve us. Combining the urge to play with the urge for gratuitous difficulty, a new generation of executives and engineers—often dressed in T-shirts
and sneakers and working from home on their own schedule—imagine
ever more sophisticated and faster ways of communicating, building, and
creating.

Even in football, winning coaches are building on opportunities for improvisation. University of Texas coach Mack Brown has said repeatedly that
his star player of the championship 2005–6 season, quarterback Vince Young,
began to excel only after Brown and his coaching team decided to back off
and let him be himself. Brown and offensive coordinator Greg Davis had
tried to mold Young into a pocket passer and to correct his sidearm delivery
when he first arrived in Texas. The effort was a disaster. "The biggest thing
was I didn't know Coach [Davis]; he was my first white coach and I was his
first black quarterback," Young said. "We weren't on the same page because
of where I'm from." Coaches Brown and Davis went so far as to listen to hip
hop with Young in an effort to understand him better.[41] Brown didn't just
become Young's supporter in postgame news conferences; he actually took
reporters to task for what he perceived as racial bias in describing Young's
style. "Vince Young is every bit as good at reading defenses as any quarterback
in the country and he doesn't seem to have gotten the same praise for that
as he should," Brown complained to a reporter. "Vince needs to start getting
credit for being a great quarterback, not just the guy that made the plays."[42]
Brown wanted reporters to recognize the decision-making process underlying Young's seemingly freeform play. When Young went pro, his first-year
performance quarterbacking the Tennessee Titans earned him a Rookie of the
Year award, justifying his former coach's faith in his intellectual improvisation on the field.

There are moments in jazz and blues and gospel, and even in basketball, in
which a player suddenly defies time and space and human limitations with a
bit of gratuitous difficulty that transcends the human condition. Earlier I used
Olly Wilson's term "soul focal moment." Ralph Ellison's name for it was a
"true jazz moment." In The Blue Devils of Nada, Albert Murray calls it the "Moment of Truth," meaning "that disjuncture that should bring out your personal
best."[43] The Moment of Truth fills one's auditory or visual consciousness
with such complete elaboration and refinement that there is, at that moment,
nothing more to be said. In retrospect, it might be considered showing off, or

hotdogging. But in truth, at such times there is no individual or team. There is only one ecstatic consciousness that includes everyone present.

The Moment of Truth is one of calculated risk. Athletes and dancers and musicians defy human limitations in moments of unnecessary difficulty. They don't have to do what they do to score. Their virtuosic moments—the slam dunks, the runaway solos—are counterstatements, and here I quote Albert Murray from *The Omni-Americans*, "antidotes against the pernicious effects of a technological enthusiasm inadequately counter-balanced by a literary sense of the ambiguities and absurdities inherent in all human experience."[44]

Play is serious business, and art is the extension, elaboration, and refinement of play. To understand American history, we need to look at American music and dance and play: the stomping, jumping, swooping, gliding side of America. In play and art we reconnect with the "warmth, sensitivity, nonsense, vitality, and elegance" of which human beings are capable, under almost any conditions.[45] Play and art are survival technology, essential equipment for living, because the real secret of the game is to make life swing.

NOTES

PREFACE

1. Patricia Willard, notes to *Jump for Joy* (Washington, D.C.: Smithsonian Institution, 1988), 31.
2. There were many other all-black basketball teams. Sportswriter Chester Washington of the *Pittsburgh Courier* often published an informal directory based on mail-in information from his readers. A 1936 version lists fifty-one teams, from New Orleans to Buffalo, including three women's teams. "Basketball Directory," *Pittsburgh Courier*, 8 February 1936, sec. 2.
3. Arthur R. Ashe Jr., *A Hard Road to Glory—Basketball: The African-American Athlete in Basketball* (1988; reprint, New York: Amisted Press, 1993), 10.

1. SNEAKERS AND TUXES

1. Bill Russell and Taylor Branch, *Second Wind: The Memoirs of an Opinionated Man* (New York: Random House, 1979), 73.
2. Lewis A. Erenberg, "From New York to Middletown," *American Quarterly* 38 (Winter 1986): 773.
3. David W. Stowe, *Swing Changes: Big-Band Jazz in New Deal America* (Cambridge: Harvard University Press, 1994), 193.
4. Marshall Stearns and Jean Stearns, *Jazz Dance: The Story of American Vernacular Dance* (New York: Macmillan, 1968), 329.
5. Stowe, *Swing Changes*, 14.
6. Scholars Eric Lott and Scott DeVeaux have made compelling arguments for bebop as an assertion of ethnicity. See Eric Lott, "Double V, Double-Time: Bebop's Politics of Style," *Callaloo* 36 (1988): 597–605; and Scott Deveaux, "Constructing the Jazz Tradition: Jazz Historiography," *Black American Literature Forum* 25 (1991): 525–60.
7. Barry Pearson has called attention to an accelerating "tempo of black life during and after the urban migration," as well as an "upbeat sense of expanded possibility." Barry Pearson, "Jump Steady: The Roots of R&B," in *Nothing but the Blues: The Music and the Musicians*, ed. Lawrence Cohn (New York: Abbeville Press, 1993), 316–17.
8. Adam Clayton Powell Jr., "No Joe Louis Eulogy," *Amsterdam News*, 27 June 1936, emphasis added.

9. Adam Clayton Powell Jr., *Marching Blacks: An Interpretive History of the Rise of the Black Common Man* (New York: Dial Press, 1945), 15.

10. Ibid., 88.

11. Ibid., 101.

12. Ibid., 104–7.

13. Jervis Anderson, *This Was Harlem: A Cultural Portrait, 1900–1950* (New York: Farrar Straus Giroux, 1982), 7.

14. Cheryl Lynn Greenberg, *"Or Does It Explode?" Black Harlem in the Great Depression* (New York: Oxford University Press, 1991), 5.

15. Ibid., 6.

16. John Hope Franklin, *From Slavery to Freedom: A History of Negro Americans* (1947), 3rd ed. (New York: Alfred A. Knopf, 1968), 499.

17. Stephen Henderson, *Understanding the New Black Poetry: Black Speech and Black Music as Poetic References* (New York: William Morrow, 1973), 44.

18. Albert Murray, *Stomping the Blues* (1976; reprint, New York: DaCapo, 1987), 12.

19. Ray Oldenburg, *The Great Good Place: Cafés, Coffee Shops, Community Centers, Beauty Parlors, General Stores, Bars, Hangouts, and How They Get You Through the Day* (New York: Paragon House, 1989), 16.

20. Ibid., 11.

21. Melvin D. Williams, *On the Street Where I Lived* (New York: Holt, Rinehart, and Winston, 1981), 82.

22. Michael Henry Adams, *Harlem Lost and Found: An Architectural and Social History* (New York: Monacelli Press, 2002), 249; Michael Henry Adams, "Renaissance Ballroom and Casino—What Is a Casino? Playing Politics with Harlem's Landmarks," www.harlemonestop.com/organization.php?id=564 (18 November 2007); John Hareas, "Remembering the Rens," *NBA Encyclopedia Playoff Edition*, www.nba.com/history/encyclopedia_rens_001214.html (19 October 2007).

23. Trudier Harris, "The Barbershop in Black Literature," *Black American Literature Forum* 13, no. 3 (Fall 1979): 113.

24. Johnny Otis, *Upside Your Head! Rhythm and Blues on Central Avenue* (Hanover: University Press of New England, 1993), 32.

25. Samuel B. Charters and Leonard Kunstadt, *Jazz: A History of the New York Scene* (New York: Doubleday, 1962), 25.

26. In dancehalls black and white youth drew together to flout the conventions and restrictions of middle-class society in a harmony of the underclasses that scholars such as W. T. Lhamon and Dale Cockrell argue has existed since at least the

eighteenth century. See W. T. Lhamon Jr., *Raising Cain: Blackface Performance from Jim Crow to Hip Hop* (Cambridge: Harvard University Press, 1998); and Dale Cockrell, *Demons of Disorder: Early Blackface Minstrels and Their World* (New York: Cambridge University Press, 1997).

27. Joel Dinerstein, *Swinging the Machine: Modernity, Technology, and African American Culture between the World Wars* (Amherst: University of Massachusetts Press, 2003), 5.

28. "Duke Sets the Pace in Themes," *Afro-American*, 2 July 1938, 10; cited in John Edward Hasse, *Beyond Category: The Life and Genius of Duke Ellington* (1993; reprint, New York: Da Capo Press, 1995), 217.

29. Neil Leonard, *Jazz and the White Americans: The Acceptance of a New Art Form* (Chicago: University of Chicago Press, 1962), 124, 139; Hasse, *Beyond Category*, 197.

30. Lewis A. Erenberg, *Swingin' the Dream: Big Band Jazz and the Rebirth of American Culture* (Chicago: University of Chicago Press, 1999), 48.

31. Ibid., 49.

32. Charters and Kundstadt, *Jazz*, 259. Dancer Frankie Manning recalls the night, the outcome, and Krupa's reaction similarly. Frankie Manning and Cynthia R. Millman, *Frankie Manning: Ambassador of Lindy Hop* (Philadelphia: Temple University Press, 2007), 73.

33. Charters and Kundstadt, *Jazz*, 259.

34. Manning and Millman, *Frankie Manning*, 74.

35. "*Something New!!* Basket Ball–Dance. Labor Temple, . . . $1.00 / DANCING After the Game / Music by Bennie Moten's Orchestra," *Kansas City Call*, 12 January 1923.

36. Steven A. Riess, *City Games: The Evolution of American Urban Society and the Rise of Sports* (Urbana: University of Illinois Press, 1989), 108; Robert W. Peterson, *Cages to Jump Shots: Pro Basketball's Early Years* (New York: Oxford University Press, 1990), 122.

37. John Taylor, *The Rivalry: Bill Russell, Wilt Chamberlain, and the Golden Age of Basketball* (New York: Random House, 2005), 105. Chickie Passon is incorrectly identified as "Passion" in this source.

38. "Elks Out to Extend Victory Streak," *Pittsburgh Courier*, 21 December 1935; "Elks Five in Opening Game at Pythian Temple Sunday," *Pittsburgh Courier*, 14 December 1935.

39. Joe Jares, *Basketball: The American Game* (Chicago: Follett, 1971), 38; Peterson, *Cages to Jump Shots*, 119.

40. Frank Marshall Davis, *Livin' the Blues: Memoirs of a Black Journalist and Poet*, ed. John Edgar Tidwell (Madison: University of Wisconsin Press, 1991), 52.

41. Cum Posey, "Posey's Points," *Pittsburgh Courier*, 28 January 1939.

42. Chester L. Washington, "Ches' Sez," *Pittsburgh Courier*, 2 January 1937.

43. Cum Posey, "Posey's Points," *Pittsburgh Courier*, 18 January 1936.

44. Ron Thomas, *They Cleared the Lane: The NBA's Black Pioneers* (Lincoln: University of Nebraska Press, 2002), 7.

45. Peterson, *Cages to Jump Shots*, 97–98.

46. Ralph Ellison, "Homage to Duke Ellington on His Birthday," in *Going to the Territory* (New York: Random House, 1987), 220.

47. Rex William Stewart, *Jazz Masters of the Thirties* (1972; reprint, New York: Da Capo Press, 1985), 164.

48. "Cab Calloway's Basketball Team to Play Miles Brothers, Local Champs, for Charity," unidentified newspaper clipping (ca. January 1935) from the Cab Calloway scrapbooks, Cab Calloway archives, Boston University.

49. *Amsterdam News*, 21 November 1936, ibid.

50. Manning and Millman, *Frankie Manning*, 129.

51. Chester L. Washington, "Rens Keep on Rollin'," *Pittsburgh Courier*, 30 January 1937.

52. Cited in Nelson George, *Elevating the Game: Black Men and Basketball* (New York: Harper Collins, 1992), 40.

53. Wendell Smith, "Smitty's Sport Spurts," *Pittsburgh Courier*, 8 April 1939.

54. Chester L. Washington, "Rens on a Rampage," *Pittsburgh Courier*, 7 January 1939.

55. Arthur R. Ashe Jr., *A Hard Road to Glory—Basketball: The African-American Athlete in Basketball* (1988; reprint, New York: Amisted Press, 1993), 10.

56. Peterson, *Cages to Jump Shots*, 98.

57. Clarence Gaines, telephone conversation with author, 5 March 1996.

58. Manning and Millman, *Frankie Manning*, 54.

59. Albert Murray, conversation with author, 30 August 1996.

60. Murray, *Stomping the Blues*, 230.

61. Stowe, *Swing Changes*, 255 n. 47.

62. Stanley Dance, *The World of Swing* (New York: C. Scribner's Sons, 1974), 277.

63. Lewis A. Erenberg, "News from the Great Wide World: Duke Ellington, Count Basie, and Black Popular Music, 1927–1943," *Prospects* 18 (1993): 483.

64. Editor Frank Bolden in remarks addressed to the American Studies Association Conference, Pittsburgh, 10 November 1995.

65. Richard Wright, "Joe Louis Uncovers Dynamite," *New Masses*, 8 October 1935, 163.

66. Roy Wilkins with Tom Mathews, *Standing Fast: The Autobiography of Roy Wilkins* (New York: Viking Press, 1982), 163–64.

67. Lewis A. Erenberg, *The Greatest Fight of Our Generation: Louis vs. Schmeling* (New York: Oxford University Press, 2006), 9.

68. Paula Pfeffer, *A. Philip Randolph: Pioneer of the Civil Rights Movement* (Baton Rouge: Louisiana State University Press, 1990), 33.

69. Lawrence W. Levine, *The Unpredictable Past: Explorations in American Cultural History* (New York: Oxford University Press, 1993), 209.

70. Wilkins and Matthews, *Standing Fast*, 127.

71. Franklin, *From Slavery to Freedom*, 527.

72. See Richard Polenberg, *One Nation Divisible: Class, Race, and Ethnicity in the United States since 1938* (New York: Viking Press, 1980), 32–34.

73. Doris Kearns Goodwin, *No Ordinary Time* (New York: Simon and Schuster, 1994), 162–63.

74. Ibid., 163.

75. Ibid., 164.

76. "Roosevelt Sweeps Entire Country," *Pittsburgh Courier*, 7 November 1936, sec. 1. For a summary of Du Bois's assessment of the Roosevelt years, see Arnold Rampersad, *The Art and Imagination of W. E. B. Du Bois* (Cambridge: Harvard University Press, 1976), 225.

77. Kevin K. Gaines, *Uplifting the Race: Black Leadership, Politics, and Culture in the Twentieth Century* (Chapel Hill: University of North Carolina Press, 1996), 251.

2. UP, UP, AND AWAY

1. Billy Rowe, "What Is This Thing Called Swing?" *Pittsburgh Courier*, 20 February 1937. Rowe reported on entertainment for the *Courier*; he left in 1954 to become deputy police commissioner for the city of New York.

2. Stanley Dance, *The World of Swing* (New York: C. Scribner's Sons, 1974), 1.

3. Joel Dinerstein, *Swinging the Machine: Modernity, Technology, and African American Culture between the World Wars* (Amherst: University of Massachusetts Press, 2003).

4. Ann Douglas, *Terrible Honesty: Mongrel Manhattan in the 1920s* (New York: Farrar, Straus and Giroux, 1995), 456.

5. "Hubert Julian," *Microsoft Encarta Africana 2000*, ed. Kwame Anthony Appiah and Henry Louis Gates Jr.; Douglas, *Terrible Honesty*, 457–61.

6. Hannibal B. Johnson, *Black Wall Street: From Riot to Renaissance in Tulsa's Historic Greenwood District* (Austin: Eakin Press, 1998), 17.

7. A. Scott Berg, *Lindbergh* (New York: Berkley Books, 1998), 122–30.

8. Ibid., 137.

9. Ibid., 153–57.

10. Ibid., 150–51.

11. The first "Skyscraper" was not a building but a fast horse—the winner of the 1789 Epsom Derby. The next application of the word was to the uppermost sail on a ship's mast, hoisted to catch strong winds and propel the ship even faster through the water.

12. Le Corbusier, *When the Cathedrals Were White: A Journey to the Country of Timid People* (1936; reprint, New York: Reynal and Hitchcock, 1947), 42.

13. Rem Koolhaas, *Delirious New York: A Retroactive Manifesto for Manhattan* (New York: Oxford University Press, 1978), 68.

14. Christopher Gray, "Streetscapes/The Haugwout Building; Restoring a Richly Sculpted Venetian Palace," *New York Times*, 1 January 1995.

15. Le Corbusier, *When the Cathedrals Were White*, 45.

16. Quoted in Neil Bascomb, *Higher: A Historic Race to the Sky and the Making of a City* (New York: Doubleday, 2003), 194.

17. "An Architectural Dream," *New York Times*, 11 February 1929; cited in Bascomb, *Higher*, 195.

18. Quoted in Bascomb, *Higher*, 268.

19. Quoted ibid., 271.

20. Le Corbusier, *When the Cathedrals Were White*, 41.

21. Irving Pond, *The Meaning of Architecture: An Essay in Constructive Criticism* (Boston, 1918), 202; cited in Thomas A. P. van Leeuwen, *The Skyward Trend of Thought: The Metaphysics of the American Skyscraper* (1986; reprint, Cambridge, Mass.: MIT Press, 1988), 133.

22. Claude Bragdon, *The Frozen Fountain, Being Essays on Architecture and the Art of Design in Space* (New York: Alfred A. Knopf, 1932), 724; cited in van Leeuwen, *Skyward Trend of Thought*, 133.

23. Eliel Saarinen, "A New Architectural Language for America," *The Western Architect* 32, no. 2 (February 1923): 13; cited in van Leeuwen, *Skyward Trend of Thought*, 139.

24. Quoted in van Leeuwen, *Skyward Trend of Thought*, 51.

25. Louis H. Sullivan, "The Tall Office Building Artistically Considered," in *Kindergarten Chats and Other Writings*, ed. Isabella Athey (1947; reprint, New York: Wittenborn Art Books, 1976), 206; cited in van Leeuwen, *Skyward Trend of Thought*, 122.

Sullivan put these ideas into his tall buildings: the Wainwright Building (1891), the Chicago Stock Exchange Building (1893–94), and the Guaranty Building (1895), all in Chicago, and in the New York Bayard-Condict Building (1897–99).

26. Le Corbusier, *When the Cathedrals Were White*, 36.

27. Ibid., 42.

28. Dinerstein, *Swinging the Machine*, 40–41.

29. For a discussion of Superman in 1930s America, see Lawrence W. Levine, *The Unpredictable Past: Explorations in American Cultural History* (New York: Oxford University Press, 1993), 227.

30. http://xroads.virginia.edu/ffiUG02/yeung/actioncomics/cover.html (20 October 2007).

31. To be precise, one-eighth of a mile is 660 feet. But it is not clear whether this claim of clearing a twenty-story building takes into account the kinetic energy (velocity) necessary to jump this high. For an extensive discussion, see James Kakalios, *The Physics of Superheroes* (New York: Gotham, 2005).

32. Jerry Siegel and Joe Shuster, *Action Comics* no. 1 (June 1938), 1; http://xroads.virginia.edu/ffiUG02/yeung/actioncomics/cover.html (20 October 2007).

33. Koolhaas, *Delirious New York*, 73.

34. *Chicago Defender*, 10 June 1933; cited in William J. Baker, *Jesse Owens: An American Life* (New York: Free Press, 1986), 31–32.

35. Chester L. Washington, "A Runner with Rhythm," *Pittsburgh Courier*, 18 July 1936, sec. 2.

36. "Meet the Fast-Flying Rens—in Civies," photo caption, *Pittsburgh Courier*, 6 February 1937; Chester L. Washington, "Rens' Circus Comes to Town," *Pittsburgh Courier*, 11 November 1936, sec. 2.

37. "Ski-Scraper," *Pittsburgh Courier*, 7 March 1936, sec. 2.

38. Chester L. Washington, "A Runner with Rhythm," *Pittsburgh Courier*, 18 July 1936, sec. 2.

39. David Margolick, *Beyond Glory: Joe Louis vs. Max Schmeling, and a World on the Brink* (New York: Alfred A. Knopf, 2005), 76.

40. Duke Ellington, "From Where I Lie," in *The Duke Ellington Reader*, ed. Mark Tucker (New York: Oxford University Press, 1993), 131.

41. Le Corbusier, *When the Cathedrals Were White*, 161, 159.

42. Robert Goffin, "Hot Jazz," in *The Louis Armstrong Companion: Eight Decades of Commentary*, ed. Joshua Berrett (New York: Schirmer, 1999), 60.

3. THE 1936 OLYMPICS

1. Scott Holland, "First We Take Manhattan, Then We Take Berlin: Dietrich Bonhoeffer's New York," *Crosscurrents*, www.crosscurrents.org/hollandf20.htm (19 September 2006).

2. Roy Wilkins with Tom Mathews, *Standing Fast: The Autobiography of Roy Wilkins* (New York: Viking Press, 1982), 175.

3. Arthur R. Ashe Jr., *A Hard Road to Glory: A History of the African-American Athlete, 1919–1945*, vol. 2 (New York: Warner Books, 1988), 74.

4. Quoted in Ashe, *A Hard Road to Glory*, 80.

5. In 1958, Gourdin was named the first African American Superior Court Justice in Massachusetts.

6. Ashe, *A Hard Road to Glory*, 78–79.

7. *Chicago Defender*, 5 August 1933; cited in William J. Baker, *Jesse Owens: An American Life* (New York: Free Press, 1986), 35.

8. Chester L. Washington, "Owens Thrills Penn Relays," *Pittsburgh Courier*, 2 May 1936, sec. 2.

9. Roi Ottley, *Amsterdam News*, 18 July 1936; cited in Jon Entine, *Taboo: Why Black Athletes Dominate Sports and Why We Are Afraid to Talk About It* (New York: Public Affairs, 2000), 176.

10. *Call and Post*, 1 August 1935; cited in Baker, *Jesse Owens*, 74.

11. "Joe Louis Performed Like a Master Surgeon," *Pittsburgh Courier*, 21 December 1935, sec. 2.

12. *Pittsburgh Courier*, 18 July 1936, sec. 1.

13. Paul Lowry, "Colored Boys Sports Threat," *Los Angeles Times*, 31 July 1932; cited in Entine, *Taboo*, 175.

14. Elmer A. Carter, "The Negro in College Athletics," *Opportunity* (July 1933).

15. Ashe, *Hard Road to Glory*, 85. There is some confusion as to how many African American athletes were on the team. Most sources list eighteen African American Olympians. Ashe's history cites the names of ten track and field men, two women, and five boxers; the names of the two weightlifters are not given.

16. *New York Amsterdam News*, 18 July 1936; cited in Baker, *Jesse Owens*, 71.

17. Quoted in Peter Hain, "The Politics of Sport and Apartheid," in *Sport, Culture, and Ideology*, ed. Jennifer Hargreaves (London: Routledge and Kegan Paul, 1982), 233.

18. "N.A.A.C.P. Asks A.A.U. to Abandon Olympics," *Pittsburgh Courier*, 14 December 1935, sec. 2.

19. "Joe Louis vs. Jim-Crow," *Pittsburgh Courier*, 29 February 1936, sec. 2.

20. Lewis A. Erenberg, *The Greatest Fight of Our Generation: Louis vs. Schmeling* (New York: Oxford University Press, 2006), 104.

21. Ibid.

22. Baker, *Jesse Owens*, 84.

23. "African American Athletes: African American Medalists," United States Holocaust Memorial Museum, www.ushmm.org/museum/exhibit/online/olympics/zcd065.htm.

24. Robert L. Vann, "Dave Albritton, Mack Robinson, Metcalfe Place," *Pittsburgh Courier*, 8 August 1936, sec.1.

25. Robert L. Vann, " 'Proud I'm an American,' Owens Says," *Pittsburgh Courier*, 8 August 1936, sec. 1.

26. Cited in Chris Mead, *Champion: Joe Louis, Black Hero in White America* (New York: Viking Penguin, 1986), 105.

27. Chester L. Washington, "A Runner with Rhythm," *Pittsburgh Courier*, 18 July 1936, sec. 2.

28. Robert L. Vann, "Dave Albritton, Mack Robinson Place," *Pittsburgh Courier*, 8 August 1936, sec. 1.

29. Jesse Owens with Paul Neimark, *Jesse, the Man Who Outran Hitler* (New York: Fawcett Gold Medal, 1978), 93.

30. Leni Riefenstahl, *The Sieve of Time: The Memoirs of Leni Riefenstahl* (London: Quartet, 1992), 196.

31. Clarence E. Gaines with Clint Johnson, *They Call Me Big House* (Winston-Salem: John F. Blair, 2004), 128.

32. Dean B. Cromwell, *Championship Technique in Track and Field* (New York: Whittlesey House/McGraw-Hill, 1941), 6.

33. Harry F. V. Edward, *Amsterdam News*, 29 August 1936; cited in Entine, *Taboo*, 178.

4. THE LINDY HOP TAKES TO THE AIR

1. Carl Van Vechten, *Parties: Scenes from Contemporary New York Life* (1930; reprint, New York: Bard, 1977), 158.

2. Ibid.

3. Frankie Manning and Cynthia R. Millman, *Frankie Manning: Ambassador of Lindy Hop* (Philadelphia: Temple University Press, 2007), 49.

4. Marshall Stearns and Jean Stearns, *Jazz Dance: The Story of American Vernacular Dance* (New York: Macmillan, 1968), 325. According to the Stearnses, the Lindy owes its

origins to the "Texas Tommy," introduced in 1913, consisting of a kick and hop three times on each foot (323).

5. Chip Defaa (quoting Norma Miller), in conversation with A. Scott Berg, 10 July 1990; cited in A. Scott Berg, *Lindbergh* (New York: Berkley Books, 1998), 151.

6. Stearns and Stearns, *Jazz Dance*, 316.

7. Terry Monaghan, "George Snowden," http://www.savoyballroom.com/exp/ dancefloor/savoydancers/shorty.htm (23 October 2007).

8. Thomas E. Parson, "News from New York," *American Dancer* 8 (September 1934): 10; cited in Howard Spring, "Swing and the Lindy Hop: Dance, Venue, Media, and Tradition," *American Music* 15, no. 2 (Summer 1997): 191.

9. Spring, "Swing and the Lindy Hop," 183.

10. Stanley Dance, *The World of Duke Ellington* (New York: Charles Scribner's Sons, 1970), 13.

11. "Eddie Barefield," Oral History Project, Institute of Jazz Studies, Rutgers University, Newark, N.J., 49; cited in Spring, "Swing and the Lindy Hop," 192.

12. Dance, *The World of Duke Ellington*, 13.

13. Stanley Dance, *The World of Swing* (New York: Charles Scribner's Sons, 1974), 124.

14. Andy Kirk quoted in the documentary *Born to Swing*, dir. John Jeremy, BBC Productions, 1973; quoted in Joel Dinerstein, *Swinging the Machine: Modernity, Technology, and African American Culture between the World Wars* (Amherst: University of Massachusetts Press, 2003), 59.

15. Dicky Wells and Stanley Dance, *The Night People: The Jazz Life of Dicky Wells* (Washington, D.C.: Smithsonian Institution Press, 1991), 91.

16. Quoted in Dance, *The World of Swing*, 124.

17. Rex William Stewart, *Boy Meets Horn*, ed. Claire P. Gordon (Ann Arbor: University of Michigan Press, 1991), 138.

18. The history of the term "jitterbug" is hard to pin down. Some say that black dancers called white Lindy Hoppers "jitterbugs," while others assert just the opposite. Terry Monaghan argues that the jitterbug was actually a descendant of the original Lindy (when it still resembled the Charleston) called the "collegiate/shag." William Barlow writes that among African American blues musicians the term "jitterbug" referred to the slide guitar. In an article appearing in the *New York City Enquirer* (15 November 1938) Cab Calloway (absurdly) claimed to have coined the word. Another article appearing in the *Brooklyn Eagle* (3 December 1938) stated that the word originally applied to anyone who was a lover of Calloway's music. Whatever the application, the origins of the word are certainly African American.

19. Gunther Schuller, *The Swing Era: The Development of Jazz, 1930–1945* (New York: Oxford University Press, 1989), 223.

20. Manning and Millman, *Frankie Manning*, 80–81.

21. Ibid., 74.

22. Ibid., 62.

23. Ibid., 71. Norma Miller also discusses this: "At the Savoy . . . white girls was always dancing with the black fellers. It's the way the Savoy was." Norma Miller with Evette Jensen, *Swingin' at the Savoy: The Memoir of a Jazz Dancer* (Philadelphia: Temple University Press, 1996), 78.

24. Manny Fernandez, "Where Feet Flew and the Lindy Hopped," *New York Times*, 12 March 2006.

25. Jervis Anderson, *This Was Harlem: A Cultural Portrait, 1900–1950* (New York: Farrar Straus Giroux, 1982), 308.

26. Manning and Millman, *Frankie Manning*, 62.

27. Anderson, *This Was Harlem*, 310.

28. Frankie Manning in *Savoy Style Lindy of Frankie Manning*, produced by Jerry Goralnick for the New York Swing Dance Society, dir. Mark Faulkner, 1996.

29. Some scholars claim that air steps had long been a part of African American social dance but had been prohibited at dancehalls because they were dangerous to dancers and observers. Given the detail of Manning's recollection, similar tales by Norma Miller, who was stunned to see the first air step when she returned from a European tour, the absence of any other such record, and the difficulty Manning describes in mastering a step he had never seen any one else perform, this suggestion is hard to accept. See Dinerstein, *Swinging the Machine*, 380–81 n. 18.

30. Until recently, conventional wisdom has held the year to be 1936; one 2006 article on the Savoy Ballroom gives the year as 1935, although I can find no film or photographic documentation of this claim. Fernandez, "Where Feet Flew and the Lindy Hopped." Manning does not give a definitive date in his account, but it had to have been very late 1935 or early 1936, since he remembers working on it for several weeks, beginning "sometime after the 1935 Harvest Moon Ball," which took place in August. Manning and Millman, *Frankie Manning*, 94.

31. Ibid., 97.

32. Frank Manning in *Swingin' at the Savoy: Frankie Manning's Story*, produced by Rosemary Hemp, Living Traditions, Seattle, 1995.

33. Manning and Millman, *Frankie Manning*, 99; Manning in *Swingin' at the Savoy*.

34. The Stearnses state that the old guard of the Lindy—Leon James, Leroy Jones, and Shorty Snowden—disapproved of air steps. They link the transition to an airborne Lindy to a night at the Savoy in 1937 when one of the younger generation—Al Minns—confronted Leon James with his new air steps. Stearns and Stearns, Jazz Dance, 326–27. But Manning says that Minns, who later admitted he had no idea who introduced the air step, was not yet dancing at the Savoy when Manning performed his airstep, and Leon James, who was on tour in Europe, also missed seeing Manning's showstopper. Manning and Millman, Frankie Manning, 102.

35. Manning and Millman, Frankie Manning, 102, 176.

36. Morgan and Marvin Smith photographed Manning throwing Ann Johnson over his head while dancing at Big George's Tavern, Corona, Long Island, New York. The photograph appeared in Life, 8 July 1940.

37. Miller, Swingin' at the Savoy, 62.

38. Manning and Millman, Frankie Manning, 101.

39. Miller, Swingin' at the Savoy, 71.

40. Manning and Millman, Frankie Manning, 75.

41. Ibid., 255. Most of these films are included in the Ernie Smith Jazz Film Collection 1894–1979, Archives Center, National Museum of American History, which includes others not listed in Manning's book or in other sources I have consulted and referenced in this chapter. In reviewing this extensive collection of dance films, I saw none with air steps dating from before 1936.

42. Miller, Swingin' at the Savoy, 62.

43. Manning and Millman, Frankie Manning, 142.

44. Amsterdam News, 10 April 1937; cited in Thomas Cripps, Slow Fade to Black: The Negro in American Film, 1900–1942 (New York: Oxford University Press, 1977), 262.

45. Manning and Millman, Frankie Manning, 153.

46. Manning and Millman, Frankie Manning, 89–90.

47. Robert P. Crease, "Last of the Lindy Hoppers," Village Voice, 25 August 1987.

48. Manning and Millman, Frankie Manning, 165.

49. William Murtha, "20,000 See Engaged Couple Win Ball Title," New York Daily News, 29 August 1940; "20,000 See Ball Finals; Big Winners to Wed," New York Daily News, 27 August 1942; cited in Dinerstein, Swinging the Machine, 274.

50. David W. Stowe, Swing Changes: Big-Band Jazz in New Deal America (Cambridge: Harvard University Press, 1994), 41.

51. Neil Leonard, *Jazz and the White Americans: The Acceptance of a New Art Form* (Chicago: University of Chicago Press, 1962), 143.

52. Stearns and Stearns, *Jazz Dance*, 323.

53. " 'Jitterbug' Dying Out, Dance Masters Agree," *New York Times*, 1 August 1939, emphasis added.

54. John Martin, *New York Times*, 10 January 1943.

55. Jerry Wexler and David Ritz, *Rhythm and the Blues: A Life in American Music* (New York: Knopf, 1993), 23.

56. Stearns and Stearns, *Jazz Dance*, 329, 330.

57. Press release, Edna Guy Programs, Dance Collection, New York Public Library; cited in Julia L. Foulkes, *Modern Bodies: Dance and American Modernism from Martha Graham to Alvin Ailey* (Chapel Hill: University of North Carolina Press, 2002), 65, 199 n. 45.

58. *Life*, 8 August 1938, 57; *New York Times*, 30 May 1938, and 31 May 1938.

59. E. B. White, *One Man's Meat* (New York: Harper and Row, 1944), 62.

60. *Pittsburgh Courier*, 28 January 1939.

61. "Building Quivers as Jitterbugs Vie," *New York Times*, 21 May 1939, sec.1.

62. Dinerstein, *Swinging the Machine*, 303.

63. Playbill, Harvard Theatre Collection, Nathan Marsh Pusey Library, Cambridge, Mass.

64. Ibid.

65. Ibid.

66. Stearns and Stearns, *Jazz Dance*, 332; Manning and Millman, *Frankie Manning*, 161.

67. Stearns and Stearns, *Jazz Dance*, 327; Jacqui Malone, *Steppin' on the Blues: The Visible Rhythms of African American Dance* (Chicago: University of Illinois Press, 1996), 103–4.

68. *Life*, 28 December 1936, 30–31.

69. *Life*, 23 August 1943.

70. Van Vechten, *Parties*, 157.

71. Manning and Millman, *Frankie Manning*, 54.

72. "The Lindy Hop," *Life*, 23 August 1943, 43–44.

73. Dinerstein, *Swinging the Machine*, 277.

74. Joel Dinerstein, "Backfield in Motion: The Transformation of the NFL by Black Culture," in *In the Game: Race, Identity, and Sports in the Twentieth Century*, ed. Amy Bass (New York: Palgrave, 2005), 169.

75. William Carlos Williams, *In the American Grain* (1925; reprint, New York: New Directions, 1956), 209.

5. THE JOINT IS JUMPING

1. Gunther Schuller, *The Swing Era: The Development of Jazz, 1930–1945* (New York: Oxford University Press, 1989), 772.

2. Gunther Schuller, *Early Jazz: Its Roots and Musical Development* (1968; reprint, New York: Oxford University Press, 1986), 284.

3. Ibid., 289.

4. Ibid., 287.

5. On tour in the East following this battle, in which the Moten band did not do well, Moten bought forty arrangements by Benny Carter and Horace Henderson, which greatly affected the band's development. Ibid., 295, 305–6.

6. Ibid., 316.

7. Schuller, *Swing Era*, 226.

8. Quoted in Albert Murray, *Stomping the Blues* (New York: 1976; reprint, Da Capo, 1987), 170. According to Schuller, "Six or Seven Times" is featured in the Chocolate Dandies 1929 recording, arranged by Don Redman, with Fats Waller at the piano. Schuller, *The Swing Years*, 237. In the documentary film *The Last of the Blue Devils*, Joe Turner claims that the piece was based on a Basie standard called "Blue Balls," which for obvious reasons Basie renamed. Neil Leonard, in *Jazz and the White Americans* (Chicago: University of Chicago, 1962), says a "large part" of the piece "was taken from a Don Redman arrangement" (124).

9. Sadly, Basie had signed a contract with no provision for royalties and earned nothing from record sales. John Hammond in Bill Crow, *Jazz Anecdotes* (New York: Oxford University Press, 1993), 63.

10. Brian Rust, *Jazz Records, 1897–1942* (1969; reprint, Chigwell, Essex: Storyville Publishers, 1975); *Jazz and Ragtime Records, 1897–1942*, 6th ed., with CD-ROM (Highlands Ranch, Colo.: Mainspring Press, 2007).

11. Louis Jordan made a career of jump tunes and pieces that relied on a "shuffle" beat, achieved by subdividing each beat into three and emphasizing the first and third segments of the beat. The terminology disappeared from titles by the 1940s, but the shuffle beat remained in tunes called "jump" tunes.

12. "A lot of tunes were called stomps, and a lot of bands were called stomp bands," according to Count Basie. Albert Murray, *Good Morning Blues: The Autobiography of Count Basie* (New York: Random House, 1985), 6.

13. Ibid., 120.

14. "Parlor Social Stomp" (1926), "Jubilee Stomp" (1928), "Cotton Club Stomp" (1929), "Swanee Shuffle" (1929), "Syncopated Shuffle" (1929), "Tough Truckin' " (1935), and "Showboat Shuffle" (1935) are but a few instances of the Ellington stomp, truckin', and shuffle repertory.

15. Murray, *Stomping the Blues*, 97. In conversation Murray recalled some tunes that seemed more like jumps than stomps, even when they weren't called "jumps." Earl Hines's 1933 "Cavernism," for instance, is an upbeat, riff-based, hard-driving piece with a jumping bass line. Albert Murray, conversation with author, 30 August 1996; Earl Hines, "Cavernism," Archives of Jazz 3801022 (1933). The Earl Hines band broadcast from Chicago as far as Kansas City, where he could very well have influenced Kansas City musicians.

16. Encyclopedias are universally unspecific in defining "jump." Hugues Panassié and Madeleine Gautier's *Guide to Jazz*, trans. Desmond Flower (Boston: Houghton Mifflin, 1956), calls it a "synonym for 'swing' " (156). Barry Kernfeld in the *New Grove Dictionary of Jazz* (London: Macmillan Press, 1988) calls it a "style of jazz related to swing . . . a precursor of rhythm and blues" (639).

17. John Chilton, *Let the Good Times Roll: The Story of Louis Jordan and His Music* (London: Quartet Books, 1992), 63.

18. Murray, *Good Morning Blues*, 196.

19. Frankie Manning and Cynthia R. Millman, *Frankie Manning: Ambassador of the Lindy Hop* (Philadelphia: Temple University Press, 2007), 132.

20. Dizzy Gillespie with Al Fraser, *To Be or Not . . . to Bop: Memoirs of Dizzy Gillespie* (1979; reprint, New York: Da Capo, 1985), 166.

21. Burt Korall, *Drummin' Men: The Heartbeat of Jazz, The Swing Years* (New York: Schirmer Books, 1990), 168.

22. Albert Murray, conversation with author, 30 August 1996.

23. Brian Priestley, in *Jazz: the Essential Companion*, suggests that the jump bands were the "first to start emphasizing the up-beat . . . which [was] more pronounced in what became rhythm-and-blues." Ian Carr, Digby Fairweather, and Brian Priestley, *Jazz: The Essential Companion* (New York: Prentice Hall Press, 1987), 274.

24. Jerry Wexler and David Ritz, *Rhythm and the Blues* (New York: Knopf, 1993), 79.

25. David W. Stowe, *Swing Changes: Big-Band Jazz in New Deal America* (Cambridge: Harvard University Press, 1994), 194.

26. Schuller, *Swing Era*, 214.

27. Ibid., 715–16, 424, 461. Schuller also makes note of Skeets Tolbert and his

musicians, who recorded forty sides between 1939 and 1941, calling them a "well-disciplined clean-playing jump band" (776).

28. Wexler, *Rhythm and the Blues*, 63.

29. Chilton, *Let the Good Times Roll*, 61, 63.

30. Charles Keil, *Urban Blues* (Chicago: University of Chicago Press, 1966), 64.

31. All cited in Chilton, *Let the Good Times Roll*, 138, 136, 126.

32. Wexler, *Rhythm and the Blues*, 63.

33. Quoted in Stanley Dance, *The World of Swing* (New York: Charles Scribner's Sons, 1974), 278.

34. Johnny Otis, *Upside Your Head! Rhythm and Blues on Central Avenue* (Hanover: University Press of New England, 1993), 112.

35. Ibid., 111–12.

36. George Lipsitz, "Creating Dangerously: The Blues Life of Johnny Otis," ibid., xxiv.

6. "THAT'S NOT BASKETBALL"

1. The Original Celtics were formed in 1918 from a disbanded New York Celtics team; they are unrelated to the Boston team of the same name.

2. Robert W. Peterson, *Cages to Jump Shots: Pro Basketball's Early Years* (New York: Oxford University Press, 1990), 116.

3. Jon Entine, "The 'Scheming, Flashy Trickiness' of Basketball's Media Darlings, the Philadelphia 'Hebrews,'" http://www.jewishmag.com/45mag/basketball/basketball.htm (28 October 2007).

4. Peterson, *Cages to Jumpshots*, 114.

5. James Naismith, *Basketball: Its Origin and Development* (Lincoln: University of Nebraska Press, 1996), 44.

6. Ibid., 46.

7. Ibid., 50.

8. Ron Thomas, *They Cleared the Lane: The NBA's Black Pioneers* (Lincoln: University of Nebraska Press, 2002), 5.

9. Peterson, *Cages to Jump Shots*, 84, 37.

10. Ibid., 110.

11. The National Basketball Committee governed college sports, and professional teams tended to follow the college rules changes. The National Basketball League gave the home team the option of using the center jump in the 1937–38 season, but without it the higher scores and faster pace proved to increase the game's appeal.

12. Arthur R. Ashe Jr., *A Hard Road to Glory: The African-American Athlete in Basketball* (New York: 1988; reprint, Amistad, 1993), 12.

13. Naismith, *Basketball*, 86.

14. Ibid., 63.

15. John B. McLendon Jr., *Fast Break Basketball: Fundamentals and Fine Points* (West Nyack, N.Y.: Parker Publishing Company, 1965), 3.

16. Naismith, *Basketball*, 80.

17. McLendon, *Fast Break Basketball*, 5.

18. Ibid., 18.

19. Ibid., 10.

20. Ellsworth, "The Secret Game: Defying the Color Line," in *Perspectives*, http://www.dukemagazine.duke.edu/alumni/dm6/secret_txt.html (28 October 2007).

21. Ibid.; "The Secret Game of 1944," *Duke University Medical Alumni News*, Spring 1998, http://development.mc.duke.edu/medalum/man/sp98/man1_5.html.

22. Originally a football player, Gaines was the head football coach from 1946 to 1949, when he became the head basketball coach.

23. Clarence E. Gaines with Clint Johnson, *They Call Me Big House* (Winston-Salem: John F. Blair, 2004), 127.

24. Calvin Irvin, telephone interview with author, 11 March 1996.

25. Gaines, *They Call Me Big House*, 89–90.

26. Thomas, *They Cleared the Lane*, 166.

27. Gaines, *They Call Me Big House*, 122.

28. Ibid., 122.

29. Clarence Gaines, telephone interview with author, 5 March 1996.

30. Coaches Piggy Lambert at Purdue and Frank Keaney at Rhode Island are sometimes said to have developed fast break basketball in the 1920s and 1930s, but it is difficult to imagine the fast break prior to 1937, when basketball was still essentially a half-court game. Neil D. Isaacs, *All the Moves: A History of College Basketball* (New York: J. B. Lippincott, 1975), 57–60.

31. *Pittsburgh Courier*, 11 January 1940.

32. Ibid.

33. "Elks Show Class as Rens Win, 40–30," *Pittsburgh Courier*, 14 December 1935; Chester L. Washington, "Rens on a Rampage," *Pittsburgh Courier*, 7 January 1939. Fifty years later people used the same words to describe Michael Jordan.

34. Frank Marshall Davis, *Livin' the Blues: Memoirs of a Black Journalist and Poet*, ed. John Edgar Tidwell (Madison: University of Wisconsin Press, 1991), 232.

35. "Keeping Ball Over 6 Minutes Rens' All-Time Holding Record?" *Pittsburgh Courier*, 7 January 1939.

36. "John Isaacs on 2005 Hall of Fame Ballot," http://www.blackathlete.net/artman/publish/article_0471.shtml.

37. Bill Russell and Taylor Branch, *Second Wind: The Memoirs of an Opinionated Man* (New York: Random House, 1979), 64–65.

38. Peterson, *Cages to Jump Shots*, 109.

39. Quoted ibid.

40. Quoted ibid.

41. Walter Meanwell, *The Science of Basketball for Men* (1924; reprint, Madison: University of Wisconsin, 1942); J. Craig Ruby, *Coaching Basketball: A Textbook by J. Craig Ruby* (self-published, 1931); Forrest C. Allen, *Better Basketball: Technique, Tactics, and Tales* (New York: McGraw Hill, 1937).

42. Quoted in "Many's the One," *Sports Illustrated*, 12 February 1996, 20.

43. Stephen R. Fox, *Big Leagues: Professional Baseball, Football, and Basketball in National Memory* (New York: William Morrow, 1994), 19, 21.

44. Isaacs, *All the Moves*, 115.

45. John Christgau, *The Origins of the Jump Shot: Eight Men Who Shook the World of Basketball* (Lincoln: University of Nebraska Press, 1999), 201, 204.

46. Isaacs, *All the Moves*, 262.

47. Ibid., 222.

48. "Paul Joseph Arizin," *NBA Encyclopedia: Playoff Edition*, http://www.nba.com/history/players/arizin_bio.html.

49. Cristgau, *Jump Shot*, 28.

50. Ibid., 53.

51. For instance, a story about a 1937 Virginia State College win reads: "The second half was a repetition of the first, with the lanky Trojans out-reaching and out-jumping the shorter Shaw team to make all sorts of hair-raising baskets." "Bailey Leads Va. State to Victory," *Pittsburgh Courier*, 30 January 1937.

52. *Pittsburgh Courier*, 8 April 1939.

53. Thomas, *They Cleared the Lane*, 18.

54. Cum Posey, "Posey's Points," *Pittsburgh Courier*, 28 January 1939.

55. *Pittsburgh Courier*, 6 March 1937.

56. Ashe, *Hard Road to Glory: Basketball*, 20; Thomas, *They Cleared the Lane*, 14.

57. Ashe, *Hard Road to Glory: Basketball*, 24. In 2000 King was inducted into the Long Island University Hall of Fame.

58. *Pittsburgh Courier*, 13 March 1937.

59. " 'Doc' Kelker Scores 39 Points in 2 Games for Reserve '5,' " *Pittsburgh Courier*, 27 February 1937; "Kelker Helps Western Reserve," *Pittsburgh Courier*, 26 December 1936.

60. Harry Walker, "Kelker Stars on Court for Reserve," *Pittsburgh Courier*, 26 December 1936.

61. "Pittsburgh's Strong 'Y' Five," *Pittsburgh Courier*, 28 January 1939.

62. Cristgau, *Origins of the Jump Shot*, 92.

63. Clarence Gaines, telephone interview with author, 5 March 1996.

64. Ibid.

65. Ibid.

66. Charles Salzberg, *From Set Shot to Slam Dunk: The Glory Days of Basketball in the Words of Those Who Played It* (1987; reprint, New York: Dell Publishing, 1990), 51, emphasis added. Davies also describes the "midwestern style of play, which was run and go." Davies came from Pennsylvania ("the Midwest . . . was considered just outside of New York"), where he played "full-court basketball. In the East, they were bringing the ball down slowly, which made it half-court basketball." Ibid.

67. Alex Sachare, *The Naismith Memorial Basketball Hall of Fame's 100 Greatest Basketball Players of All Time* (New York: Byron Preiss Multimedia, 1997), 64.

68. Quoted in Ken Shouler, *The Experts Pick Basketball's Best 50 Players in the Last 50 Years* (Lenexa, Kans.: Addax Publishing, 1998), 60.

69. http://www.nba.com/history/players/maravich_bio.html (12 November 2007).

70. Russell, *Second Wind*, 63–65.

71. Walt Frazier and Ira Berkow, *Rockin' Steady: A Guide to Basketball and Cool* (New York: Warner, 1974), 105.

72. Ibid.

73. John Taylor, *The Rivalry: Bill Russell, Wilt Chamberlain, and the Golden Age of Basketball* (New York: Random House, 2005), 42, 46.

74. Ibid., 80.

75. Shirley Povich, "Basketball Is for the Birds," *Sports Illustrated*, 8 December 1958; cited in Taylor, *The Rivalry*, 80.

76. Taylor, *The Rivalry*, 55; Russell, *Second Wind*.

77. Taylor, *The Rivalry*, 78.

78. Ibid., 26–31.

79. Thomas, *They Cleared the Lane*, 88–92.

80. John Edgar Wideman, *Brothers and Keepers* (1984; reprint, New York: Vintage Books, 1995), 226.

81. Nelson George, *Elevating the Game: Black Men and Basketball* (New York: Harper Collins, 1992), xviii.

82. Gaines, conversation with author, 6 March 1996.

83. George, *Elevating the Game*, xv.

84. Kareem Abdul-Jabbar and Peter Knobler, *Giant Steps* (New York: Bantam, 1983), 160.

85. Pete Axthelm, *The City Game: Basketball from the Garden to the Playgrounds* (Cutchogue, N.Y.: Buccaneer Books, 1970), 127.

86. Fran Blinebury, "Glory Road," Houston Chronicle, 10 January 2006.

87. Gaines, *They Call Me Big House*, 219.

88. Dave Krieger, "Sports Better for Pair's Bond," Rocky Mountain News, 10 January 2006.

89. Steve Kelley, "Texas Western's Crown Helped Open Doorways," Seattle Times, 10 January 2006.

90. Gene Menez, "Scorecard: A Night to Remember," Sports Illustrated, 23 January 2006, 20–21.

91. Tim Dahlberg, "Glory Road Looks at a Team Trying to Win, Not Make a Statement," Associated Press, 10 January 2006, National Association of Basketball Coaches, http://nabc.cstv.com/sports/m-baskbl/spec-rel/011006aac.html.

92. Ibid.; "Enid Honors Legendary Basketball Coach," Associated Press, 13 October 2005.

93. Nevil Shed, in conversations with author at the University of Texas at San Antonio, 1999–2000.

94. Pat Riley, interviewed in Dahlberg, "Glory Road."

95. Jon Robinson, "Starting Five: The True Story behind Glory Road and the Texas Western Miners," http://sports.ign.com/articles/679/679216p1.html (6 December 2007).

96. Andrew Bagnato, "Who's Hall of Famer Wooden Rooting For? The Old School," Austin American-Statesman, 30 March 2000, sec. C.

97. See "Be Like Mike? Michael Jordan and the Pedagogy of Desire," in *Signifyin(g), Sanctifyin', and Slam Dunking*, ed. Gena Dagel Caponi (Amherst: University of Massachusetts Press, 1999), 407–16.

98. Wilson's remarks on the "soul focal moment" were made at a conference of the Center for the Study of Black Music, New Orleans, 1994. See Olly Wilson, "Black

Music as an Art Form," *Black Music Research Journal* 3 (1983): 1–22; Olly Wilson, "The Association of Movement and Music as a Manifestation of a Black Conceptual Approach to Music-making," in *More Than Dancing: Essays on Afro-American Music and Musicians*, ed. Irene V. Jackson (Westport, Conn.: Greenwood Press, 1985), 9–23.

99. Taylor, *The Rivalry*, 61.

100. Cited in Greil Marcus, *Dead Elvis: A Chronicle of a Cultural Obsession* (Cambridge: Harvard University Press, 1991), 38.

101. Ralph Ellison, "The Charlie Christian Story," *Shadow and Act* (1953; reprint, New York: Vintage Books, 1972), 234.

102. Much of this argument, and some of its phrasing, results from conversation and correspondence with Clark Dougan of the University of Massachusetts Press, particularly in e-mails on 21 and 22 May 2007.

7. THE BROWN BOMBER

1. Quoted in David Margolick and Douglas Century, "Fight Club," *Notebook: A New Read on Jewish Culture*, http://www.nextbook.org/cultural/feature.html?id=220 (29 October 2007).

2. Chris Mead, *Champion: Joe Louis, Black Hero in White America* (New York: Viking Penguin, 1986), 20.

3. Ibid., 23.

4. Joe Louis, with Edna and Art Rust Jr., *Joe Louis: My Life* (New York: Harcourt Brace Jovanovich, 1978), 32.

5. Lewis A. Erenberg, *The Greatest Fight of Our Generation: Louis vs. Schmeling* (New York: Oxford University Press, 2006), 23–24.

6. Ibid., 30.

7. Richard Bak, *Joe Louis: The Great Black Hope* (1996; reprint, New York: Da Capo, 1998), 38.

8. Louis, *My Life*, 32.

9. Erenberg, *The Greatest Fight*, 30.

10. Louis, *My Life*, 37.

11. Mead, *Champion*, 6.

12. Louis, *My Life*, 39.

13. Ibid., 41.

14. Ibid., 48–49.

15. Mead, *Champion*, 50–51.

16. Ibid., 49.

17. Louis, *My Life*, 55.

18. Mead, *Champion*, 38.

19. Louis, *My Life*, 50.

20. Adapted from Mead, *Champion*, 52.

21. David Margolick, *Beyond Glory: Joe Louis vs. Max Schmeling, and a World on the Brink* (New York: Alfred A. Knopf, 2005), 81–83.

22. Cited in Mead, *Champion*, 62–63.

23. Erenberg, *The Greatest Fight*, 41.

24. Cited in Mead, *Champion*, 64.

25. Cited ibid., 68.

26. "Joe Favored to Stop Basque: See $150,000 Gate," *Pittsburgh Courier*, 14 December 1935, sec. 2.

27. "Joe Louis Hailed as 'Perfect Fighter' Following 4-Round Knockout of Uzcudun; Cancel Bout in Cuba," *Pittsburgh Courier*, 21 December 1935, sec. 1.

28. "Joe Louis Performed Like a Master Surgeon," *Pittsburgh Courier*, 21 December 1935, sec. 2.

29. Nat Fleischer, "Better Get Those White Hopes Ready!" *Ring* 14 (September 1935): 14; cited in Erenberg, *The Greatest Fight*, 43–44.

30. Cited in Mead, *Champion*, 118–19.

31. Louis, *My Life*, 109.

32. "Lunceford Is My Favorite," *Pittsburgh Courier*, 25 January 1936, sec. 2.

33. "Taps for Basque—and the Joe Louis 'Truck,'" *Pittsburgh Courier*, 21 December 1935, sec. 1.

34. S. T. Holland, "The Inside Story of How John Roxborough Met Louis Bared," *Pittsburgh Courier*, 1 February 1936, sec. 2.

35. "Hotel Rates and Food Costs Take Wings Suddenly," *Pittsburgh Courier*, 20 June 1936, sec. 1.

36. Edgar T. Rouzeau, "Harlem in Mourning over Louis Setback; Deny Disturbances," *Pittsburgh Courier*, 26 June 1936, sec. 2.

37. Edgar T. Rouzeau, "'Joe Agreed to Stall for 3 Rounds,' Says Trainer," *Pittsburgh Courier*, 27 June 1936, sec. 2.

38. Louis, *My Life*, 90.

39. "Louis-Braddock Bout Nears O.K. Stage," *Pittsburgh Courier*, 28 November 1936.

40. Cited in Mead, *Champion*, 120.

41. Louis, *My Life*, 108.

42. Erenberg, *The Greatest Fight*, 123; Margolick, *Beyond Glory*, 225.

43. Louis, *My Life*, 114.

44. William G. Nun, "'Jim in a Fog,' Declares Nunn," *Pittsburgh Courier*, 26 June 1937.

45. Ibid.; Chester L. Washington, "Dynamite Right Too Much for 'Irish Terror,'" *Pittsburgh Courier*, 23 June 1937.

46. Louis, *My Life*, 119.

47. William G. Nunn, "Nunn Describes South Side As It Goes Mad after Joe Louis Victory," *Pittsburgh Courier*, 26 June 1937, sec. 1.

48. Louis, *My Life*, 118–19.

49. Cited in Mead, *Champion*, 137.

50. Margolick, *Beyond Glory*, 91.

51. Erenberg, *The Greatest Fight*, 143.

52. Mead, *Champion*, 140–45.

53. Erenberg, *The Greatest Fight*, 140.

54. Margolick, *Beyond Glory*, 7.

55. Ibid., 288–89.

56. Erenberg, *The Greatest Fight*, 142.

57. Margolick, *Beyond Glory*, 293.

58. *Chicago Defender*, 2 July 1938; cited in Margolick, *Beyond Glory*, 295.

59. *New Orleans Item*, 27 June 1938; cited in Margolick, *Beyond Glory*, 293.

60. Doris Kearns Goodwin, *No Ordinary Time* (New York: Simon and Schuster, 1994), 240.

61. Margolick, *Beyond Glory*, 5, 289–91.

62. *Pittsburgh Courier*, 2 July 1938; cited in Margolick, *Beyond Glory*, 297.

63. Erenberg, *The Greatest Fight*, 145.

64. *Pittsburgh Courier*, 2 July 1938; cited in Margolick, *Beyond Glory*, 321.

65. Mead, *Champion*, 153.

66. Cited ibid., 153–54.

67. Ibid., 157–58.

68. Ibid., 158.

69. "Fight of the Century—Joe Louis vs [sic] Jim-Crow," *Pittsburgh Courier*, 29 February 1936, sec. 2.

70. Margolick, *Beyond Glory*, 316–17.

71. Ibid., 314.

72. Wright, "High Tide in Harlem," *New Masses*, 28 July 1938, 18–19.

73. Erenberg, *The Greatest Fight*, 148–49.

74. Ibid., 149.

75. Mead, *Champion*, 174.

76. Ibid., 218.

77. Erenberg, *The Greatest Fight*, 52–53.

78. "Joe Louis and Jesse Owens," *The Crisis*, August 1935, 241.

79. Cited in Mead, *Champion*, 201.

80. Gerald Early, "The Hero of the Blues," in *Signifyin(g), Sanctifyin', and Slam Dunking*, ed. Gena Dagel Caponi (Amherst: University of Massachusetts Press, 1999), 383.

81. Ibid., 382.

82. Mead, *Champion*, ix.

83. Chester L. Washington, "Ches' Sez," *Pittsburgh Courier*, 29 February 1936, sec. 2.

84. E. Franklin Frazier, *Negro Youth at the Crossways: Their Personality Development in the Middle States* (1940; reprint, New York: Schocken, 1967), 178–79.

85. George Schuyler, *Pittsburgh Courier*, 27 June 1936, sec. 1.

86. Louis, *My Life*, 63.

87. Cited in Mead, *Champion*, 196.

88. Hazel Rowley, "Richard Wright: The Life and Times," http://www.jerryjazz musician.com/linernotes/richard_wright.html#"King%20Joe" (30 October 2007).

89. Quoted in Richard Bak, "Joe Louis: The Great Black Hope," 1996, http://www .cyberboxingzone.com/boxing/joebak.htm (16 November 2006).

90. Richard Wright, "Joe Louis Uncovers Dynamite," *New Masses*, 8 October 1935, 162, 163.

91. Mead, *Champion*, 197–98.

92. Rouzeau, "Harlem in Mourning."

93. Maya Angelou, *I Know Why the Caged Bird Sings*; cited in Mead, *Champion*, 191–92.

94. Gerald Early, *Tuxedo Junction: Essays on American Culture* (New York: Ecco Press, 1989), 179.

95. Joe Louis Barrow Jr. and Barbara Munder, *Joe Louis: Fifty Years An American Hero* (New York: McGraw Hill, 1988), 143.

96. William L. Van Deburg, *Black Camelot: African-American Culture Heroes in Their Times, 1960–1980* (Chicago: University of Chicago Press, 1997), 100.

97. Dizzy Gillespie with Al Fraser, *To Be or Not . . . to Bop: Memoirs of Dizzy Gillespie* (1979; reprint, New York: Da Capo, 1985), 289.

98. Quoted in David Shields, *Black Planet: Facing Race During an NBA Season* (New York: Crown, 1999), 84. For a discussion of political awareness in the Louis post-victory

celebrations, see Erenberg, *The Greatest Fight*, 153–54; Lawrence W. Levine, *Black Culture and Black Consciousness* (New York: Oxford University Press, 1977), 433–40.

99. Mead, *Champion*, 159.

8. RACIAL UPLIFT AND CULTURAL PERMISSION

1. Hannibal B. Johnson, *Black Wall Street: From Riot to Renaissance in Tulsa's Historic Greenwood District* (Austin: Eakin Press, 1998), 4.

2. *Daily Oklahoman*, 2 June 1921; cited ibid., 51.

3. Ibid., 46, 48.

4. Ibid., 47.

5. Ibid., 53.

6. Kinney Booker, interview with Terry Gross, "Fresh Air," National Public Radio, 23 February 2000; other information from Brent Staples, "Unearthing a Riot," *New York Times Magazine*, 19 December 1999, 62–69.

7. Walter White, "Defending Home and Hearth: Walter White Recalls the 1906 Atlanta Race Riot," History Matters: The U.S. Survey Course on the Web, http://www.historymatters.gmu.edu/d/104/ (29 September 2006).

8. Russell Baker, *Growing Up* (1982; reprint, New York: Signet, 1984), 260.

9. Richard Wright, "The Ethics of Living Jim Crow," in *American Stuff: An Anthology of Prose and Verse by Members of the Federal Writers' Project* (New York: Viking Press, 1937), 44.

10. For discussion and examples of early resistance, see Robin D. G. Kelley, " 'We Are Not What We Seem': Rethinking Black Working-Class Opposition in the Jim Crow South," and Kenneth W. Goings and Gerald L. Smith, " 'Unhidden' Transcripts: Memphis and African American Agency, 1862–1920" *New African American Urban History*, ed. Kenneth W. Goings and Raymond A. Mohl (Thousand Oaks, Calif.: Sage Publications, 1996), 187–239, 142–66.

11. In the lives and culture of oppressed groups is a "hidden transcript" of "daily conversations, folklore, jokes, songs, and other cultural practices" that challenges those in power and often arises in disguised form "on stage," in public spaces controlled by the powerful. See James C. Scott, *Domination and the Arts of Resistance: Hidden Transcripts* (New Haven: Yale University Press, 1991); also Scott, *Weapons of the Weak: Everyday Forms of Peasant Resistance* (New Haven: Yale University Press, 1985).

12. Quoted in Jervis Anderson, *This Was Harlem: A Cultural Portrait, 1900–1950* (New York: Farrar Straus Giroux, 1982), 74.

13. Ralph Matthews, "The Negro Theatre—A Dodo Bird," in *Negro: An Anthology*, ed. Nancy Cunard (1933; reprint, New York: Frederick Ungar Publishing Company, 1970), 195. Surveying Harlem, the white heiress Nancy Cunard praised the Lindy Hop in terms terrifying to those espousing dignity for the good of the race. "The Lindy is the more astounding as it is as violent (and as beautiful)," she wrote. Nancy Cunard, "Harlem Reviewed," ibid., 49.

14. Frank Marshall Davis, *Livin' the Blues: Memoirs of a Black Journalist and Poet*, ed. John Edgar Tidwell (Madison: University of Wisconsin Press, 1991), 34.

15. Countee Cullen, "Review of *The Weary Blues*," *Opportunity*, February 1926, 73–74.

16. Cited in Richard K. Barksdale, *Langston Hughes: The Poet and His Critics* (Chicago: American Library Association, 1977), 25.

17. Langston Hughes, "The Negro Artist and the Racial Mountain," *The Nation*, June 1926; cited in Nathan Irvin Huggins, ed., *Voices from the Harlem Renaissance* (New York: Oxford University Press, 1976), 308.

18. Morroe Berger, "Jazz: Resistance to the Diffusion of a Culture Pattern," in *American Music: From Storyville to Woodstock*, ed. Charles Nanry (New Brunswick, N.J.: Transaction Books, 1972), 16. In the same article Berger noted, "The most prominent chroniclers of Negro achievement in America, Benjamin Brawley, W. E. B. Du Bois and Edwin R. Embree, scarcely mention jazz in their books" (16).

19. Ibid., 15.

20. For a full discussion of uplift ideologies, see Kevin K. Gaines, *Uplifting the Race: Black Leadership, Politics, and Culture in the Twentieth Century* (Chapel Hill: University of North Carolina Press, 1996).

21. Hughes, "The Negro Artist and the Racial Mountain," 300.

22. Quoted in Julia L. Foulkes, *Modern Bodies: Dance and American Modernism from Martha Graham to Alvin Ailey* (Chapel Hill: University of North Carolina Press, 2002), 74.

23. Foulkes, *Modern Bodies*, 166.

24. *New York Times*, 19 June 1988; cited ibid., 167.

25. *Amsterdam News*, 29 April 1944; cited in Julia L. Foulkes, "Dancing in America: Modern Dance and Cultural Nationalism, 1925–1950" (Ph.D. diss., University of Massachusetts, 1997), 153.

26. Martha Graham, "The American Dance," in *Modern Dance*, ed. Virginia Stewart (New York: E. Weyhe, 1935), 103–4; cited in Joel Dinerstein, *Swinging the Machine: Modernity, Technology, and African American Culture between the World Wars* (Amherst: University of Massachusetts Press, 2003), 36.

27. Lawrence W. Levine, *The Unpredictable Past: Explorations in American Cultural History* (New York: Oxford University Press, 1993), 92.

9. JUMP JIM CROW

1. See Samuel A. Floyd Jr., *The Power of Black Music: Interpreting Its History from Africa to the United States* (New York: Oxford University Press, 1995), 70; Albert J. Raboteau, *Slave Religion: The "Invisible Institution" in the Antebellum South* (New York: Oxford University Press, 1978), 225.

2. John S. Wright, "The New Negro Poet and the Nachal Man: Sterling Brown's Folk Odyssey," *Black American Literature Forum* 23 (Spring 1989): 104.

3. Stephen Henderson, *Understanding the New Black Poetry: Black Speech and Black Music as Poetic References* (New York: William Morrow, 1973), 44.

4. David Stowe writes, "Defining swing required recourse to the social setting in which the music was performed or consumed, or to the political ideas it seemed to express." David W. Stowe, *Swing Changes: Big-Band Jazz in New Deal America* (Cambridge: Harvard University Press, 1994), 5.

5. Clarence Major, *Dictionary of Afro-American Slang* (New York: International Publishers, 1970), 72; Edward Kennedy Ellington, *Music Is My Mistress* (Garden City, N.Y.: Doubleday and Company, 1973), 179. In his introduction to the anthology *Understanding the New Black Poetry* (44), Stephen Henderson coined the term "mascon" to describe words such as "jump"—words with "*a massive concentration of Black experiential energy which powerfully affects the meaning of Black speech,* Black song, and Black poetry."

6. Quoted in Margaret McKee and Fred Chisenhall, *Beale Black and Blue* (Baton Rouge: Louisiana State University Press, 1981), 34–35; cited in Shane White and Graham White, *Stylin': African American Expressive Culture from Its Beginnings to the Zoot Suit* (Ithaca: Cornell University Press, 1998), 167.

7. Bessie Jones and Bess Lomax Hawes, *Step It Down: Games, Plays, Songs, and Stories from the Afro-American Heritage* (1972; reprint, Athens: University of Georgia Press, 1972), 44.

8. Ibid., 10.

9. "Miss Lucy! / Mama say to send a chew tobacco, / She'll pay you back tomorrow. / Hooray! Let's jump!" Ibid., 173.

10. Ibid., 53, 61.

11. It might be worthwhile to explore connections to jumping rope. Roger Abrahams noted in his *Jump-Rope Rhymes: A Dictionary* (Austin: University of Texas Press,

1969) that until relatively recently the pastime of jumping rope was exclusively a boys' activity.

12. Charles W. Chesnutt, "The Goophered Grapevine," in *Collected Stories of Charles W. Chesnutt* (New York: Penguin, 1992), 9, emphasis added.

13. Cited in Arthur R. Ashe Jr., *A Hard Road to Glory: A History of the African American Athlete, 1619–1918*, vol. 1 (New York: Amistad Press, 1993), 58.

14. Jomo Kenyatta, *Facing Mount Kenya* (1938), in *Microsoft Encarta Africana 2000*, ed. Kwame Anthony Appiah and Henry Louis Gates Jr., emphasis added.

15. "Glimpse of an Old Dutch Town," *Harper's Monthly Magazine* 63 (March 1881): 525–26, 535–36; cited in Shane White, " 'It Was a Proud Day: African Americans, Festivals, and Parades in the North, 1741–1834," in *New African American Urban History*, ed. Kenneth W. Goings and Raymond A. Mohl (Thousand Oaks, Calif.: Sage Publications, 1996), 32.

16. Cited in Ashe, *Hard Road to Glory*, 59.

17. See Appiah and Gates, *Microsoft Encarta Africana 2000*, for the sources cited throughout this discussion: Henry Walton Bibb, "A Fruitless Effort for Education"; Solomon Northrup, *Twelve Years a Slave: Narrative of Solomon Northup, a Citizen of New-York, Kidnapped in Washington City in 1841, and Rescued in 1853, from a Cotton Plantation near the Red River, in Louisiana* (Auburn, N.Y., 1853), 80–81; Frank J. Webb, *The Garies and Their Friends* (New York: G. Routledge & Co., 1857), 8; Olaudah Equiano, *The Interesting Narrative of the Life of Olaudah Equiano*, chap. 2; Nancy Prince, *A Narrative of the Life and Travels of Mrs. Nancy Prince, Written by Herself* (1853; originally published in Boston, 1850), 6–7; "Saint Kitts and Nevis"; Williams Wells Brown, *Clotel; or, the President's Daughter: A Narrative of Slave Life in the United States* (London: Partridge & Oakey, 1853),10.

18. Lester B. Shippee, ed., *Bishop Whipple's Southern Diary, 1843–1844* (Minneapolis, 1937), 51; cited in William D. Piersen, "African-American Festive Style," in *Signifyin(g), Sanctifyin', and Slam Dunking*, ed. Gena Dagel Caponi (Amherst: University of Massachusetts Press, 1999), 420.

19. Mura Dehn, "The Spirit Moves: Jazz Dance from the Turn of the Century to 1950," manuscript in Dance Collection, New York Public Library.

20. William D. Piersen, *Black Legacy: America's Hidden Heritage* (Amherst: University of Massachusetts Press, 1993), 176–77; Eugene D. Genovese, *Roll, Jordan, Roll: The World the Slaves Made* (1972; reprint, New York: Vintage, 1976), 475–81.

21. Anna Louise Burton, *Memories of Childhood's Slavery Days* (Boston, 1909), 5, in Appiah and Gates, *Microsoft Encarta Africana 2000*.

22. Charles Dickens, *American Notes and Pictures from Italy* (1842; reprint, New York: W. W. Norton, 1966), 90–91.

23. Gilbert Chase, *America's Music: From the Pilgrims to the Present* (New York: McGraw-Hill, 1966), 260.

24. Dale Cockrell, "Of Gospel Hymns, Minstrel Shows, and Jubilee Singers: Toward Some Black South African Musics," *American Music* 5 (Winter 1987): 418.

25. See Robert C. Toll, *Blacking Up: The Minstrel Show in Nineteenth-Century America* (New York: Oxford University Press, 1974); Thomas L. Riis, *Just Before Jazz: Black Musical Theater in New York, 1890 to 1915* (Washington, D.C.: Smithsonian Institution, 1989); Eric Lott, *Love and Theft: Blackface Minstrelsy and the American Working Class* (New York: Oxford University Press, 1993).

26. Dale Cockrell, "Jim Crow, Demon of Disorder," *American Music* 14 (Summer 1996): 161.

27. W. T. Lhamon Jr., *Raising Cain: Blackface Performance from Jim Crow to Hip Hop* (Cambridge: Harvard University Press, 1998), 180, 181.

28. W. T. Lhamon Jr., *Jump Jim Crow: Lost Plays, Lyrics, and Street Prose of the First Atlantic Popular Culture* (Cambridge: Harvard University Press, 2003), 95–96.

29. Chase, *America's Music*, 265.

30. Harold Courlander, "Dance and Dance Drama in Haiti," in *The Function of Dance in Human Society*, ed. Franziska Boas (New York: Boas School, 1944), 42; cited in Lynne Fauley Emery, *Black Dance in the United States from 1619 to 1970* (Palo Alto: National Press Books, 1972), 56.

31. Munah Mayo, "All That Glitters," in *Jump Up and Say! A Collection of Black Storytelling*, ed. Linda Goss and Clay Goss (New York: Simon and Schuster, 1995), 48.

32. Chase, *America's Music*, 264.

33. Carl Wittke, *Tambo and Bones: A History of the American Minstrel Stage* (Durham: Duke University Press, 1930), 27; cited in Marshall Stearns and Jean Stearns, *Jazz Dance: The Story of American Vernacular Dance* (New York: Macmillan, 1968), 43.

34. Cockrell, "Jim Crow, Demon of Disorder," 169.

35. Stearns and Stearns, *Jazz Dance*, 42.

36. Cited in Lott, *Love and Theft*, 3.

37. *Barbadoes v. Bolcolm*, reported in the *Boston Post*, 30 March 1840; cited in Cockrell, "Jim Crow, Demon of Disorder," 175.

38. Ibid., 176.

39. Ibid., 168; C. Vann Woodward, *The Strange Career of Jim Crow* (1955; reprint, New York: Oxford University Press, 1964), 7.

40. Dale Cockrell, conversation with author, 6 March 1997.

41. Molly Niederlander Ramshaw, "Jump, Jim Crow!" *Theatre Annual* 17 (1960): 44, 45.

42. Lhamon, *Raising Cain*, 152, 181.

43. Stearns and Stearns, *Jazz Dance*, 232.

44. Ibid., 41.

45. Lhamon, *Raising Cain*, 255 n. 30.

46. Stearns and Stearns, *Jazz Dance*, 100.

47. Harold Courlander, *Negro Folk Music, U.S.A.* (New York: Columbia University Press, 1963), 201.

48. Stearns and Stearns, *Jazz Dance*, 26.

49. Lydia Parrish, *Slave Songs of the Georgia Sea Islands* (1942; reprint, Athens: University of Georgia Press, 1992), 111.

50. Ibid., 27.

51. Courlander, *Negro Folk Music U.S.A.*, 202, emphasis added.

52. Jones and Hawes, *Step It Down*, 55–56.

53. Stearns and Stearns, *Jazz Dance*, 41.

54. Marian Hannah Winter, "Juba and American Minstrelsy," in *Chronicles of the American Dance*, ed. Paul Magriel (New York: H. Holt, 1948), 40; cited in Stearns and Stearns, *Jazz Dance*, 40.

55. Joseph Ireland, *Records of the New York Stage from 1750 to 1860* (New York: B. Blom, 1867), 55–56; cited in Ramshaw, "Jump, Jim Crow!" 36.

56. Stearns and Stearns, *Jazz Dance*, 41.

57. See Sterling Stuckey, *Slave Culture: Nationalist Theory and the Foundations of Black America* (New York: Oxford University Press, 1987), chap. 1; Dena Epstein, *Sinful Tunes and Spirituals: Black Folk Music to the Civil War* (Urbana: University of Illinois Press, 1977), 278–86.

58. James Weldon Johnson, "From Preface to *The Books of American Negro Spirituals*," in Caponi, *Signifyin(g), Sancifyin', and Slam Dunking*, 64.

59. Epstein, *Sinful Tunes and Spirituals*, 357.

60. Here Abrahams is referring to one of the principles Robert Farris Thompson illuminates as defining African music and dance in "The Cool Aesthetic"; cited in Jacqui Malone, *Steppin' on the Blues: The Visible Rhythms of African American Dance* (Urbana: University of Illinois Press, 1996), 5–6.

61. Ebenezer Davies, *American Scenes, and Christian Slavery: A Recent Tour of Four Thousand Miles in the United States* (London: John Snow, 1849), 198–99; cited in Shane White and Graham White, *The Sounds of Slavery* (Boston: Beacon Press, 2005), 103.

62. Daniel Alexander Payne, *Recollections of Seventy Years* (1886; reprint, New York: Arno Press, 1969), 256; cited in Piersen, *Black Legacy*, 173. As for jumping itself as a physical expression of joy, I offer this note: "[James W. C.] Pennington, describing his feelings when he realized that he must be near free soil, said that 'my spirits were so highly elated, that I took the whole of the road to myself; I ran, hopped, skipped, jumped, clapped my hands, talked to myself.' [In *The Adventures of Huckleberrry Finn*, Twain transforms the passage so that] Huck tells us that Jim, seeing one last light that looks like Cairo, says, 'We's safe, Huck, we's safe! Jump up and crack yo' heels, dat's de good ole Cairo at las', I jis knows it.'" Lucinda MacKethan, "Huck Finn and the Slave Narratives: Lighting Out as Design," *Southern Review* 20 (1984): 247–64; cited in Shelley Fisher Fishkin, *Was Huck Black? Mark Twain and African-American Voices* (New York: Oxford University Press, 1993), 200 n. 68.

63. Frederick Law Olmsted, *The Cotton Kingdom*, 2 vols. (New York, 1861), 1:311; cited in Piersen, *Black Legacy*, 174.

64. Courlander, *Negro Folk Music U.S.A.*, 195.

65. Frankie Manning and Cynthia R. Millman, *Frankie Manning: Ambassador of Lindy Hop* (Philadelphia: Temple University Press, 2007), 36–37.

66. Stearns and Stearns, *Jazz Dance*, 37.

67. Dizzy Gillespie with Al Fraser, *To Be or Not . . . to Bop: Memoirs of Dizzy Gillespie* (1979; reprint, New York: Da Capo, 1985), 31.

68. Timothy J. Nelson, *Every Time I Feel the Spirit: Religious Experience and Ritual in an African American Church* (New York: New York University Press, 2005), 151–52.

69. Ibid., 152.

70. Ibid., 159.

71. Parrish, *Slave Songs of the Georgia Sea Islands*, 227.

72. Stearns and Stearns, *Jazz Dance*, 31.

73. Carl Van Vechten, *Parties: Scenes from Contemporary New York Life* (1930; reprint, New York: Bard, 1977), 158.

74. Minstrelsy scholar William J. Mahar believes that it must have been athletic to attract as much attention as it did. Mahar also suggests that it bore the influence of stepping groups, for in some acts the dance was called "Stepping Jim Crow." William J. Mahar, conversation with author, 24 March 1996.

75. "National Negro Congress Gets Endorsement," *Pittsburgh Courier*, 28 December 1935, sec. 1. Poster on display in National Civil Rights Museum, Memphis, Tennessee.

10. UPWARD MOBILITY

1. Larry Tye, *Rising from the Rails: Pullman Porters and the Making of the Black Middle Class* (New York: Henry Holt, 2004), 61.

2. E. B. White, "Progress and Change," in *One Man's Meat* (New York: Harper and Row, 1944), 28.

3. Tye, *Rising from the Rails*, 83.

4. Ibid., 79.

5. Roy Wilkins with Tom Mathews, *Standing Fast: The Autobiography of Roy Wilkins* (New York: Viking Press, 1982), 41.

6. Tye, *Rising from the Rails*, 81.

7. Ibid., 83.

8. Ibid., 183.

9. Paula F. Pfeffer, *A. Philip Randolph, Pioneer of the Civil Rights Movement* (Baton Rouge: Louisiana State University Press, 1990) 22.

10. Quoted in "The Reminiscences of A. Philip Randolph," transcript interview by Wendell Wray, 1972, Oral History Research Office, Columbia University, 327; cited ibid., 21.

11. Doris Kearns Goodwin, *No Ordinary Time* (New York: Simon and Schuster, 1994), 162.

12. Pfeffer, *A. Philip Randolph*, 25.

13. Tye, *Rising from the Rails*, 167.

14. G. James Fleming, "Pullman Porters Win Pot of Gold," *Crisis* (November 1937); cited in Tye, *Rising from the Rails*, 163.

15. Pfeffer, *A. Philip Randolph*, 29.

16. See Melinda Chateauvert, *Marching Together: Women of the Brotherhood of Sleeping Car Porters* (Champaign: University of Illinois Press, 1998).

17. Ibid., 33.

18. Wilkins and Mathews, *Standing Fast*, 147.

19. Jervis Anderson, *A. Philip Randolph: A Biographical Portrait* (New York: Harcourt Brace Jovanovich, 1973), 248.

20. Pfeffer, *A. Philip Randolph*, 46.

21. Goodwin, *No Ordinary Time*, 246–47.

22. Pfeffer, *A. Philip Randolph*, 46.

23. Goodwin, *No Ordinary Time*, 165.

24. Ibid., 169.

25. Franklin Delano Roosevelt, statement, Office File 93, Franklin D. Roosevelt Presidential Library, Hyde Park, N.Y.; cited ibid., 171.

26. Cynthia Taylor, A. Philip Randolph: The Religious Journey of an African American Labor Leader (New York: New York University Press, 2006), 130.

27. A. Philip Randolph, Chicago Defender, 12 June 1943; cited in Goodwin, No Ordinary Time, 248.

28. Pfeffer, A. Philip Randolph, 48.

29. Transcript, A. Philip Randolph, Oral History Interview 1, with Thomas H. Baker, 29 October 1969, 4, LBJ Library, http://www.lbjlib.utexas.edu/johnson/archives.hom/oralhistory.hom/RandolpA/randolp.asp (22 August 2006).

30. Ibid., 5.

31. Ibid.

32. Pfeffer, A. Philip Randolph, 31.

33. Randolph, Oral History Interview, 5.

34. Ibid., 6

35. Ibid.

36. Chicago Defender, 25 June 1941, 2; cited in Goodwin, No Ordinary Time, 253.

37. Eleanor Roosevelt, "My Day," 13 July 1943; cited ibid., 447.

38. Taylor, A. Philip Randolph, 158–59, 165.

39. Ibid., 175.

40. Ibid., 165.

41. "President and Public Pressure: 'For a Redress of Grievances,' " Section B: "Truman, A. Philip Randolph, and the Desegregation of the Armed Services," http://www.whitehousehistory.org/04/subs/04_a03_d02.html (23 August 2006).

42. Memo for Matt Connelly, January 20, 1948, "Desegregation of the Armed Forces," Truman Presidential Library and Museum, http://www.trumanlibrary.org/whistlestop/study_collections/desegregation/large/documents/index.php?documentdate=1948–01–20&documentid=59&studycollectionid=deseg&pagenumber=1 (23 August 2006).

43. Randolph, Oral History Interview, 13.

44. Ibid., 14.

45. Ibid.

46. Lillie Patterson, A. Philip Randolph: Messenger for the Masses (New York: Facts on File, 1996), 84.

47. Pfeffer, A. Philip Randolph, 140.

48. Letter from Grant Reynolds and A. Philip Randolph to President Truman, 29 June 1948, Truman Presidential Library and Museum, Independence, Mo.; cited in Pfeffer, A. Philip Randolph, 142.

49. Executive Order Establishing the President's Committee on Equality of Treatment and Opportunity in the Armed Services, 26 July 1948, Truman Presidential Library and Museum, http://www.trumanlibrary.org/photos/9981a.jpg (23 August 2006).

50. "Desegregation of the Armed Forces: Chronology," Truman Presidential Library and Museum, http://www.trumanlibrary.org/whistlestop/study_collections/ desegregation/large/index.php?action=chronology (23 August 2006).

51. Wilkins and Mathews, Standing Fast, 292.

52. Ibid., 293.

53. Tye, Rising from the Rails, 221.

54. James C. Scott, Domination and the Arts of Resistance: Hidden Transcripts (New Haven: Yale University Press, 1990), 288.

11. JUMP FOR JOY!

1. See "The Recordings of Jimmie Rodgers," a discography, in Nolan Porterfield, Jimmie Rodgers: The Life and Times of America's Blue Yodeler (Urbana: University of Illinois Press, 1979), 388–422.

2. David Hajdu, Lush Life (New York: North Point Press, 1996), 53, 55.

3. Albert Murray, Stomping the Blues (New York: Da Capo, 1976), 124.

4. Joel Dinerstein, Swinging the Machine: Modernity, Technology, and African American Culture between the World Wars (Amherst: University of Massachusetts Press, 2003), 68, 71.

5. Patricia Willard, Jump for Joy (Washington, D.C.: Smithsonian Institution, 1988), 3.

6. Ibid., 1; Stuart Nicholson, Reminiscing in Tempo: A Portrait of Duke Ellington (Boston: Northeastern University Press, 1999), 231.

7. Patricia Willard (Jump for Joy, 1) quotes Kuller as saying that the budget was $42,000. John Edward Hasse, in Beyond Category: The Life and Genius of Duke Ellington (1993; reprint, New York: Da Capo Press, 1995), 246, says the show cost $52,000, of which $10,000 was contributed by Garfield.

8. Edward Kennedy Ellington, Music Is My Mistress (Garden City, N.Y.: Doubleday and Company, 1973), 175.

9. Ibid. Jump For Joy has its roots in the Hollywood Theatre Alliance's "Negro

Revue." Arnold Rampersad, *The Life of Langston Hughes*, vol. 2, 1941–1967 (New York: Oxford University Press, 1988), 26.

10. Willard, *Jump for Joy*, 3.

11. Nicholson, *Reminiscing in Tempo* , 234.

12. Later spelled "Ivie" Anderson. I have chosen to use "Ivy" as it appears in the original Mayan Theatre billing, in Ellington's *Music Is My Mistress*, and in notes for *Jump for Joy*, Smithsonian Collection of Recordings, selected by Martin Williams and annotated by Patricia Willard (Washington DC 20560). All selections were taken from the original 1941 production, as listed in the program reprinted in *Music Is My Mistress*.

13. Willard, *Jump for Joy*, 6.

14. Ibid., 9.

15. Ibid., 11.

16. Rex William Stewart, *Boy Meets Horn*, ed. Claire P. Gordon (Ann Arbor: University of Michigan Press, 1991), 211.

17. Willard, *Jump for Joy*, 13.

18. Paul Webster, Ray Golden, and Hal Borne, "I've Got a Passport from Georgia," Duke Ellington Collection, Archives Center, National Museum of American History, Smithsonian Institution (hereafter cited as Duke Ellington Collection, Smithsonian Institution). I thank Ann Kuebler and Deborra Richardson at the Smithsonian Institution for their assistance.

19. "Uncle Tom's Cabin Is A Drive-In Now," Duke Ellington Collection, Smithsonian Institution.

20. "Tentative Outline of Jump for Joy: A Musican Revue," Duke Ellington Collection, Smithsonian Institution.

21. Paul Webster, Sid Kuller, and Duke Ellington, "Jump for Joy" (1941), Duke Ellington Collection, Smithsonian Institution.

22. Willard, *Jump for Joy*, 17, 31.

23. Ibid., 21.

24. Frank Marshall Davis, *Livin' the Blues: Memoirs of a Black Journalist and Poet*, ed. John Edgar Tidwell (Madison: University of Wisconsin Press, 1991), 49.

25. Cited in Willard, *Jump for Joy*, 17–18.

26. Ibid., 19.

27. Ibid., 21.

28. Ibid., 20.

29. W. E. Oliver, *Los Angeles Evening Herald-Express*, 8 August 1941; cited ibid., 22.

30. Hasse, *Beyond Category*, 248; Willard, *Jump for Joy*, 28.

31. Untitled typescript running order, Duke Ellington Collection, Smithsonian Institution.

32. Willard, *Jump for Joy*, 29; Ellington, *Music Is My Mistress*, 180.

33. Ellington, *Music Is My Mistress*, 460.

34. Willard, *Jump for Joy*, 31.

35. Murray, *Stomping the Blues*, 196.

AFTERWORD: JUMPING AS PLAY

1. Alain LeRoy Locke, *The New Negro* (1925; reprint, New York: Atheneum, 1968), 1–2.

2. For a survey of intellectual positions on this issue in the 1930s, see Richard Pells, *Radical Visions and American Dreams: Culture and Social Thought in the Depression Years* (New York: Harper and Row, 1973), 96–150.

3. George Schuyler, *Pittsburgh Courier*, 14 December 1935, sec. 1.

4. Warren I. Susman, *Culture as History* (New York: Pantheon, 1985), 162.

5. Gena Dagel Caponi, "Introduction: The Case for an African American Aesthetic," in *Signifyin(g), Sanctifyin,' and Slam Dunking: A Reader in African American Expressive Culture*, ed. Gena Dagel Caponi (Amherst: University of Massachusetts Press), 1–44.

6. Albert J. Raboteau, *A Fire in the Bones: Reflections on African-American Religious History* (Boston: Beacon Press, 1995), 151.

7. Essays by some of these scholars appear in Caponi, *Signifyin(g), Sanctifyin', and Slam Dunking*.

8. Roger Pryor Dodge, *Hot Jazz and Jazz Dance: Collected Writings, 1929–1964* (New York: Oxford University Press, 1995), 143.

9. Robert Farris Thompson, "An Aesthetic of the Cool: West African Dance," in Caponi, *Signifyin(g), Sanctifyin', and Slam Dunking*, 72–86; John Miller Chernoff, *African Rhythm and African Sensibility: Aesthetics and Social Action in African Musical Idioms* (Chicago: University of Chicago Press, 1979).

10. Marshall Stearns and Jean Stearns, *Jazz Dance: The Story of American Vernacular Dance* (New York: Macmillan, 1968); Jaqui Malone, *Steppin' on the Blues: The Visible Rhythms of African American Dance* (Urbana: University of Illinois Press, 1996).

11. Richard Crawford, *America's Musical Life: A History* (New York: W. W. Norton & Company, 2001), xi.

12. David W. Stowe, *Swing Changes: Big-Band Jazz in New Deal America* (Cambridge: Harvard University Press, 1994), 9.

13. Albert Murray, *Stomping the Blues* (1976; reprint, New York: Da Capo, 1987), 196.

14. Albert Murray, telephone conversation with author, 14 October 1998.

15. Friedrich Schiller, *On the Aesthetic Education of Man* (1795), trans. Reginald Snell (New York: Frederick Ungar, 1965), 80.

16. Brian Sutton-Smith, *The Ambiguity of Play* (Cambridge: Harvard University Press, 1997), 148.

17. Johan Huizinga, *Homo Ludens: A Study of the Play Element in Culture* (Boston: Beacon Press, 1960), 198.

18. Ibid., foreword, 211.

19. Ibid., 9.

20. Sutton-Smith, *The Ambiguity of Play*, 78–80.

21. Roger Caillois, *Man, Play, and Games* (1958), trans. Meyer Barash (New York: Free Press of Glencoe, 1961), 13.

22. Ibid., 27.

23. Albert Murray, conversation with author, 14 October 1998.

24. Murray, *Stomping the Blues*, 158.

25. Ibid., 45, 87, 98.

26. Ibid., 70.

27. Ibid., 50.

28. Albert Murray, *The Omni-Americans* (New York: Vintage 1970), 90.

29. Bill Russell and Taylor Branch, *Second Wind: The Memoirs of an Opinionated Man* (New York: Random House, 1979), 100.

30. Walt Frazier and Ira Berkow, *Rockin' Steady: A Guide to Basketball and Cool* (New York: Warner, 1974), 88.

31. Clarence Gaines, telephone interview with author, 5 March 1996.

32. Frederick Douglass, *My Bondage and My Freedom* (1855; reprint, New York: Dover, 1969), 98–100; Sidney Bechet, *Treat It Gentle* (1960; reprint, New York: Da Capo, 1975), 3.

33. Murray, *Stomping the Blues*, 65.

34. Ibid., 189.

35. Murray, *Omni-Americans*, 32–33.

36. Ibid., 98.

37. Ibid., 95–96.

38. Ibid., 84.

39. Ralph Ellison, "What America Would Be Like without Blacks," *Time*, 6 April 1970.

40. See, for example, Peter F. Drucker, *Managing in a Time of Great Change* (New York: Dutton, 1995), 98–101.

41. Ted Miller, "Glory Road Paved for Young," *Seattle Post-Intelligencer Reporter*, 7 January 2006.

42. Ibid.

43. Albert Murray, *The Blue Devils of Nada: A Contemporary American Approach to Aesthetic Statement* (New York: Pantheon Books, 1996), 16.

44. Murray, *Omni-Americans*, 17.

45. Ibid., 98.

INDEX

AAU (Amateur Athletic Union), 36, 37–38, 42, 45, 97

ABA (American Basketball Association), 2, 81, 86, 102, 106

Abott, Cleveland, 37–38

Abrahams, Roger, 155, 227–28n11, 230n60

accommodation, 17, 18

Action Comics, 31–32

Adams, "Jumpin' Johnny," 95

Adler, Renata, 133–34

The Adventures of Huckleberry Finn (Twain), 231n62

Aerial Experiment Association, 22

aeronautics. *See* aviation

aesthetic. *See* African American aesthetic

AFL (American Federation of Labor), 165, 166

Africa: athletic competitions in, 147; and blues music, 195, 196; buzzards in, 153; call and response in music of, 188; dance of, 51, 63, 141–43, 147, 153, 185, 189–90, 192; expressive culture of, 188–90; jump in, xvii, 141, 146, 147–49, 153; minstrelsy in, 149–50

African American aesthetic: in basketball, xiv, 2, 89–92, 96, 100–101, 103–5, 109–10; characteristics of, 109–10, 188; contribution of, to popular culture, 1–3, 20, 21, 65–66, 197

African American holiness or sanctified churches, 156–57

African Ceremonial (dance), 143

The African (Courlander), 153

Afro-American, 139

After Seben, 51

Agricultural Adjustment Act, 19

Air Mail Special, 59

airplanes. *See* aviation

air steps: first instance of, in Lindy Hop, xiii, 57–58, 211nn29–30, 212n34; as jumping steps generally, 1, 21, 195; and Manning, 55, 57–59, 194, 211nn29–30, 212n34; and popularity of Lindy Hop, 65; prohibition of, in ballrooms and nightclubs, 211n29; types of, 58–61, 65; by Whitey's Lindy Hoppers in *A Day at the Races*, 60–61

Akron Firestones (basketball team), 81, 93

Akron Goodyear Wingfoots (basketball team), 81

Alabama State Hornets (basketball team), 12, 15

Albritton, Dave, 33, 40, 41, 43, 46, 47

Alhambra Ballroom, 56, 60

Allan, Lewis, 143

Allen, Forrest "Phog," 86, 92

Amateur Athletic Union (AAU), 36, 37–38, 42, 45, 97

America Dances, 143

American Basketball Association (ABA), 2, 81, 86, 102, 106

American Basketball League, 11–12, 14, 84, 86, 90

American Federation of Labor (AFL), 165, 166

American Revue Theatre, 177–78

American Stuff (Federal Writers' Project), 138

America's Musical Life (Crawford), 190

Amsterdam News, 40, 42, 61, 129, 143

Anderson, Ivy, 122, 178, 180–83, 185, 235n12

Anderson, Marian, 19, 132

Angelou, Maya, 132, 133

anti-lynching legislation, 19, 43, 170, 171

Apache Minstrels, 150

Apollo Theater, 10, 60, 72

Appalachian State College, 93

"The Apple Jump," 65, 70

architecture. *See* skyscrapers; *specific architects and buildings*

Arizin, Paul, 94, 102

armed forces: and basketball, 83, 93–94, 95, 98; desegregation of, xv, xvii, 171–72; segregation of, 113, 133, 170, 171–72, 185

Armstrong, Louis, 9, 34, 65, 122, 163

Ashe, Arthur, 97

Astaire, Fred, 61

athletic clubs, 36

athletics. *See* basketball; boxing; Olympics; track and field; *specific players*

Atlanta, Ga., 5

Atlanta Journal, 128

Atlanta riots (1906), 137

Attali, Jacques, 192